# Governing Telecommunications and the New Information Society in Europe

# Governing Telecommunications and the New Information Society in Europe

*Edited by*

Jacint Jordana

*Associate Professor of Political Science, Universitat Pompeu Fabra, Barcelona, Spain*

*In association with Universidade de Santiago de Compostela, Vicerrectorado de Extension Cultural*



**Edward Elgar**

Cheltenham, UK • Northampton MA, USA

Published by
Edward Elgar Publishing Limited
Glensanda House
Montpellier Parade
Cheltenham
Glos GL50 1UA
UK



Edward Elgar Publishing, Inc.
136 West Street
Suite 202
Northampton
Massachusetts 01060
USA



A catalogue record for this book
is available from the British Library

**Library of Congress Cataloguing in Publication Data**

Governing telecommunications and the new information society in Europe / edited by Jacint Jordana.
p. cm.
"In association with Universidade de Santiago de Compostela, Vicerrectorado de Extensión Cultural."
Includes bibliographical references and index.
1. Telecommunication policy—Europe. 2. Information society—Europe. I. Jordana, Jacint, 1962–

HE8081.G68 2003
384′.094—dc21

2002072156

ISBN 1 84064 757 4

Printed and bound in Great Britain by Biddles Ltd, *www.biddles.co.uk*

# Contents

## PART II CREATING NEW POLICIES FOR A EUROPEAN INFORMATION SOCIETY

# Figures

# Tables

# Contributors

**Antonio Alabau** Department of Communications, Universitat Politècnica de València, Valencia, Spain.

**Johannes M. Bauer** Department of Telecommunication, Michigan State University, United States

**Martin Cave** Centre for Management under Regulation, Warwick Business School, University of Warwick, United Kingdom

**Massimo G. Colombo** Department of Economics, Università degli Studi di Pavia, Pavia, and CIRET, Politecnico de Milano, Milan, Italy

**Marco Delmastro** Department of Economics, Università degli Studi di Pavia, Pavia, Italy

**Jacint Jordana** Department of Political and Social Sciences, Universitat Pompeu Fabra, Barcelona, Spain

**David Sancho** Department of Political and Social Sciences, Universitat Pompeu Fabra, Barcelona, Spain

**Volker Schneider** Department of Politics and Managment, Universität Konstanz, Constance, Germany

**Joan Subirats** Department of Political Science and Public Law, Universitat Autònoma de Barcelona, Bellaterra, Spain

**Mark Thatcher** Department of Government, London School of Economics and Political Science, London, United Kingdom

**Raymund Werle** Max Planck Institute for the Study of Societies, Cologne, Germany

# Preface

This volume had its origins in a conference on Telecommunications Policy and Information Society in Europe held in the city of Santiago de Compostela (Galicia, Spain), 13–14 April 2000. The main focus of the conference was to analyze the recent transformations of the telecommunications regulatory regime in Europe, the market developments, and its implications for the development of a European Information Society. This conference formed part of a program entitled *Europa Mundi*, that included a seminar series dealing with diferent political, economic and social aspects of European integration, coordinated by the Universidade de Santiago. These series of seminars were a contribution from the academic community to the Santiago's de Compostela mandate of European City of Culture for the Year 2000. The initiative was conceived and developed by Ramón Máiz, Dean of the Universidade de Santiago Political Sciences School, and generously funded by a grant from the Consorcio da Cidade de Santiago de Compostela.

This volume consists of the revised versions of the papers presented at the conference, some of which have evolved considerably, and in many cases in response to the excellent discussions and contributions of the seminar participants during the two day session. I thank Daniel Blanch, a graduate student from the Universidade de Santiago Political Science Department, who handled most of the organization of the conference, helping to make the conference the success it was. I am also indebted to the people who assisted me during the process of preparing this book. For linguistic revision I thank Andrew Spencer and Paris von Lockette, and for editing assitance, Yanina Welp. I would also like to thank Ángel Ligero Fraile, Manager of the Consorcio da Cidade de Santiago de Compostela, who helped a lot to facilitate the financial assitance for the whole project. Finally, I am especially indebted to Ramón Máiz for his continued suport and feedback both during the process of organizing the conference and editing this volume.

# Abbreviations

| | |
|---|---|
| ACTS | Advanced Communications Technologies and Services |
| AGCOM | Autorità per le Garanzie nelle Communicazioni |
| ASST | Azienda di Stato per i Servizi Telefonici |
| ARPA | Advanced Research Projects Agency |
| ART | Autorité de Régulation des Télécommunications |
| ATM | Asynchronous Transfer Mode |
| AT&T | American Telephone and Telegraph |
| BIC | Business Innovation Centres |
| BT | British Telecom |
| CATV | Cable Television |
| CcTLD | Country code Top-Level Domains |
| CERN | European Organization for Nuclear Research |
| CF | Cohesion Fund |
| CISI | Comité interministériel pour la Société de l'Information |
| CMT | Comisión del Mercado de Telecomunicaciones |
| CN | Comunicaçoẽs Nacionais |
| COSINE | Cooperation for Open Systems Interconnection Networking in Europe |
| CPE | Customer Premises Equipment |
| CTNE | Compañìa Telefónica Nacional de España |
| CTP | Correios e Telecomunicaçoes de Portugal |
| DGT | Direction Générale des Télécommunications |
| DGIV | The former European Commission Directorate General for Competition Policy |
| DGXIII | The former European Commission Directorate General Enterprise and Information Society |
| EARN | European Academic and Research Network |
| ECPR | Efficient Component Pricing Rule |
| EC | European Community |
| EIN | European Informatics Network |
| ERDF | European Regional Development Fund |
| ESF | European Social Fund |
| ESPRIT | EU Information Technologies Program |
| ETSI | European Telecommunications Standards Institute |

| | |
|---|---|
| EU | European Union |
| DBP | Deutsches Bundespost |
| DGT | Direction Genérale des Télécommunications (France) |
| FCC | Federal Commission of Communications (US) |
| GAC | Governmental Advisory Committee (ICANN) |
| GATT | General Agreement on Tariffs and Trade |
| GSM | Global System for Mobile Communications |
| HLCG | High-Level Communications Group (representatives of EU NRA) |
| HTML | Hypertext Markup Language |
| HTTP | Hypertext Transfer Protocol |
| IBM | International Business Machines Co. |
| ICANN | Internet Corporation for Assigned Names and Numbers |
| ICP | Instituto das Comunicacoês de Portugal |
| ICT | Information and Communication Technology |
| IPO | Initial Public Ofering |
| IRISI | Inter-Regional Information Society Initiative |
| ISDN | Integrated Services Digital Network |
| ISI | Information Society Initiative (United Kingdom) |
| ISO | International Standardization Organization |
| ISP | Internet Service Provider |
| ISPAs | Internet Service Providers Associations |
| ISPA | Pre-accession Structural Policy Instruments |
| IST | Information Society and Technology (EC program) |
| ITT | International Telephone and Telegraph |
| ITU | International Telecommunications Union |
| LOT | Ley de Ordenación de las Telecomunicaciones |
| Marconi | Companhía Portuguesa Rádio Marconi |
| MCI | Microwave Communications of America |
| MIT | Massachusetts Institute of Technology |
| NBS | National Bureau of Standards |
| NPL | National Physical Laboratory |
| NRA | National Regulatory Authority |
| NSF | National Science Foundation (US) |
| NSCA | National Center for Supercomputer Applications |
| NTBF | New Technology-Based Firms |
| OECD | Organisation for Economic Cooperation and Development |
| Oftel | Office of Telecommunications (United Kingdom) |
| ONP | Open Network Provision |
| OSI | Open Systems Interconnection |
| PAGSI | Programme d'action gouvernmental pour préparer l'entreé de la France dans la Societé de l'Information |

| | |
|---|---|
| PT | Portugal Telecom |
| PTO | Public Telecommunications Operators |
| PTT | Post, Telegraph and Telecommunications |
| RACE | R&D in Advanced Communications technologies in Europe (EC program) |
| RARE | Réseaux Associés pour la Récherche Européenne |
| RegTP | Regulierungsbehörde für Telekommunikation und Post |
| RISI | Regional Information Society Initiative |
| RPI | Retail Price Index (RPI – X represents a formula for profits that substracts X from the RPI) |
| RTDF | Research and Technological Development Fund |
| SME | Small and Medium Enterprises |
| SNA | Systems Network Architecture (IBM computer network) |
| STAR | Modernization of services and networks in less developed and peripheral regions (EC program) |
| TCP/IP | Transmission Control Protocol/ Internet Protocol |
| TDP | Teledifusora de Portugal |
| TEN | Trans-European Networks |
| TLD | Top Level Domain |
| TLP | Telefones de Lisboa e Porto |
| TP | Telecom Portugal |
| ULL | Unbunded Local Loop |
| URL | Uniform Resource Locator |
| USO | Universal Service Obligations |
| WTO | World Trade Organization |
| WWW | World Wide Web |

# 1. Introduction: Regulating telecommunications and enforcing the Information Society in Europe

**Jacint Jordana**

Researchers often encounter difficulties in analysing public policy, however the telecommunications field poses an additional hurdle: the breakneck pace of technological, social and economic change in the sector over the last few decades. Such a rapid transformation makes it very difficult to analyse the phenomenon in depth, discuss hypotheses or indeed attempt an intellectual debate regarding its fundamental features. Nevertheless, it is precisely this challenge which makes this field of research so exciting. There are few recent examples of such a rapid and radical change in policies occurring on a global scale. Studying telecommunications policy change is not only an intellectual task worthy of public policy analysts but also concerns a sector which fuels world economic development and has become a driving force behind globalisation and social change.

This introductory chapter contains four sections. The first covers the themes analysed and the contributions contained in the book. A brief guide is provided on the transformations of the telecommunications sector in Europe during the 1990s, which are discussed in detail by the contributors to this book. The following section sets out the analytical problems associated with trying to explain this enormous transformation. One of the main concerns of the authors in this volume is to analyse the specific features of the phenomenon in Europe and the national variations exhibited. The contributors have adopted different theoretical approaches for this purpose and the analytical perspectives employed are briefly sketched in this section. The third section sets out the reasons for combining both contributions on telecommunications policies and on public strategies to foster the Information Society in Europe. It will be argued that public policy formulation in Europe over the last few decades has linked the two themes much more than elsewhere. The chapters in this book clearly reveal the multiple facets of this complex and changeable interrelationship. The last section covers the contributions as a whole, identifies links between them and how they bear on the main issues.

## AN ENORMOUS TRANSFORMATION

In broad terms, one can say that the transformation of the telecommunications sector began in the 1980s. It began with small changes in regulation of the industry which then spilled over to institutions and policies as the process gathered steam. In less than two decades, the sector leapt from nationally organised monopolistic regimes (whether private or public) to a free market system operating on an international scale and based on private property for both the provision of infrastructure and services. New specialised public institutions appeared on the scene once the operators had split away from the public sector. These institutions were charged with regulating the industry and promoting public policies befitting the new context. Changes were slow at first and limited to a few countries (United States, United Kingdom) but accelerated rapidly later, as other countries followed suit and introduced new regulatory frameworks for the sector (Hills 1986; Davies 1994; Brock 1994; Schneider, Chapter 2 this volume). Thus, by the end of the 1990s, virtually the whole industry operated under a completely new global, competence driven regime despite the fact that some developing countries maintained a monopoly of basic telecommunication services (OECD 2001).

In Europe, the European Commission (henceforth, the Commission) gave a clear lead in the process of institutional change and the radical shift in policies, advocating market liberalisation and the dismantling of State monopolies from the 1980s onwards. There were important debates between the Member States and the Commission as the Commission shifted its stance on these issues. The resulting tensions led to matters being taken to the European Court of Justice. The Court finally decided in favour of the Commission in 1991, recognising the latter's powers to promote Community Directives in the telecommunications field (Schmidt 1998). From then on, conflicts between the Member States and Commission abated, with the most reticent countries accepting the decision-making role of European institutions in this field. These developments, along with the firm line taken by the Commission, led to a new state of affairs which some analysts consider as laying the path to 'Europeanisation' of telecommunications policies and a curtailment of the powers of Member States (Sandholtz 1993; Fuchs 1994)

Europeanisation of telecommunications continued apace throughout the decade with the drafting and implementation of numerous EC Directives. This led to a European-wide strategy which focused almost exclusively on market regulation aspects – something which was seen as an example of negative integration in the EU (Scharpf 1999). What is somewhat surprising is that the relationship between various levels of government had undergone such a sea change by the late 1990s, contrasting with the conflict-ridden period of the early 1990s. The tensions between Member States and the Commission disappeared and while the former transferred EC directives into their national legislation, the latter focussed on overseeing the introduction of competition on a European scale. Everything seemed to point to the emergence of a supranational telecommunications regime (Sandholtz 1998).

The Commission began monitoring the implementation of the regulatory model established in each country from 1998 onwards, once liberalisation Directives had been passed into the legislation of Member States. The Commission's study of regulation and competition in each Member State revealed a complex picture, which was more heterogeneous than expected. Progress towards a truly competitive open market was patchy (European Commission 2000b). It became clear that each Member State had set incentives and also applied Directives in way designed to suit its own ends - an approach which casts a less rosy light on the much-vaunted liberalisation of the telecommunications sector and the emergence of a European market (Eliassen and Svojaag 1999; Hulsink 1999; Thatcher, Chapter 4 this volume). Some analysts considered that the interplay between Member States and the Commission gave rise to embedded national policies within a loose European framework (Levi-Faur 1999).

A good example of national differences was the regulation of e-commerce (Piazolo 2001); yet another was the range of models applied by national governments in granting third generation cell phone licences during 2000 and 2001 (auctions, tenders, and so on) - an issue which created a great deal of controversy in Europe. Nevertheless, one can say that the various newly established national markets showed very similar basic characteristics given that these all stemmed from the implementation of EU Directives. In any event, one needs to assess the importance and origins of the differences and similarities found in each country. This is a controversial issue which generates many debates and is tackled in depth by several of the contributions to this volume.

Not surprisingly, matters did not rest there. The difficulties encountered in making the transition to open markets and the wide differences in national implementation led the Commission to propose a new regulatory scheme from 1999 onwards. This was intended to simplify and harmonise telecommunications in Europe and was gradually brought into effect over the following years. In drawing up the new regulatory framework, the Commission wagered on convergence between the audio-visual, telecommunications, and information technology fields. In so doing, the Commission took a neutral stance with regard to technological alternatives when introducing new regulatory measures designed to reduce the need for direct public intervention in the sector (European Commission 2000a, 2001). The conceptual framework employed by the Commission was no longer 'telecommunications' but rather 'electronic communications'. The aim was to emphasise the range of alternative technologies available for managing communications and the homogeneity represented by a universal digital/binary format.

The concept of the Information Society began to catch on while the transformation of the telecommunications sector was under way. The 'Information Society' was an umbrella term which took in the likely social and economic changes produced by the development of ICT (Information and Communication Technologies) (Steinfeld and Salvaggio 1989). In this respect, it should be noted that the term was used more as a handy catch-all when considering the broad consequences of the spread of computing and electronic communications than as part of a well-structured discourse on social change. One of the factors which probably did most to make the term popular was its enthusiastic adoption by the Commission as a convenient umbrella term for the changes and innovations it wished to foster throughout Europe. Thus the seminal Green Book, published in 1987, mentioned the need for profound changes in the State-guided telecommunications regime in order to dynamise society (European Commission 1987).

The Commission published a white book on growth, competitiveness and employment six years later, once the main decisions regarding telecommunication liberalisation had been taken. The publication, which came to be known as the Delors Report, drew links between new technologies, economic growth and the creation of jobs (European Commission 1993). Another important step was the Bangemann Report, in which a group of experts was asked by the European Commission to study and make recommendations to advance the Information Society in Europe. The report findings included a range of public policy initiatives for fostering and disseminating ICT applications and services in all socio-economic and policy fields, including a strong commitment to rapid liberalisation of the whole telecommunications sector (European Commission 1994a). The reasoning behind these recommendations was that Europe could not remain on the fringes of the technological revolution already underway. It was argued that public authorities should foster technological change by adopting pro-active policies in all fields, as well as providing by ensuring a suitable regulatory environment. The message was enthusiastically echoed throughout Europe during the 1990s by a coalition of public and private actors, inspiring public initiatives in most of the Member States (Servaes and Burgelman 2000).

## INTERPRETING POLICY VARIATIONS

New telecommunications networks and associated interactive services and applications are changing the face of the world and opening up new frontiers. Although there is a trend towards standardisation as technology spreads worldwide, there are still many special features of the way each society uses and adapts ICT. Many factors play a role in the form ICT takes in each country and include a nation's economic development, cultural idiosyncrasies and previous track record on markets for products and services. We shall not analyse the factors producing diversity here but rather simply make the point that globalisation of markets is compatible with specific adaptations to world economic and social change. One of the features of this diversity is the varying style and content of telecommunications public policies in different countries, and the EU as a whole. The way in which governments either promoted or reacted to change varied widely. Their actions and reactions depended on how each one read the international context; resolved internal conflicting interests and pursued its own strategies and visions of the future. Such responses ranged from passive to active measures and differed in both their sophistication and the results obtained (Eliasen and Sjovaag 1999). Nevertheless, it is interesting to note that where governments enjoy some freedom in drawing up policies, their initiatives tend to take on a life of their own and affect the way global trends are expressed in local and national markets. In this respect, understanding national telecommunications policies helps one grasp how our societies are changing, the way in which policies are formulated and how decisions are taken.

The contributions in this book focus on two policy fields in the EU and its Member States: (1) the formulation and implementation of telecommunications policies and (2) measures designed to foster the Information Society. Analysing the sources of variation in each case involves identifying the path followed in liberalising telecommunications and pursuing technological innovation in the EU as well as examining the existing diversity found in the Member States. Armed with this information, one can then discuss issues such as the degree of national policy variations in liberalising telecommunications markets in the EU. Given that market liberalisation occurred within a multi-level governmental context, it is essential to examine what was happening simultaneously at national and EU government levels. Both levels of government form part of Europe's complex institutional architecture and together provide the most interesting source of variations. Once these aspects were made clear, it would be then possible identify the institutional mechanisms that effectively work in the European *scene* (understanding both EU and Member States) for decision-making processes in these policy fields.

Broadly speaking, one can readily concede that policy differences between Member States were less marked than those between the EU and other areas of the world. The strong role which the Commission played in this policy area from the 1980s onwards in drawing up and implementing a new regulatory framework was undoubtedly the cause of the lesser variation found between Member States. Nevertheless, it is highly likely that other factors contributed to the similarities observed in various European countries. One such factor was the previous existence of public monopolies in the industry. These and many other themes give rise to interpretative nuances and the adoption of different theoretical perspectives. Not surprisingly, this has given rise to a certain amount of controversy regarding the elements producing distinctive policy and institutional changes in the sector in Europe.

The discussion on the range of national variations in telecommunications policies in Europe has produced a similar but possibly more complex debate. The questions posed by various contributions in this book follow the same thread: to what extent was the Commission's role a determining one in producing the policy and institutional changes in the sector? How much did the Commission direct hierarchically the course of the changes implemented by Member States or were other factors more important? If we can explain the various sources of variation at both national and European levels, we will understand public actors' institutional framework in taking decisions and hence be in a better position to assess the results of their actions in greater detail. In more general terms, the question implicitly touches on the institutional mechanisms involved in policy change (Pierson 2000a). In this respect, the transformation of the telecommunications sector constitutes an excellent laboratory for examining the way some decision-making procedures change in parallel to the process of policy change.

The answers to these questions may take several forms as both themes become better-defined and the issues are tackled using different theoretical approaches. Thus a detailed analysis of the strategies followed by national actors sometimes reveals a different range of interests in each policy network, depending on the particular configuration of a given policy arena in a country. By the contrary, when one looks at each country's regulatory framework in isolation, the homogeneity of change processes is much greater, leading one to believe that actors' scope for manoeuvre is much more limited *vis-à-vis* external factors (as EC guidance). Most of the contributions in this volume take into account the specific roles played by institutions and actors in policy formulation. More specifically, many of the contributions tend to either explicitly or implicitly emphasise the role of existing institutions (whether national or European) in explaining the limitations on actors and the opportunities they faced in fostering new policies for the industry. Although all the contributions in this book focus on the role of institutions, some authors tend to stress the importance of major international trends over purely policy and institutional considerations. Others, by contrast, emphasise variables, which show greater national scope for manoeuvre with regard to policy formulation and institutional change. Accordingly, significant emphasis is placed on Member States' policymaking behaviour changed at different junctures in the light of the great global changes taking place.

One should note that a more detailed discussion of the degree of national variations in Europe poses a theoretical issue. The institutional approaches to this issue can be divided into two types. The first approach considers policy changes as local adaptations to global changes. Here, the idea of path-dependency holds sway in which existing institutions and past decisions mould the way change is dealt with. Such path-dependency arises from the hidden costs which would be incurred if such idiosyncratic features were not taken into account (Pierson 2000b). This interpretation underlines the difficulties each country has in transforming institutions and policies and indicates that national adaptation to change is strictured by a nation's institutional past. Thus changes are only possible under certain circumstances, for example, when general trends (technology, regulatory frameworks, and so on) open windows of opportunity, which facilitate policy changes or the renewal of national institutions (Cortell and Peterson 1999).

Researchers adopting this perspective look for and measure variables which highlight national variations and identify their special features. An example of this kind of work can be found in theories on the continuing importance of nation-states in the context of globalisation. It is argued that governments have partially maintained their own traditions of intervention, largely as a consequence of path-dependency. It is merely that methods of control have changed in response to new conditions. However, such changes do not necessarily mean that governments' control over their respective countries' economic development has lessened at all (Vogel 1996; Evans 1997). Thus the range of state traditions is reflected in the persistence of various forms of government intervention (whether more or less active) in both the economy as a whole and in particular markets. Such intervention is the fruit of a mix of continuity and change in institutions, which needs to be clearly analysed in each case (Weiss 1998). With regard to telecommunications policy, the argument runs that states – and especially strong states – far from being overwhelmed by global forces, have managed to find a new role as agents fostering consensus and as arbitrators. In the process, they have imposed their own criteria on the development of new national markets (especially in cases where there was a strong tradition of state intervention) and they also introduced active policy measures such as those aimed at promoting the Information Society. Finally, one can also say that the external pressure exercised by the Commission was seized upon by states to overcome domestic resistance to government initiatives. National governments used EC directives to build coalitions of actors to help them to re-shape the role of state institutions in the telecommunications sector in their respective countries.

The second type of analytical approach considers institutional and policy changes as an example of the way policies are transferred between countries or derive from developments at an international level. Some institutional mechanism can emerge to impulse these processes of policymaking, defining different modes of how policy is managed in a multilevel government environment. From hierarchical guidance to mutual adjustment, or joint decision-making, or also intergovernmental negotiations, there is an array of specific interaction modes that can provide us with interpretative models to understand how each sectorial policy is defined and managed (Scharpf 1997, 2001). This perspective applies equally to policy instruments and to institutional guidelines and design. Also, when multi-level institutional mechanisms seems to have no role in policymaking, some policy transfer effects would be on the way. These crop up in one country and are then either imitated or applied elsewhere. International bodies (such as the European Union) transmit new conceptual models and frameworks, reinforcing interaction and imitation between various countries (Evans and Davies 1999; Dolowitz and Marsh 1996, 2000; Radaelli 2000). The fact that imitative and institutionalised (coercive, joint-decision, and so on ) processes often co-exist makes analysis in our policy fields a particularly complex task. Hence analysts' interest is identifying the institutional mechanisms at work, and also measuring the links and similarities in innovative policies adopted by different countries. This involves gauging the influence and relative importance of both sources of policy innovation and transmission.

An examination of telecommunications policy in Europe from this perspective is illuminating. The role of the Commission in fostering new regulatory models in the sector during the 1990s occurred at the same time as the transfer of policies and institutional schemes between EU Member States. In addition, American ideas and models were also taken on board in Europe given that the United States led the world in revolutionising the industry. The simultaneous combination of these factors was transmitted in various ways to the national levels to shape markets through the key actors in each country. In conclusion, policy change mechanisms coupled a complex mix of coercion, imitation and self-imposed limitations to the vision of the telecommunications sector which was shared by leading public and private actors in each national environment.

## THE INFORMATION SOCIETY AND TELECOMMUNICATIONS POLICY

Strong long-term links between telecommunications policy and measures aimed at promoting the Information Society constituted another general source of variation in Europe. Both strands became interwoven in the formulation of public policy during the transition from national monopolies to the free market during the 1990s. Special features of the European scene helped bring this about, such as the way in which the debate on technological innovation and its role in economic development was conducted (Kaitatzi-Whitlock 2000).

The Commission's discourse on the need to liberalise telecommunications markets in Europe, as a pre-condition for the Information Society was particularly important in this respect. The Bangemann Report (European Commission 1994a) marked a milestone in this debate. Another strand in this argument was the way Europe lagged behind the United States and Japan in technology. The Commission considered that the dead hand of telecommunications monopolies in Europe was one of the main reasons why the continent trailed behind its two major competitors and had made so little progress towards the Information Society. These ideas became the focal point for a network of European actors (basically business interests) committed to changing the regulatory framework and able to act at both national and European levels (Schneider, Dang-Nguyen and Werle 1994; Bartle 1999).

However, the Commission's discourse scarcely mentioned other factors such as the conversion of European public monopolies (whose transformation into international corporations occurred in tandem with market liberalisation). Nevertheless, one should remember that this conversion was carefully planned and vigorously defended by each national government for its respective telecommunications operator throughout the 1990s. Other points in the Commission's discourse on the Information Society were filled in by various action plans aimed at disseminating relevant technologies (European Commission 1994b, 1996). When the Commission drew up plans, it centred on policies for boosting productivity and supporting the development of applications and contents. By contrast, it did little to stimulate mass demand for these applications and services. In this respect, policies promoting universal services, the development of new infrastructure and intensive public training in the new digital culture were given short shrift (Soete 1999).

If one were to ask what the results were of using the relationship between the Information Society and telecommunications - policies at the nexus of the debate on new European institutions and policies for the sector - the answer would probably be very little. The debate proved largely opportunistic, even if it was not intended to be so. Its purpose was to overcome resistance by several national actors and to convince the general public that the changes in telecommunications policies and institutions were solely aimed at ensuring a better transition to the new Information Society. Unfortunately, other vital issues in these critical years relating to the Information Society were relegated in importance as a result.

The validity of the link made between the need to change the telecommunications framework in Europe and the development of the Information Society is not disputed here. Our purpose is simply to briefly summarise the argument used to justify some of the new telecommunications policies in Europe during the 1990s – a critical decade in the transition to a free market, as the Commission's priorities focused clearly on market liberalisation. The concentration on liberalisation meant that other measures took a back seat. Even though policies for introducing the Information Society formed part of the general discourse, their discussion was conspicuously absent in political debates. The Commission's discourse on the Information Society made very little impact during virtually the whole of the 1990s and focused almost exclusively on regional development and science and technology issues. Meanwhile, other countries around the world (including several in Europe) embarked upon ambitious initiatives to familiarise their populations with the challenges and opportunities of the Information Society (Kahin and Wilson 1997). The Commission's policy remained unchanged until the belated launch of the eEurope initiative at the end of 1999. It was only then that the Commission began to make serious efforts to address the issue (European Council and European Commission 2000).

Europe's failure to deploy more ambitious policies for promoting the Information Society during the 1990s is somewhat surprising, especially considering the Community's tradition of public intervention in all policy spheres (whether at a national level, Community level or combinations thereof). The issue provides an interesting analytical challenge. A possible explanation for this lack of policy may lie in the fact that the main actors in each country were essentially (and had been for decades) the public telecommunications operators and, in some cases, related industrial groups providing technological backing. These actors found themselves in totally new circumstances in the mid 1990s as they lost their role in setting public policy and were forced to change their priorities. Policies aimed at introducing the Information Society were pursued against a background of a policy network turbulence in which both public and private actors were redefining their roles. Those actors which had hitherto shown most interest in the subject now found they had their hands full with adapting to a new telecommunications market. The network of actors became increasingly differentiated during the decade, but it took time to digest these changes. Late in the decade, a more specialised policy network emerged which was centred on Information Society issues and capable of facing new policy challenges. Thus it was only with the dawning of the twenty-first century that a new set of both private and public actors found themselves in a position to press ahead with policies fostering the Information Society. Moreover, for this emerging network of actors, the issue of an Information Society was not an important part of the telecommunications debate at either national or Community levels. In this respect, the gap between actors, discourses and issues linking telecommunications policy and Information Society issues tended to widen as policy gradually took shape.

This sketched interpretation reveals that the roles played by the main actors

– national governments, the Commission, and operators – during the telecommunications liberalisation process was critical in deciding which policies were adopted. The concern of most of these traditional actors to influence the new rules of game during a period of profound institutional change effectively thrust other (arguably equally important) matters such as fostering the Information Society into the shade. The links between telecommunications policy and the discourse on the Information Society are a common thread running throughout the contributions in this volume. Each author takes different considerations into account, some focusing heavily on particular policies while others analyse general strategies. However, they all show the strong interrelationship between ideas on social change and policy decisions, epitomised by the rhetoric on the Information Society. However, these are not the only themes explored by the authors and it is for this reason that the book has been divided into two parts, depending on the main focus of each chapter. The first part covers telecommunications policies while the second examines policies for promoting the Information Society. A short summary follows below of the themes dealt with in each case, the main arguments made and the questions posed by the respective author(s).

## CONTRIBUTIONS IN THIS VOLUME

The first part of the volume begins with several chapters addressing the way European transformation of the sector evolved during the 1980s and 1990s. These are followed by chapters focusing on more specific cases and issues, introducing the national level in the analysis. Chapter 2, written by Volker Schneider, aims to provide a global analysis of the telecommunications sector over the last few decades. It discusses the behaviour of EU Member States detail during the transition process. Schneider's contribution begins by setting forth two large-scale technological trends which underlay changes in the industry. First, there was the growth of large multinational corporations with worldwide networks which used the air transport and communications methods emerging from the Second World War to operate its subsidiaries in a co-ordinated fashion. These organisations spurred demand for worldwide telecommunications services – demand which national monopolies found increasingly difficult to satisfy. Second, there were the technological advances in the industry occasioned by the union between computing and telecommunications (and with it the birth of packet switching). In this case, technological convergence led to plummeting costs and in the process removed some of the barriers to entry which helped maintain monopolies. Competitive pressures began to build in various sectors of the market as a result.

Schneider analyses the reasons for the institutional changes which began in the United States in the early 1980s and highlights the structuring of business interests and the institutional context which made regulatory changes much more likely. He also notes the mechanisms for disseminating new liberalising policies, particularly international bodies such as the OECD, GATT (later to become the WTO) and the European Community. The role of European institutions in defining a new policy for the sector was of key importance in fostering innovation in the Member States (particularly in those opposing change, for whatever reasons). Thus Schneider considers Europeanisation of telecommunications policy, both catalysed and oriented domestic changes. This policy not only exerted external pressure on national actors but also ensured that variations on the basic theme were limited, thanks to a common decision-making framework and an unequivocal commitment to a single market.

The opening of the European telecommunications market in 1998 marked a watershed given its implications for consumer choice and the disappearance of state monopolies in the sector. Nevertheless, the transition to a free market was highly complex and various features were carried over from the previous regime which were gradually altered over time. Martin Cave's chapter focuses on this context, analysing the main difficulties in introducing a truly European telecommunications market and detailing the national variations found. The specific regulations implemented in each country emanated from European directives but, as Cave indicates, showed significant variations which revealed the gap between Commission theory and state practice regarding liberalisation.

The first point Cave makes is the way the process of regulatory change influenced corporate expectations of investment opportunities. An evolving regulatory framework provides no guarantees and increases the degree of uncertainty in corporate decision making, thus favouring opportunistic behaviour. Cave analyses five key instruments used by the regulators which effectively hindered new companies in entering the new market. Ironically, the original purpose of these regulations was to stop unfair competition by the former monopoly operator. These instruments are: interconnection charges, the charge for rented lines, the cost allocation for universal service, the start date for commencing operations, and the regulation of prices charged by the dominant operator (which determined the prices which could be charged by new entrants to the market). A further twist to the story occurred when the New Regulatory Authorities (NRAs) took over control of these policy instruments from 1988 onwards with the advent of market liberalisation. In many cases, these new agents were semi-independent bodies created in parallel to the implementation of the Commission's framework for telecommunications liberalisation.

One of the biggest sources of national variation was the system for granting licences since both their allocation and use had historically varied considerably among the Member States. Nevertheless, the most significant aspect regarding the way national markets worked was the power granted NRAs to regulate prices, particularly inter-connection prices. The regulator's use of various methods allowed great influence to be exerted on specific markets and to encourage or hinder competition. For example, barriers could prevent new entrants from concentrating on the most profitable market segments. Cave also stresses that the Commission kept an eye on the progress of liberalisation through its annual reports but was relatively toothless when it came to forcing national governments to act in a particular way.

The Commission's heavy involvement in liberalising the European telecommunications market during the 1990s concealed the significant powers retained by Member States. The national variations analysed by Cave reveal that despite appearances to the contrary, the opening up of the sector to competition did not mean thoroughgoing Europeanisation. Rather, following Schneider's interpretation, the result has been a fundamental change in the way Member States have prosecuted their own policies regarding telecommunications and promotion of the Information Society. The new regulations designed by the European Community have been implemented by Member States but in a way which reflects national policy objectives. European national governments have retained control over many of the key regulatory instruments, the form taken by the regulatory body, and privatisation of the former state-owned monopolies. In this sense, it could be said that the lack of a European body regulating telecommunications has strengthened national autonomy in the field, limiting the Commission's ability to influence the future development of the industry.

Mark Thatcher's chapter analyses the influence of European institutions on the behaviour of Member States over the last few years, arguing that the latter have maintained considerable scope for manoeuvre during the liberalisation process. In this context, Thatcher distinguished three ways in which the EC had an impact on Member States: direct, indirect and legitimating. Each way influenced domestic policies in a different manner. Four countries (the United Kingdom, France, Germany and Italy) are analysed in assessing the ways in which this influence was felt. Thatcher coincides with Schneider in stating that there may have been other non-EC influences on national policies which the EC subsequently chose to express and legitimise.

Thatcher's review of the impact of EC regulation on liberalisation and competition from the viewpoint of the four nations begins in the early 1980s when state monopolies held sway and the Commission had just begun to make timid proposals for change. These proposals were hotly disputed by some Member States and the issue was take to the European Court of Justice. The

Commission's proposals in the 1990s were more open-ended and general, proposing complete liberalisation of services and infrastructure. The author argues that this liberalisation strategy helped national governments and operators pursuing similar aims and overcome serious internal opposition to reforms. The domestic reasons for overhauling institutions in the sector did not necessarily stem from the new regulatory ideas being put forward by the Commission. Their roots often lay in state decision-making concerns such as privatisation of publicly owned operators as a way of reducing the national debt or the opportunity of opening up international markets. Thatcher considers that national variations are important in this context, offsetting the EC's attempt to standardise the sector by issuing directives.

My chapter follows Thatcher's emphasis on nation-states by analysing Spain and Portugal, which both present fairly similar cases. The starting point for these Southern European countries embarking on liberalisation was quite different from that in other Member States. As mentioned earlier, Member States had accepted a European liberalisation policy during the early 1990s. Nevertheless, the least developed countries in Southern Europe initially had serious reservations. It was not that they disagreed with the final aims of this policy – it was simply that they were worried that telecommunications giants from more advanced countries would conquer their relatively backward markets and take up unassailable positions. Nevertheless, both countries changed their respective positions once liberalisation got under way, taking a very active role in the whole process. This change of attitude was undoubtedly a response to the accelerating institutional change in the sector identified by Schneider.

Although the transition to a market economy in Spain and Portugal seems very different at first sight, I argue that the approach to telecommunications policies in both nations was pretty similar. Indeed, one can speak of a 'Southern European' approach to regulatory reform in the telecommunications sector. It is true that the pace of liberalisation was different in both cases (Portugal took two years longer than Spain), as was the attitude to granting licenses (Spain took a much more active approach). However, despite these and other differences, the strategies followed by both countries and the final outcome (that is consolidation of national business consortia in the face of foreign competition) was very similar. These similarities undoubtedly have something to do with the cultural affinities in both countries and, in particular, with the fact that both Spain and Portugal found themselves in the throes of socio-economic modernisation during the 1990s which strengthened the state's hand when it came to policymaking.

The use of the whole range of policymaking instruments during transition to a market economy (and even after liberalisation) was what allowed Southern European countries to follow an interventionist approach for the first time in the telecommunications field. These strategies also clearly reveal the considerable scope for manoeuvre which EC initiatives gave European Member States in shaping their markets. This implied a tacit division of responsibilities at national and European levels during the transition to a free market. However, one should note that this national scope for manoeuvre was conditioned by EC Directives for securing a free market and which necessarily implied less public intervention in the telecommunications sector.

Johannes Bauer's chapter provides an in-depth study of the market model drawn up by EU institutions. Bauer details how the concept of the Information Society caught on in Europe from the mid 1990s onwards and inspired various strategies fostering innovation, regulatory changes and ICT development. Taking the entrenched values which inspired telecommunications policies in Europe for decades (with regard to the service model and as an economic and industrial policymaking tool), Bauer shows how changes were introduced from the 1970s onwards, gradually creating a new consensus on the need for competition operating in a free market. In this respect, the Commission took an ever greater role from the 1980s onwards in making proposals designed to open up EU national markets to competition - a policy which was intended to breathe new life into the industry. These strategies are then analysed after the demise of the large telecommunications monopolies in 1998. Bauer also reviews the new regulatory framework proposed by the Commission in 1999, particularly from the viewpoint of the its new normative values. With regard to universal service, he argues that things stand very much as they did before liberalisation.

Bauer asks why the EU has followed this market model and why public debate on these issues was conspicuously absent, with policy focusing heavily on business interests. In his view, this state of affairs mirrored a policy which stressed the overriding importance of a free market and which set out to minimise public intervention. Service improvements and price reductions in the 1990s seem to endorse that policy. However, Bauer points out that further deregulation will not necessarily benefit consumers in the future: the duplication of infrastructure, the fragmentation of networks, marketing costs and so on may destroy the gains made to date. He recalls that the obsession with deregulation was particularly evident in the Reagan and Thatcher administrations and influenced many other countries to take a similar course. Unfortunately, the persistence of such ideas reinforces prejudices against public intervention. For this author, this bias has blinded many to the limitations implicit in the telecommunications network-based markets.

Bauer also states that the notion of 'public interest' has almost disappeared from European debates on the new regulatory framework. In this context, the Information Society concept has been frequently presented as a justification for telecommunications policy, despite the vague way it is used to describe a ragbag of ideas for promoting ICT. It is precisely in order to discuss these broad issues that the second part of this book looks at the policies and initiatives aimed at promoting the Information Society. These policies can be found in Europe at all levels of government, from the local one to the European. However, it it has to be said that in many European countries such policies during most of the 1990s were generally poorly implemented and lacked political impetus.

The Internet is nowadays one of the main pillars in the development of the Information Society. Nevertheless, the policies designed to promote its use in Europe during the 1990s were both timid and unconvincing and were not directly linked to a telecommunications policy which then focused narrowly on the transition to a free market. Raymund Werle examines this paradox and introduces one of the most exciting fields linking technological innovation and telecommunications policies. The paradox presented by the author is of even greater importance: the building of computer networks, including the protocols used for Internet and the World Wide Web (TCP/IP) were both created in Europe. Nevertheless, it was the United States which took these ideas up and developed applications on a massive scale. Werle highlights the institutional hurdles and policy failures which stopped European politicians from seeing the Internet's potential for far too long. It was only with changes to the regulation of telecommunications throughout the 1990s that a window of opportunity opened for Europe in this field, giving rise to policies fostering the growth of the Internet.

World growth of the Internet during the 1990s was unplanned. No public policy or national strategy lay behind the phenomenon. Its unexpected growth was due to the fact that the network was decentralised and non-proprietary and that the hypertext philosophy (Berners-Lee 1999) facilitated connection between computers. However, the success of the Internet also owed something to fortune, with a series of almost 'accidental' decisions by the United States science establishment - such as the National Science Foundation - which facilitated its organisation and subsequent rapid growth.

How was it that serendipity failed in Europe? Werle argues that the type of telecommunications institutions which dominated in the Old Continent were both hierarchical and monopolistic. Accordingly, their view of the future of network computing was based on hierarchical systems rather than the open-ended solution provided by the Internet. National divisions presented an additional hurdle - each country vied with others in the EU in promoting its own interests rather than co-operating on a European scale. According to Werle, the possibilities of policy alternatives in Europe were therefore more limited than in the United States. In Europe, the public sector took a strong role in defining a connection standard within the Community and European institutions were committed to deciding on a given option. This contrasted with United States' institutions which had not made a strategic decision and took a much more passive role in the fight among private companies to extend their proprietary standards. Thus, when the Europeans realised that another standard was taking root, they had to backtrack and rethink their policies - something which did not occur in the United States.

Antonio Alabau's chapter introduces the policies promoting the Information Society and analyses the strategies and procedures developed by the Commission during the 1990s. In this context, regional policies, despite the range of regional government types in Europe, became of key importance in implementing Commission policy in this field (along with science and technology policy in general). This was because most of the funding instruments at the EC's disposal formed part of the Community's development funds, many of which were linked to regional development. Regions' identification of their respective needs and management of the funds they receive is very important in this context. The poorest regions get preferential treatment when it comes to allocating EC development funds. Alabau analyses the way in which European Regional Development Funds were used to promote the Information Society through particular programmes. He points out that the strategy began in the 1980s as part of the FEDER plan, with programmes such as STAR (1986) and TELEMATIQUE (1988), which were followed up in the 1990s with new initiatives like IRISI (later RISI). Strategic plans were drawn up and implemented to encourage regional actors to promote the Information Society in their own areas.

Another basic requirement for building the Information Society is the consolidation of new ICT companies. Innovative entrepreneurs are of signal importance in extending a new economy based on networks and innovation. There was considerable concern about Europe's capacity for innovation during the 1990s and this led to both the EU and other levels of government instituting new policies to address the issue. Measures aimed at strengthening links between business and science were particularly notable in this respect and helped the emergence of technologically innovative start-ups. In this context, Massimo Colombo and Marco Delmastro's chapter analyses the position of companies based on new technology in Europe.

Colombo and Delmastro's study is based on a survey of Italian entrepreneurs which highlighted significant differences between European companies, with features which distinguish businesses in Southern Europe from their counterparts in the rest of the EU. The new entrepreneurs involved in Internet-based activities were also different from those operating in other parts of the ICT sector. Internet entrepreneurs were younger and less well trained and had relatively little professional experience in comparison with those working in the industrial side of ICT. These findings led the authors to conclude that the policy measures promoting business activities in the industry need to take account of this diversity and focus on specific needs.

Colombo and Delmastro propose various measures to encourage the emergence of new entrepreneurs and help them consolidate their businesses. These proposals include indirect financial support, tax reductions and better regulation of the way scientific discoveries are used for commercial purposes. With regard to Internet-based companies, the authors note that there is no shortage of business initiatives in Europe - the real problem lies in the consolidation of these enterprises. In this respect, they argue that stimulation of B2B (Business to Business) and B2C (Business to Consumer) demand should be a policy priority (particularly with regard to local and national goods and services rather catering to world demand). This approach to public policies provides a better understanding of the big initiatives for promoting the Information Society in Europe at regional, national and EU levels. These measures are based on rapid extension of the Internet, fostering the network of ICT businesses as a way of creating employment and wealth.

While Commission initiatives made a modest contribution to the advancement of the Information Society since the 1980s, the process only began to really get underway in Member States in the mid 1990s. The belief that the public sector ought to take an active role in disseminating ICT took hold late in Europe and was partly a reaction to the lack of initiative shown by private companies. Big national initiatives first began in the mid 1990s; however, it was not until towards the end of the decade that promotion schemes became more widespread and sophisticated. The measures adopted by virtually all European countries included: collaboration programmes involving business and society at large; setting up co-ordination schemes between different branches of government with a view to enhancing the effectiveness of policies; and taking high profile political initiatives to promote the sector. Some of these measures showed national variations, reflecting institutional differences between countries. Nevertheless, there was a certain degree of convergence in policy style and the aims pursued.

David Sancho's chapter analyses this process and the policies carried out by four countries (the United Kingdom, Germany, France and Spain) for fostering the Information Society. His contribution also reviews the role of European institutions during the period as standard-bearers for the Information Society and in defining new policies for getting Europe's various levels of government involved in promotion initiatives. In this respect, Sancho's work complements Alabau's analysis. Sancho examines how European initiatives, particularly after the Prodi Commission's *e*Europe plan in 1999, prompted convergence in national plans and measures by indicating the main priorities and introducing a common yardstick for measuring the impact of ICT on the economy and society at large. However, EU institutions were not the only factor creating convergence. Sancho points to the considerable horizontal transfer of policies between countries in which ideas were freely copied from inside and outside Europe. An entirely new ambit for public policy, with its own policy network, was being created in Europe, for which there was no specific precedent. Perhaps this was why collective learning by governments and copying of measures adopted by other countries were so rapid. Indeed, in many cases these initiatives aimed at promoting the Information Society ran counter to traditional national approaches to policy formulation.

Sancho identifies another interesting source of variation within the Community framework. In this case there appears to be a certain correlation between the effort made by Member States to liberalise their respective telecommunications markets and the introduction of policies fostering the Information Society. Thus, countries which were quicker off the mark in making the transition to free competition were also those which were first to adopt policies for promoting the dissemination of IT. By contrast the foot-draggers on liberalisation also trailed behind when it came to creating an institutional framework for orchestrating government and social participation in the new policies. The two extremes in this case are the United Kingdom and Spain, with the former leading and the latter trailing the field.

The last chapter, written by Joan Subirats, turns from policy analysis to the discussion of a polity issue. It could be quite surprising to find a chapter like this in a sound policy-oriented volume, but the reason lies behind the nature of the Information Society policy debates. The chapter focuses on the form government could take in an Information Society. At the moment, the Internet revolution seems to have had little effect on politics, at least with regard to its most formal aspects, despite the general dissatisfaction with the lack of political participation found in modern democracies. Nevertheless, new opportunities are opening up, as the Internet becomes more universal. Clearly, this represents a window of opportunity to establish new polity goals, but this type of new developments seems to be unattractive to the political process. However, the question remains open: are Information Society developments limited only to deliver public policies in a more efficient way, or could they also influence the way decisions about public policies are made?

The chapter discusses some of the institutional polity changes possible in Europe with the help of ICT. The analysis starts from several innovative experiments to stimulate political participation at the local level, and explores its generalisation to broader levels. The author of this chapter considers that these initiatives should be taken in fostering wider participation by citizens in policy formulation and decision-making. In this respect, ICT might provide a way of extending public participation in politics which until now have been confined to the local level for reasons of physical proximity.

In Subirat's view, the political and institutional sphere in EU countries (particularly with regard to Community institutions) is ripe for innovation. He suggests initiatives which complement existing decision-making processes and employ a general system of direct voting. The aim would be to stimulate public participation in wide-ranging debates on key issues. Without doubt, Subirats chapter is far removed from the main themes in this book, focusing instead on a much wider issue in EU politics. In general, the other authors' contributions in this volume basically are empirically grounded policy oriented, analysing telecommunications regulation and the Information Society. However, Subirats' concern is how to use the instruments made available by the Information Society to transform the way government functions and policies are formulated. Although these ideas are purely exploratory, they represent an interesting reflection on the way in which advances towards the Information Society may improve standards of European democracy. Additionally, attracting more theoretical thinking to the field of policy analysis, where implementation is always a matter of high consideration, could be useful for two reasons. First, it could help more public policy-oriented readers to think about ways of polity innovation, and second, it could introduce more attention - having the case this chapter deals with as example - to the importance of polity objectives for policy annalists.

## FINAL REMARKS

Despite the wide range of themes dealt with by the contributions in this book, there are still many others which deserve attention in this field. However, the main questions concerning how regulation of the telecommunications sector underwent a transformation in Europe during the period are addressed and the main policies designed to encourage the emergence of the Information Society are also analysed. New questions are posed, opening up debate on the mechanisms underlying institutional change in the telecommunications industry and the way public policies are formulated in the EU's multi-level system of governance.

One can conclude by saying that the contributions in this volume shed different lights on the political process which has led Europe - both as a whole and at the level of individual nations - towards the Information Society since the 1980s. The remarkable changes which have taken place were fuelled by a complex interaction of technology, international developments, and policy which provided national actors with limited scope for manoeuvre yet which was wide enough to permit national variations. The architecture of EU institutions gave the whole process a unique stamp. One should also recognise that the process is far from over and that the future development of the telecommunications sector and the Information Society are difficult to discern.

One cannot say that there is a stable framework of actors and institutions or ideas and values which might suggest policy continuity in these sectors. On the contrary, after 15 years of rapid change, the only constant in Europe appears to be change itself. At the beginning of the twenty-first century, with respect to telecommunications, new regulatory institutions are becoming well-established and their policies are currently being drawn up or redefined; with respect to Information Society policies, new institutions and policy networks are still in formation. Thus, it becomes clear that the continual emergence of new actors and ideas in the sector means the issues regarding the shape the Information Society and the definition of electronic communications policy should take remain as open for the future as it was in the previous decades.

## REFERENCES


Bartle, Ian (1999), 'Transnational interests in the European Union: globalization and changing organization in telecommunications and electricity', *Journal of Common Market Studies*, **37** (3), 363–83.

Berners-Lee, Tim (1999), *Weaving the Web: The Original Design and Ultimate Destiny of the World Wide Web*, San Francisco: Harper.

Brock, Gerald W. (1994), *Telecommunications Policy for the Information Age: From Monopoly to Competition*, Cambridge, US: Harvard Business School Press.

Cortell, Andrew P. and Susan Peterson (1999), 'Altered states: explaining domestic institutional change', *British Journal of Political Science*, **29**, 177–203.

Davies, Andrew (1994), *Telecommunications and Politics*, London: Francis Pinter.

Dolowitz, David D. and David Marsh (1996), "Who learns what from whom? A review of the policy transfer literature', *Political Studies*, **44**, 343–57.

Dolowitz, David D. and David Marsh (2000), 'Learning from abroad: the role of policy transfer in contemporary policy-making', *Governance*, **13** (1), 5–24.

Eliassen, K. and M. Svojaag (1999), *Liberalising European Telecommunications*, London: Routledge.

European Commission (1987), *Towards a Dynamic European Economy – Green Paper on the Development of the Common Market for Telecommunications Services and Equipment*, Brussels, 30 June 1987, COM(87)290.

European Commission (1993), *Growth, Competitiveness, Employment. The Challenges and Ways Forward in the 21st Century*, Brussels, Commission of the European Communities (Delors White Paper).

European Commission (1994a), *Europe and the Global Information Society: Recommendations to the European Council and the European Commission*, Brussels, 26 May 1994 (Bangemann Report).

European Commission (1994b), *Action Plan on Europe's Way to the Information Society*, Brussels,19 July 1994, COM(94)347.

European Commission (1996), *Europe at the Forefront of the Global Information Society. A Rolling Action Plan*, Brussels.

European Commission (2000a), *Sixth Report on the Implementation of Telecommunications Regulatory Package*, Communication from the Commission to the European Parliament, the Council, the Economic and Social Committee and the

Committee of the Regions, Brussels, 7 December 2000, COM(2000)814.
European Commission (2000b), *The Results of the Public Consultation on the 1999 Communications Review and Orientation for the New Regulatory Framework*, Communication from the Commission, Brussels, 26 April 2000, COM(2000)239 final.
European Commission (2001), *Amended Proposal for a Directive of the European Parliament and of the Council on a Common Regulatory Framework for Electronic Communications Networks and Services*, Brussels, 4 July 2001, COM(2001)380.
European Council and European Commission (2000), *eEurope. Action plan. An Information Society for All*, Brussels, 14 June 2000.
Evans, Peter (1997), 'The eclipse of the state? Reflections on stateness in an era of globalization', *World Politics*, **50** (1), 62–87.
Evans, Mark and Jonathan Davies (1999), 'Understanding policy transfer: a multi-level, multi-disciplinary perspective', *Public Administration*, **77** (2), 361–85.
Fuchs, Gerhard (1994), 'Policy-making in a system of multi-level governance – the Commission of the European Community and the restructuring of the telecommunications sector', *Journal of European Public Policy*, **1** (2), 177–94.
Hills, J. (1986), *Deregulating Telecoms: Competition and Control in the United States, Japan and Britain*, London: Francis Printer.
Hulsink, Willem (1999), *Privatisation and Liberalisation in European Telecommunications*, London: Routledge.
Kahin, Brian and Ernest J. Wilson III (eds) (1997), *National Information Infrastructure Initiatives. Vision and Policy Design*, Cambridge, MA: MIT Press.
Kaitatzi-Whitlock, Sophia (2000), 'A "redundant information society" for the European Union?', *Telematics and Informatics*, **17**, 39–75.
Levi-Faur, David (1999), 'Governing Dutch telecommunications reform: state-business interactions in the transformation of national policy regimes to (European) embedded policy regimes', *Journal of European Public Policy*, **6** (1), 102–22.
Organisation for Economic Co-operation and Development (2001), *Communications Outlook. Information Society*, Paris: OECD.
Pierson, Paul (2000a), 'The limits of design: explaining institutional origins and change', *Governance*, **13** (4), 475–99.
Pierson, Paul (2000b), 'Increasing returns, path dependency, and the study of politics' *American Political Science Review*, **94** (2), 251–68.
Piazolo, Daniel (2001), 'Multilateral and European response to E-Commerce', *European Integration Online Papers* (EioP), 5 (4); http://eiop.or.at/eiop/texte/2001-004a.htm
Radaelli, Claudio M. (2000), 'Policy transfer in the European Union: institutional isomorphism as a source of legitimacy', *Governance*, **13** (1), 25–43.
Sandholtz, Wayne (1993), 'Institutions and collective action. The new telecommunications in Western Europe', *World Politics*, **45**, 242–70.
Sandholtz, Wayne (1998), 'The emergence of a supranational telecommunications regime', in W. Sandholtz and Alec Stone Sweet (eds), *European Integration and Supranational Governance*, Oxford: Oxford University Press.
Scharpf, Fritz (1997), *Games Real Actors Play. Actor-Centered Institutionalism in Policy Research*, Boulder, Co: Westview,
Scharpf, Fritz (1999), *Governing in Europe. Effective and Democratic?*, Oxford: Oxford University Press.
Scharpf, Fritz (2001), 'Notes toward a theory of multilevel governing in Europe', *Scandinavian Political Studies*, **24** (1), 1–26

Schmidt, Sussane K. (1998), 'Commission activism: subsuming telecommunications and electricity under European competition law', *Journal of European Public Policy*, **5** (1), 169–84.

Schneider, Volker, G. Dang-Nguyen and Raymund Werle (1994), 'Corporate actor networks in European policy-making: harmonizing telecommunications policy', *Journal of Common Market Studies*, **32** (4), 473–98.

Servaes, J. and J.-C. Burgelman (2000), 'In search of a European model for the information society', *Telematics and Informatics*, **17** (1–2), 1–7.

Soete, Luc (1999), 'Europe and the Emerging Information Society: the Need for Policy Innovation', in Bruno Lasserre (ed.), *Governing the Information Society. Collective Action and European Interest*, Rapport de la Fondation IDATE, Paris: Hermes.

Steinfeld, C. and J.L. Salvaggio (eds) (1989), *The Information Society*, London: LEA and Hove.

Vogel, S. (1996); *Freer Markets, More Rules; Regulatory Reform in Advanced Industrial Countries*, Ithaca: Cornell University Press.

Weiss, Linda (1998), *The Myth of the Powerless State*, Ithaca: Cornell University Press.

# PART I

# The Telecommunications Policy Framework in Europe

# 2. The institutional transformation of telecommunications between Europeanization and globalization

**Volker Schneider**

## KNOWLEDGE SOCIETY, GLOBALIZATION AND INSTITUTIONAL REFORM[1]

During the last three decades the telecommunications sector has changed in an unprecedented way. It has been transformed from a marginal area of economic activities into the core infrastructure of the coming information society. Major components of this new social formation, as outlined by the American sociologist Daniel Bell (1980) in the early 1980s, are rapid changes in technology, large investment in research and development, intensive use of information and communications technology, and the growth of knowledge-intensive businesses.

What are the key factors triggering and driving this deep structural transformation? In the centre of the process are new communications and information technologies, which help in the gaining, sharing and the application of knowledge. The major entities of this new infrastructure are computers and modern telecommunications networks, for instance the Internet. The main driving force is technical progress, and a closely related pressure is the globalization of the world's largest economies. During the last decade this has fuelled technical and economic competition, while further pushing the process of economic concentration. Unprecedented fusions and takeovers have taken place in these techno-economic areas.

An important precondition for this rapid transformation and the diffusion of information technologies was the removal of former institutional restrictions in the areas of international trade and domestic competition. In most advanced industrial countries telecommunications infrastructures have been liberalized and privatized. The most important institutional transformations were:

(1) Separation of postal and telecommunications activities to avoid cross-subsidization and unfair competition;

(2) Legal privatization and, in many cases, also the selling of the incumbent operator at the stock market;
(3) Introduction of competition at various levels: initially in the terminal domain, then in services and finally in a number of cases including networks; and
(4) Creation of – more or less – independent regulatory agencies for the regulation of the new markets.

The changes since the early 1980s at the various levels have been very dynamic. While they initially started with the most advanced and important industrial countries, the shock wave of liberalization and privatization is now also reaching the developing world. Recent data from the ITU (see Table 2.1) shows that in most countries in the world during the last two decades postal and telecommunications activities have been organizationally separated; in more than 80 countries the incumbent telecommunications provider has been totally or partially privatized. In roughly the same number of countries competition has been introduced, and new independent regulatory agencies have been created.

In order to understand the depth and significance of this institutional transformation we have to remind ourselves that in almost all countries control over communications infrastructures had been an exclusive prerogative of the state for centuries. Since the rise of the modern nation state in the sixteenth century in continental Europe, state administrations have played a key role in the provision of communication infrastructures and the control of communication contents. During these ages postal and telecommunications systems had been highly relevant for military purposes as well as for internal security. For a long time the provision of long-distance communication facilities was considered to be a major component in the 'logistics of power'

*Table 2.1 Trends in telecommunications reform among the 188 ITU member countries*

| Institutional structures | New institutional model<br>No. of countries | Old institutional model<br>No. of countries |
|---|---|---|
| Posts and telecommunications | Separated: 156 | Not separated: 32 |
| Liberalization of basic service | Liberalized: 38 | Not liberalized: 150 |
| Ownership status of incumbent operator | Fully and partially privatized: 83 | State-owned: 105 |
| Regulation and operation | Separated: 147 | Integrated: 41 |

*Source*: ITU/BDT Regulatory Data Base (Bogdan-Martin 1999).

of the state (Mann 1986). Especially in geopolitical contexts such as in continental Europe, where the system of nation states originally was based on the military control over increasingly large territories, control over communications was a key aspect of growing state power. In almost all countries the provision and operation of communications systems became legally protected state monopolies, and the respective administrations and public enterprises had been important components of the public sector.

However this institutional division of labour between state and society, which had been immutable for centuries, began to change radically just within the past two decades. Many observers in the social and political sciences understand this 'retreat of the state' (Strange 1996) as a manifestation of the process of globalization and its negative effects on the erosion of state sovereignty. The general argument in this discourse is rather simple: Competitive pressure forces nation states to compete using industrial, infrastructural and tax policies to attract investment by multinational companies. National autonomy to set proper political goals and priorities is increasingly shrinking in this context. The political left is dramatizing this decline in autonomy and is suddenly discovering the nation state, 'the coldest of all monsters' (Nietzsche), as the last fortress against the unleashed and terrorizing world market, whereas neo-liberal economists are happy with this development, leading to more and broader economic freedom. System competition would reverse the hypertrophy of the public sector in advanced industrialized countries, that is to break up the 'tyranny of the status quo'.

As the World Bank stated in its Development Report of the Year 1997, the public sector in most countries expanded considerably after World War II. The size of the public sector doubled in just three and a half decades between 1960 and 1995 – when measuring public expenditures as a proportion of gross domestic product. A large part of this expansion, however, was due to welfare transfers and subsidies. Interestingly though, the growth of public expenditures has slowed down or even been reversed during the last ten years. The current worldwide initiatives to reform the public sector and to redimensionalize the state are thus largely seen as necessary adaptations to cope with these new challenges. Virtually all of the industrialized countries, as well as many those in the developing world, have launched some kind of reform or restructuring programme in their public sectors.

## GLOBALIZATION AND THE COMMUNICATIONS REVOLUTION

There are versions of the globalization story, too, in which the direction of causality is working in the opposite direction. Changes in telecommunications combined with informatization and institutional reform in this sector can also be seen as one of the major sources of globalization. During the past ten years, abundant definitions of globalization have been developed. In worldwide market integration the concept's core seems to consist of all factors of production and all sequences of a firm's value chain. The most important indicators for globalization are foreign investments, international trade and capital flows. Since the 1960s international market transactions have been increasingly facilitated by international trade liberalization through various GATT negotiations, culminating in the institutionalization of the agreements in the new WTO. In addition, since the 1980s many countries have significantly reduced or even completely abandoned international capital controls.

Some observers, however, perceive technological progress in transportation, information processing and telecommunication as the real driving force behind globalization. The ability to collect, analyse and transmit information, and to coordinate economic activities on a global scale has increased extraordinarily, while the costs of doing so have fallen dramatically (Lipsey 1997). Information and communication technologies enable multinational firms to slice up their value chain on a global scale (Krugman 1995), and the sequences of the production process can be outsourced or relocated according to a global optimization scheme. The enhanced coordination and monitoring capabilities made possible by the new information and communication technologies are fundamentally transforming the structure of inter- and intra-firm transactions (Schneider 1994). An increasing number of mega firms now operate under a global perspective and organize their development, production and distribution activities in one single 'global playing field'. A stratum of firms becomes larger and larger in size and veritably global in the scope of their operations. The turnover of the biggest companies reaches dizzying heights, even surpassing the GNP of an increasing number of nations.

As historical studies have shown, the organizational growth of multinational corporations is largely based on the growth of global transport and telecommunications networks. Just as industrial revolution and societal modernization are unthinkable without the railway, highways, telegraphy and telephony (Mayntz 1988: 234), today's global firms could not even be imaginable without the turbo jet, trans-oceanic cables, communication satellites, and international computer networks (Chandler 1986; Mulgan 1991). In this perspective the current globalization process is a long-term continuation of the internationalization process which started in the late nineteenth century and which was interrupted by the inter-war period. Between the 1920s and World War II, waves of nationalism, growing tariff barriers and spreading webs of cartels led to a significant drag in economic internationalization. Most of the existing multinational industries moved towards multi-domestic patterns of multinational companies, before becoming federations of largely autonomous national subsidiaries (Porter 1987).

A new wave was reached by growth in foreign direct investment. This started in the 1950s and accelerated still further in the 1970s. The earlier phase of this new internationalization boom was mainly driven by the first multinational corporations of American origin. Since the mid-1970s, European multinationals have also been very involved in the globalization process with the Japanese joining somewhat later. During the 1980s the United States lost its hegemonic position, only to regain it during the 1990s. In this new phase, the traditional pattern of the vertically integrated firm gave way to divisionalized forms with more loosely organized integration. This transformation was strongly influenced by strategies of product differentiation (Chandler 1990).

Quite contrary to the predictions of earlier market power theories, the new drive towards globalization turned into an intense global competition. Increasing market pressure induced multinationals to exploit the division of labour among more geographically dispersed units. Current internationalization processes do not imply only backward and forward expansion, but the globalization of all elements of a firm's value chain. Even research and development, and public relations are attaining an increasingly global touch.

The emergence of veritable 'global corporations' would be unthinkable without the communications revolution of the 1950s and 1960s, which generated international telephony, commercial jet travel, satellite communications and international computer networks (Chandler 1986). Also the relationship between multinational growth and the boom in air traffic is also of great interest (Barnet and Müller 1974). During the 1960s and 1970s, the air traffic system grew dramatically not only in scope but also in safety and reliability (La Porte 1988). Increasingly reliable and extended air traffic fostered business globalization by serving as a speedy and reliable logistical link in the transportation chain. The dramatic growth of air traffic is an indicator of this development. In addition to the movement of goods it also enables a tighter control over foreign business through higher personal contact (Chandler 1986).

The most important forms of international business communications in the 1960s and 1970s were the telephone and the teletypewriter, also known as telex. Although telephony had existed since the late nineteenth century and telex since the 1930s, the international diffusion of both systems did not become significant until the postwar period. The transatlantic telephone cables stimulated growth of international telephony in the 1950s and even more by satellite technology in the 1960s. Both technologies increased the speed and reliability of international information exchange. The role of the telex in telecommunications development is often greatly underestimated. Until the 1980s however, it was, besides telegraphy, one of the most important instruments for communications in international business. Even in the most advanced industrial countries, the growth of the telex did not reach its peak until the mid to late 1980s. Only within the last decade has the telex been replaced by computer networks and other types of corporate telecommunications networks. One of the first international computer links was set up via telex lines in 1963 when Honeywell used a telex terminal in Britain to control a computer in a plant in Massachusetts (Chandler 1986: 152).

The growth of computer networks during the 1970s was mainly based on leased telex and telegraph lines. During the same period, some global firms established their own private telecommunication systems. They were originally based on leased circuits from national telecommunications operators, but now such private networks can involve privately owned satellite systems.

Multinational corporations interested in creating their own world communication systems were important domestic social forces in the international liberalization of telecommunications (Schiller 1982). The setting up of private microwave links in the 1970s by the American firm MCI is generally seen as the key event in the eroding of the traditional telecommunications monopoly in the United States, leading finally to the break-up of the Bell system (Galambos 1988). After liberalization in the United States, similar changes occurred in many industrialized countries, which resulted in the abolishing of the major constraints for establishing private communications systems. Since then, corporate networks have grown dramatically in scope and scale (Irwin and Niman 1989; Hagström 1992; Schneider 1994). Corporate networks make the orchestration and synchronization of a firm's activity profile possible on a global scale. Development, design, manufacturing and distribution may be internationally scattered but technically integrated into one single control structure. By interfacing with global transportation systems, production processes of multinational corporations become 'geographically blind' (Irwin and Merenda 1986). The global firm may indeed operate in a global village. Modules manufactured in different places in the world, interfaced by global transport logistics and coordinated via telecommunications networks may assemble a watch, a car, a computer and even a suite. The combination of globally scattered production systems and global technical infrastructures creates 'global industrial system constellations' as predicted by Perlmutter (1972) in the early 1970s.

## INSTITUTIONAL REFORM AS TRANSNATIONAL POLICY DIFFUSION

In a techno-economical perspective one could say that institutional reform in the area of telecommunications was a necessary adaptation to globalization.

Such a functionalist explanation, however, would be incomplete if no mechanism was provided by which these needs for adjustments actually get transmitted and fulfilled. Since privatization and liberalization measures are purposeful political efforts towards institutional reform that are processed by complex actor constellations in national and international institutional settings, a more convincing explanation has to reconstruct this restructuring process from an actor-centred and institutionalist view (Scharpf 1997). Under such a perspective, the transformation and diffusion process is driven by social and political actors with specific goals, resources, and varying institutional positions. Such a conceptual perspective takes into account that national political systems, based on their specific institutional structures and actor constellations, vary considerably in their adaptive capacity to new contexts and structural constraints. In addition, political and economic interdependencies between the different national systems also create a number of links by which national policies and problem solutions get transmitted and affect each other.

In the following sections I will show how the international transformation process of national telecommunications systems with similarities in outcomes and differences in timing can be explained under a perspective of political science. It is an attempt to go beyond a functionalist account of this restructuring process, that is to show that institutional reforms are indeed related to pressures emerging from economic and technological globalization processes, which are transmitted by complex actor constellations operating within specific institutional opportunities and constraints. One possible mode of explanation is to relate the diverse changes to 'ideological' transformations. Indeed, during the late 1980s there was a deluge of literature relating the different sectoral reforms and changing power relations between dominant social groups in the United States, the United Kingdom, and Germany, expressed through the hegemony of specific anti-statist ideologies. In this respect, the institutional shift was identified with the triumph of neo-conservatism and neo-liberalism manifested by electoral turnovers during that time by the success of Reagan in the United States, Thatcher in Great Britain, and Kohl in Germany (Morgan and Webber 1986; Webber 1986; Lehmbruch et al. 1988).

Political and ideological variables have indeed been supportive of a general cutback of the state in these countries. However, this was not the major factor explaining this significant transformation. Deregulation in the United States was not merely a 'neo-conservative' or 'neo-liberal' idea. In fact it had much broader support, and was already gaining prominence even amongst democrats during the Carter era (Derthick and Quirk 1985). In other countries such as Australia and New Zealand, it can be shown that decisive reform steps also have been undertaken by Labour governments (Hills 1989). Even in

France the alternation between 'left' and 'right' governments has shown that there were no essential differences between socialist and conservative governments in this specific sectoral restructuring. In Germany the Social Democrats strongly supported the anti-reform alliance up to the mid 1990s. However this was more due to general partisan opposition behaviour in the German party system rather to ideological predispositions. If German social democrats had shared governmental responsibility at that time, they would have supported the various reform measures, too.

In my basic explanatory scheme, which I have used in a larger study (Schneider 2001a, 2001b), I will show that a number of forces and structural constraints at the transnational and at the European level – largely independent of political ideologies and political systems – were pushing all countries towards convergent institutional evolution in telecommunications:

- An important factor was the American promotion of liberalization via its trade policy and related agenda building in relevant intergovernmental organizations like the OECD (Cowhey 1989). Also supportive in this respect was the domestic alliance building of the various national affiliates of United States multinationals in Europe (Schiller 1982).
- Another force was Europeanization in telecommunications, that is the European Commission's decisions to promote the internal market goals and to develop various EU research and development programmes in this sector and several pro-competitive interventions of the European Court of Justice (Sandholtz and Zysman 1989; Schneider and Werle 1990).

A more convincing explanation is to reconstruct the overall reform process as a kind of policy chain reaction which operates in a global context. In such a perspective the major institutional transformations were ultimately triggered by global economic and technical changes being transmitted and reinforced by international organizations and other channels of policy diffusion. A core thesis developed here is that the reform policies in the most important industrial countries (Japan, the United Kingdom, Germany, France and Italy) ultimately were the effects of a global 'outbreak' which actually started by institutional changes in North American telecommunications during the 1970s and early 1980s.[2] This institutional reform then spread to several other countries by way of 'shock waves'. International organizations and trade regimes such as the OECD and GATT, and, above all, the European Commission, then played the role of 'transmitters' and 'amplifiers' in this diffusion process.

Compared to competing explanations of increasing international privatization and liberalization by diffusionist approaches (Ikenberry 1990; Vogel 1996) my *dynamic transformation* model has some essential differences. Major shortages in the approaches mentioned above are that, (1) the inter- and supranational level of politics is largely absent, and (2) diffusion is conceived as a rather continuous and 'flat' process. It is more plausible to reconstruct the overall transformation as a *dynamic* and *multilevel* process, in which pressures towards structural adaptation not only work between and through nation states, but also via inter- and supranational organizations creating hierarchical mechanisms of policy transfer beyond the nation State (Schneider 2001a).

A further aspect is that the pressures to adapt are not constant during the whole process, but increase over time by a positive feedback loop: the more countries get liberalized the stronger becomes the pressure to break up remaining monopolies. In the end the pressures and strains became so strong that even countries with extreme institutional rigidities and low governmental actions capacities were forced to adapt to the new model of liberalized markets and privatized enterprises.

In this perspective, the overall transformation was started by institutional erosion in the United States during the 1970s, which, after passing the threshold of 'criticality', grew in a self-stimulating manner like an avalanche. That this happened at this particular time and place is no coincidence but seems to be explained by the fact that during that time, the United States were technologically more advanced in this sector than other countries; had the largest telecommunications market covering about 2/3 of all telephones in the world; were the home base of most of the multinational corporations at that time; and, last but not least, the foregoing institutional structures could more easily erode or break up in this specific form of political system.

Whereas the first three factors largely stress general structural conditions and actor constellations, the last factor points to an institutional facet of the American telecommunications system which is almost unique in the world: an important reason for an early institutional erosion was that the sectoral structures in the United States were less deeply entrenched than elsewhere. In Europe and Japan, where telecommunication systems had been run as conventional publicly administrated bodies, institutional characteristics generally had been laid down in statutory laws or even within constitutions. But in the United States the dominant operator was a private firm, which was only indirectly controlled by the state. The Communications Law of 1934 delegated much of the legal framework to an independent regulatory agency, the Federal Communications Commission (FCC). In Germany, in contrast, the major aspects of the institutional structure have been determined at the constitutional level, based on a legal tradition dating back to the mid-nineteenth century.

The varying depth of the institutional entrenchment of sectoral governance structures (by constitution, by statutory law or by regulations) thus implies different degrees of adaptability and developmental flexibility (North 1990). Constitutional entrenchment clearly offered the best protection against change to institutions, although this, of course, also depends on the respective procedural rules for the modification of constitutional provisions. The legal systems in which change can occur most easily are those in which mere conventional statutory legislation is required for a given institutional change. Clearly the American system fits this category, since a regulatory agency or a court reviewing a given regulatory rule may change large parts of institutional arrangements in telecommunications unilaterally. In this case the respective policy sub-system essentially has only one 'veto player' (Tsebelis 1995). As the Bell system had the legal form of a private corporation and its monopolistic position was only protected by regulations, the institutional status could be changed more easily than in the other five cases that are studied here. In this context a powerful alliance between the computer industry and many multinational corporations, conditioned by a political decision structure, where very few actors (the FCC and courts) could make far-reaching decisions on the institutional development of the American telecommunications system, unequivocally supported the great institutional transformation.

If one tries to generalize these observations, the complete set of variables explaining different capacities for institutional transformation at the domestic level are therefore:

(1) The interest structure (essentially the interest positions of the major political actors for or against institutional changes, weighted with their power resources).
(2) The degree of institutional entrenchment (measured by the required 'transformation energy', or the effort to transform a given state, the *status quo*).
(3) The collective action capacity implied by the collective decision-making system determining and enacting these changes (roughly measured by the number of 'veto players' in this policy subsystem).

Among the six most important industrial countries, which so far have been mentioned (United States, the United Kingdom, Japan, Germany, France and Italy), the United States appeared to combine the most favourable conditions for institutional change, as shown in Table 2.2. The United States displayed a strongly reform-prone interest structure (dominantly based on corporate business), the lowest degree of collective institutional entrenchment, and the highest degree of action capacity in this sector. It is thus no coincidence that the earliest transformations occurred in the United States, initially by the way

*Table 2.2 Differential probability toward institutional change*

| Probability | Interest structure | Institutional entrenchment | Collective action capacity | External pressure | Cases / countries |
|---|---|---|---|---|---|
| High | Reform prone | Weak | High | Low | US |
| | Reform prone | Medium | High | Medium | UK, Japan |
| | Status quo prone | Medium | High | High | France |
| | Moderately reform prone | High | Medium | High | Germany |
| Low | Status quo prone | Medium | Weak | Extremely high | Italy |

of incremental institutional erosion and, finally, culminating in the famous AT&T divestiture (Coll 1986).

However in an increasingly interdependent and competitive world economy, the first step towards liberalization has serious ramifications. A move towards institutional reform in one country increases the pressure on other countries to follow this path. Seen from a trade perspective, liberalization in one country without similar efforts in all others, leads to critical competitive disadvantages. The 'first mover' in deregulation is strongly motivated to export liberalization policies to other countries - by traditional economic diplomacy or by transnational alliances with domestic groups in other states. A similar logic works in an industrial policy perspective, where regulations are seen as a competitive burden for the domestic industry if they are not internationalized. Both forms of interdependence create 'chain reactions' or 'bandwagon effects', based on self-stimulating feedback toward global deregulation and liberalization.

The 'first move' in the United States amplified the technological pressures towards institutional change in Europe. AT&T's divestiture not only opened the North American telecommunication system for new competitors but also liberated AT&T from old restrictions. Deregulation enabled it to move outside its established areas, that is into the computer business and to foreign countries. This triggered the formation of complex policy alliances. On the one hand, the United States trade administration established negotiations (through bilateral talks as well as through multilateral bargaining within the OECD and the GATT) with the highly regulated European countries in order to create fair trade conditions. On the other hand, some foreign subsidiaries of North American multinationals asked for liberalization especially in the

United Kingdom, Germany and France by generally supporting liberalizers and deregulators in Europe.

From this active international agenda setting (the push path) we can distinguish a passive form of international policy diffusion. This is based on a pull mechanism triggered by major changes in how the situation is perceived and socially constructed. In this respect a major perceptional shift can be identified during the early 1990s. After crossing a certain threshold, the global spread of liberalization and privatization, public monopolies and government-administered bodies no longer were regarded as protective shields. In fact, public status was increasingly conceived as a severe obstacle to flexible adaptation in a more and more competitive environment. A further important facet of this development process is that the pull mechanism is also operating in a self-stimulating way. The larger the privatized area of telecommunications operators becomes, that is the more an organizational ecology is populated by privatized telecommunications companies, the stronger are the pressures for privatization on the remaining public corporations or administrations. This is a kind of positive feedback known in economics since decades, which gained popularity in recent economic analysis under the notion of 'path dependency' (Arthur 1990).

This dynamic interpretation means that the 'winds of change' of the 1980s were transformed into hurricanes in the 1990s, which blew away the old order in telecommunications. The transformation process consisted in a combination of domestic interests in political reform, external pressures to reform, as well as increasing incentives towards adaptation. The more countries joined the liberalization path, the greater was the adaptation pressure for others.

## EUROPEAN POLICY MAKING

In addition to this horizontal diffusion picture, there is also an important vertical transmission channel, which makes an important difference in the global adaptation process. This effect operates through various mechanisms of supranational integration within the EU in the area of telecommunications policy.[3] Key factors in this process are the Europeanization of industrial and competition policies on the one hand, and the role of European competition law on the other.

As we have seen, the institutional transformation in some European countries – particularly in Germany and France – were influenced by United States efforts to strive for reciprocity in international trade and to open domestic markets in this sector. International institutions and organizations such as the OECD and the GATT have been used as leverage instruments for this purpose since the early 1980s. In a first phase, however, these efforts had not been very effective. The chances for a European transformation only improved when the European Commission and the European Court of Justice joined the reform alliance. The Commission entered the sector in the mid 1980s when it began to dramatize the changes in the United States and Japan. Subsequently it became an important corporate actor in this policy area through the mobilization of specific policy resources. In contrast to international organizations like the OECD, EU telecommunications policy did not only follow the preferences of the majority of its member states, but also the self-interest of its supranational institutions such as the Commission and the Court of Justice. Based on some specific policy resources, both institutions give sufficient relative autonomy to produce compliance, even in dissenting member states.[4]

In a global perspective, the changes in the United States and subsequent transformations in the United Kingdom and Japan had the effect of mobilizing the European Commission to anticipate the adaptation pressures of the coming years. The European Commission's main arguments were that European industry would lose industrial ground if their member governments were to wait too long with their necessary institutional adaptations. From the mid 1980s onwards, the Commission cultivated the view that Europe would become an industrial colony of United States and Japan if it did not join the liberalization forces to get more competitive structures.

In keeping with this strategy the European Commission entered into a kind of paradoxical 'political alliance' with the United States, supporting American requests for deregulation and liberalization, with the long-term goal of improving the European industry's competitiveness. Essentially, the European Commission promoted institutional adaptation through a strategy that combined elements of 'neo-liberalism' with 'neo-mercantilism'. The core of the strategy was a state-led adaptation of industrial sectors through the introduction of competition (Schneider and Werle 1990). The implementation of this strategy meant, on the one hand, to support the European computer and telecommunications industry by massive research and development programmes (for example ESPRIT and RACE) and, on the other hand, to promote a number of liberalization measures. The blueprint of this combined approach was published as the telecommunications Green Paper in 1987.

This strategy mix was quite successful. The promotion of liberalization was supported by a number of European Court of Justice decisions that essentially extended the principle of competition into the realm of former public monopolies and publicly administered bodies. During the early years of liberalization, the state monopolist telecommunication administrations tried to defend their status quo. However, over time they gradually changed their preferences. Due to the challenge from open competition, they increasingly considered their public status as a competitive disadvantage and tried to change their institutional structure into a private law company.

The forces unleashed by the liberalization and privatization processes in some key industrial countries (the United States, the United Kingdom and Japan), and the growing globalization of telecommunications was feeding back on telecommunications sectors at the European and the domestic levels. A key event was the decision of governments to introduce full competition in traditional telephony. In the summer of 1993, the European Council of Ministers agreed that national governments were obliged to allow competition in conventional telephony from 1998 onwards, with the exception of four less developed Member States.

There is no doubt that this move was very much influenced by the big European telecommunication operators, such as the Franco-German cooperation or the British alliance with a big American telecommunication company, who entered into international alliances in order to become global players. In the specific Franco-German attempt, which later failed, regulators in the United States as well as in Europe were linking the authorization of this cooperation to an acceleration of domestic liberalization (Schneider and Vedel 1999). When the Franco-German alliance under the code name Atlas (later Phoenix and Global One) was announced in 1993, the *Financial Times* commented: 'There is widespread concern that a Franco-German link-up before 1998, bringing together the world's second and third-largest operators, will "sew up" much of the European market in advance of 1998' (quoted in Schneider and Vedel 1999).

Thus in only one decade, telecommunications policy at the EU level has transformed from a non-issue to a central area of European Commission competition and industrial policy. From the first Council directive on mutual recognition of terminal equipment to the 1995 and 1996 directives liberalizing even networks and infrastructures, the EU decisions were not just good intentions or symbolic policy decisions, but resulted in deep structural transformations in all the member countries. An implementation report in 2000 concluded that harmonization results in telecommunications policy among member countries were 'very good' and that only minor variations existed in the transposition and final implementation of the various liberalization and harmonization directives (European Commission 2000).

This reform process resulted in a relatively high institutional convergence. Different horizontal pull and push forces of policy diffusion have been amplified by supranational forces and vertical relations, forcing institutional changes in countries that generally would not support such changes, or did not have the capacity to enforce such reform efforts. An interesting example in this case is Italy, where institutional change would have been unthinkable without pressure from Brussels. Italy only reluctantly complied with EU requirements. In the Italian political system, the dominance of status quo-oriented interests and the fragmented political decision structure created too many obstacles for a swift structural adaptation. Major inertia could only be overcome through pressures from Brussels. In effect, Europeanization prompted the government to realize that it had no choice but to change its policy strategies (Schneider 2001b).

Supranational pressures from the EU also supported and amplified the process of structural reform in Germany and France. In both countries, the European Commission actually entered into transnational alliances with domestic reformers; and in both countries, decisions of the European Court of Justice significantly improved the position of liberalizers, despite the straddling goals of their governments in the Council (Schneider, Dang-Nguyen and Werle, 1994). In the end, institutional changes in all EU member countries led to a far-ranging convergence in telecommunications industry structures. A recent EU implementation report shows that the convergence to liberalized infrastructures and harmonized regulations within the EU is almost complete. While there are still countries which did not succeed in the implementation of some of the recent directives, these seem merely to be the result of transient problems on a convergence process towards the new institutional model of competitive, internationally open markets, and private operators.

## CONCLUSION

It should be emphasized that this transformation is not restricted to a few core countries of the EU, but it has also gained momentum on a global scale. This is indeed remarkable. As shown by recent publications of the OECD (1999) and ITU (1999), this general trend of convergence exists in both advanced industrial countries as well as in the developing world, and not only within the three selected cases listed here. Further trade liberalization within the WTO and the domestic lobbying of multinational companies for infra-structural reform has transmitted the reform waves to the developing countries.

However institutional convergence does not mean homogenization. The introduction of competition, elimination of market barriers and privatization of former government administrated bodies does not mean that identical market structures will emerge in all countries. The structural outcome not only depends on the opportunity space that is created by the different reform processes at the European and national levels, but also on the way in which these new opportunities will be exploited by different national economic actors. The core message of this study, therefore, is not that globalization will generally lead to structural convergence. The analysis demonstrates rather that, under a specific set of conditions, global pressures to adaptations are becoming so strong that only a small spectrum of the structural pattern can survive in this competitive environment. Here political and economic analysis could borrow from evolution theory, in particular from ecological and macro-evolutionary concepts (Schneider and Werle 1998; Schneider 2000). In this respect the pressure to adapt is not simply a function of the degree of 'misfit', that is differences between the structure of an evolutionary unit struggling to survive in a given context (organism, technical artifact, social institution, and so on) and the relevant structures of its environment. As ecological approaches show, pressures to adapt can greatly vary according to the intensity of selection. In a particular environment, a persisting 'misfit' may be punished by extinction. In other environments, greater variation in structure might be possible. Global competition in the telecommunications sector was interpreted as pressures towards structural adaptation, which during the 1990s attained such intensity that virtually all countries have become forced to transform their sectors towards privatization and liberalization. Europeanization in this context did not create these pressures, but it certainly provided a certain kind of 'catalytic' transmission of these constraints in order to produce favourable conditions for European industry to survive in the context of increasing global competition.

## NOTES

1. I am grateful for linguistic support and research assistance by Ari Pattanayak.
2. For the analysis of telecommunications policy development in these countries see Cawson et al. (1990); Coll (1986); Grande and Schneider (1991); Grande (1989 and 1994); Hills (1986); Hulsink (1999); Humphreys (1990 and 1992); Lehmbruch et al. (1988); Morgan and Webber (1986); Schmidt (1991, 1996 and 1997); Schneider (1997 and 2001a); Schneider and Vedel (1999); Schneider and Werle (1991); Thatcher (1999); Vogel (1996); Webber (1986); and Werle (1990 and 1999).
3. For the history and political analysis of EU telecommunications policy see Schneider and Werle (1990), Bauer (1993), Schneider, Nguyen, and Werle (1994), Esser and Noppe (1996), Schneider and Vedel (1999) and Thatcher (1999).
4. Only recently the autonomous role of these actors in the process of European integration has gained more attention in the literature (Schmidt 1997).

## REFERENCES

Arthur, Brian (1990), 'Positive feedbacks in the economy', *Scientific American*, **262**, 92–9.

Barnet, Richard J. and Ronald E. Müller (1974), *Global Reach. The Power of the Multinational Corporations*, New York: Simon & Schuster.

Bauer, Johannes M. (1993), 'Telecommunications in post-1992 Europe', *International Review of Comparative Public Policy,* **5**, 109–35.

Bell, Daniel (1980), 'The Social Framework of the Information Society', in Michael L. Dertouzos and Joel Moses (eds), *The Computer Age: A Twenty-Year View*, Cambridge, MA: MIT, pp. 163–211.

Bogdan-Martin, Doreen (1999), 'Global Telecoms Reforms and BDT Sector Reforms Initiatives', Presentation at Workshop on Telecommunication Reform in Gaborone, Botswana, 3-5 May 1999.

Cawson, Alan, Peter Holmes, Webber Douglas, Kevin Morgan and Anne Stevens (eds) (1990), *Hostile Brothers*, Oxford: Clarendon Press.

Chandler, Alfred D. (1986), 'Die Entwicklung des Zeitgenössischen Globalen Wettbewerbs', in M.E. Porter (ed.), *Globaler Wettbewerb. Strategien der neuen Internationalisierung*, Wiesbaden: Gabler, pp. 467–514.

Chandler, Alfred (1990), *Scale and Scope. The Dynamics of Industrial Capitalism*, Cambridge, MA: Harvard University Press.

Coll, Steve (1986), *The Deal of the Century. The Break up of AT&T*, New York: Atheneum.

Cowhey, Peter F. (1989), 'Telecommunications and Foreign Economic Policy', in Paula R. Newberg (ed.), *New Directions in Telecommunications Policy*, London: Duke University Press, pp. 187–230.

Derthick, Martha and Paul J. Quirk (eds) (1985), *The Politics of Deregulation*, Washington, DC: The Brookings Institution.

Esser, Josef and Roland Noppe (1996), 'Private muddling through as a political programme? The role of the European Commission in the telecommunications sector in the 1980s', *West European Politics*, **19**, 547–62.

European Commission (2000), *Sixth Report on the Implementation of the Telecommunications Regulatory Package*, Communication from the Commission to the European Parliament, the Council, the Economic and Social Committee and the Committee of the Regions, Brussels, Commission of the European Communities, Brussels, 7 December 2000, COM(2000) 814.

Galambos, Louis (1988), 'Looking for the boundaries of technological determinism: a brief history of the U.S. telephone system', in R. Mayntz and T.P. Hughes (eds), *The Development of Large Technical Systems*, Frankfurt: Campus, pp. 135–54.

Grande, Edgar (1989), *Vom Monopol zum Wettbewerb? Die neokonservative Reform der Telekommunikation in Großbritannien und der Bundesrepublik Deutschland*, Wiesbaden: Deutscher Universitäts-Verlag.

Grande, Edgar (1994), 'The new role of the state in telecommunications: an international comparison', *West European Politics*, **17**, 138–57.

Grande, Edgar and Volker Schneider (1991), 'Reformstrategien und staatliche Handlungskapazitäten. Eine vergleichende Analyse institutionellen Wandels in der Telekommunikation in Westeuropa', *Politische Vierteljahresschrift*, **32**, 452–78.

Hagström, Peter (1992), 'Inside the "Wired" MNC', in C. Antonelli (ed.), *The Economics of Information Networks*, Amsterdam: North-Holland, pp.325-40.

Hills, Jill (1986), *Deregulating Telecoms: competition and control in the United States, Japan and Britain*, London: Pinter.

Hills, Jill (1989), 'Neo-conservative regimes and convergence in telecommunications policy', *European Journal of Political Research*, **17**, 95–113.

Hulsink, Willem (1999), *Privatisation and liberalisation in European telecommunications: comparing Britain, the Netherlands and France*, London: Routledge.

Humphreys, Peter (1990), 'The political economy of telecommunications in France: a case study of "telematics"', in K. Dyson and P. Humphreys (eds), *The Political Economy of Communications. International and European Dimensions*, London:

Routledge, pp. 198–228.

Humphreys, Peter (1992), 'The politics of regulatory reform in German telecommunications', in K. Dyson (ed), *The Politics of German Regulation*, Aldershot: Dartmouth, pp. 105–36.

Ikenberry, John G. (1990), 'The international spread of privatization policies: inducements, learning, and policy bandwagoning', in Ezra N. Suleiman and John Waterbury (eds), *The Political Economy of Public Sector Reform and Privatization*, Boulder: Westview Press, pp. 88–110.

Irwin, M.R. and R. Michael Merenda (1986), 'The network as corporate strategy', *Le Bulletin de l'Idate*, **25**, 609–14.

Irwin, M.R. and N.B. Niman (1989), 'The corporate telecommunications network: market transparency and state accountability', in Nicholas Garnham (ed.), *European Telecommunications Policy Research*, Amsterdam: IOS, pp. 175–82.

ITU (1999), *Trends in Telecommunication Reform 1999. Convergence and Regulation*, Geneva: ITU.

Krugman, Paul (1995), 'Increasing returns, imperfect competition and the positive theory of international trade', in Gene Grossman and Kenneth Rogoff (eds), *Handbook of International Economics*, vol. III, Oxford: Elsevier, pp. 1243–77.

La Porte, Todd R. (1988), 'The United States Air Traffic System: increasing reliability in the midst of rapid growth', in Renate Mayntz and Thomas P. Hughes (eds), *The Development of Large Technical Systems*, Frankfurt: Campus, pp. 215–44.

Lehmbruch, G., M. Döhler, E. Grande and O. Singer (1988), 'Institutionelle Bedingungen ordnungspolitischen Strategiewechsels im internationalen Vergleich', in Manfred G. Schmidt (ed.), *Staatstätigkeit. International und historisch vergleichende Analysen*, Opladen: Westdeutscher Verlag, pp. 251–83.

Lipsey, Robert (1997), 'Globalization and National Government Policies: An Economist's View', in John Dunning (ed.), *Governments, Globalization, and International Business*, Oxford: Oxford University Press.

Mann, Michael (1986), 'The Autonomous Power of the State: Its Origins, Mechanisms and Results', in J.A. Hall (ed.), *States in History*, Oxford: Basil Blackwell, pp. 109–36.

Mayntz, Renayte (1988), 'Zur Entwicklung technischer Infrastruktursysteme', in Renate Mayntz, Bernd Rosewitz, Uwe Schimank and Rudolf Stichweh (eds), *Differenzierung und Verselbständigung. Zur Entwicklung gesellschaftlicher Teilsysteme*, Frankfurt: Campus, pp. 233-59.

Morgan, Kevin and Douglas Webber (1986), 'Divergent Paths: Political Strategies for Telecommunications in Britain, France and West Germany', in Kenneth Dyson and Peter Humphreys (eds), *The Politics of the Communications Revolution in Western Europe*, London: Frank Cass, pp. 56–79.

Mulgan, Geoffry J. (1991), *Communication and Control. Networks and the New Economies of Communication*, Cambridge: Polity Press.

North, Douglass C. (1990), *Institutions, Institutional Change and Economic Performance*, Cambridge: Cambridge University Press.

OECD (1999), 'Home regulatory reform', see http://www.oecd.org

Perlmutter, Howard V. (1972), 'The multinational firm and the future', *The Annals of the American Academy of Political and Social Science*, **403**, 139–52.

Porter, Michael (1987), 'Changing Patterns of International Competition', in D.J. Teece (ed.), *The Competitive Challenge. Strategies for Industrial Innovation and Renewal*, New York: Harper & Row, pp. 27–57.

Sandholtz, Wayne and John Zysman (1989), '1992: Recasting the European Bargain',

*World Politics*, **42**, 95–128.

Scharpf, Fritz W. (1997), *Games Real Actors Play. Actor-Centered Institutionalism in Policy Research*, Boulder, CO: Westview Press.

Schiller, Dan (1982), *Telematics and Government*, Norwood, NJ: Ablex.

Schmidt, Susanne K. (1991), 'Taking the long road to liberalization. Telecommunications reform in the Federal Republic of Germany', *Telecommunications Policy*, **15** (3), 209–22.

Schmidt, Susanne K. (1996), 'Privatizing the Federal Postal and Telecommunications Services', in A. Benz and K.H. Goetz (eds), *A New Germany Public Sector? Reform, Adaptation and Stability*, Aldershot: Dartmouth.

Schmidt, Susanne K. (1997), 'Behind the Council Agenda: The Commission's Impact on Decisions', MPI Discussion paper 97/4.

Schneider, Volker (1994), 'Multinationals in Transition: Global Technical Integration and the Role of Corporate Telecommunication Networks', in Jane Summerton (ed.), *Large Technical Systems in Change*, Boulder, CO: Westview, pp. 71–92.

Schneider, Volker (1997), 'Telecommunications and the state: a historical and comparative perspective', *Trends in Communication*, **3**, 7–33.

Schneider, Volker (2000), 'Evolution in cyberspace: the adaptation of national videotext systems to the Internet', *The Information Society*, **16**, pp. 319–328.

Schneider, Volker (2001a), 'Institutional Reform in Telecommunications: The European Union in Transnational Policy Diffusion', in Maria Green-Cowles, Jim Caporaso and Thomas Risse (eds), *Europeanization and Domestic Change*, Ithaca: Cornell University Press.

Schneider, Volker (2001b), *Die Transformation der Telekommunikation*, Schriften aus dem MPI für Gesellschaftsforschung, Band 41, Frankfurt Main: Campus.

Schneider, Volker and Thierry Vedel (1999), 'Franco-German Relations in Telecommunications', in Douglas Webber (ed.), *The Franco-German Relationship in the European Union*, London: Routledge, pp. 75–92.

Schneider, Volker and Raymund Werle (1990), 'International Regime or Corporate Actor? The European Community in Tele-communications Policy', in K. Dyson and P. Humphreys (eds), *The Political Economy of Communications. International and European Dimensions*, London: Routledge, pp. 77–106.

Schneider, Volker and Raymund Werle (1991), 'Policy Networks in the German Telecommunications Domain', in B. Marin and R. Mayntz (eds), *Policy Networks. Empirical Evidence and Theoretical Considerations*, Frankfurt, Main: Campus.

Schneider, Volker and Raymund Werle (1998), 'Co-evolution and Development Constraints. The Development of Large Technical Systems in an Evolutionary Perspective', in C.E. Garcia and L. Sanz-Nenéndez (eds), *Management and Technology*, Luxembourg: Office for Official Publications of the European Communities (Cost A3 Vol. 5), pp. 12–29.

Schneider, Volker, Godefroy Dang-Nguyen and Raymund Werle (1994), 'Corporate actor networks in European policy-making: harmonizing telecommunications policy', *Journal of Common Market Studies*, **32**, 473–98.

Strange, Susan (1996), *The Retreat of the State. The Diffusion of Power in the World Economy*, Cambridge: Cambridge University Press.

Thatcher, Mark (1999), *The Politics of Telecommunications: National Institutions, Convergence, and Change in Britain and France*, Oxford: Oxford Univiversity Press.

Tsebelis, George (1995), 'Decision making in political systems: veto players in presidentialism, parliamentarism, multicameralism and multipartyism', *British*

*Journal of Political Science*, **25**, 289–325.
Vogel, Steven K. (1996), *Freer Markets, More Rules: Regulatory Reform in Advanced Industrial Countries*, Ithaca, NY: Cornell University Press.
Webber, Douglas (1986), 'Die ausbleibende Wende bei der Deutschen Bundespost. Zur Regulierung des Telekommunikationswesens in der Bundesrepublik Deutschland', *Politische Vierteljahresschrift*, **27**, 397–414.
Werle, Raymund (1990), *Telekommunikation in der Bundesrepublik*, Frankfurt, Main: Campus Verlag.
Werle, Raymund (1999), 'Liberalisation of Telecommunications in Germany', in K. Elliassen and M. Sjovaag (eds), *Liberalising European Telecommunications*, London: Routledge.

# 3. Barriers to entry in European telecommunications markets

**Martin Cave**

## 1. INTRODUCTION

This chapter is concerned with the degree to which barriers to entry are restraining the operation of competitive telecommunications markets in the EU (European Union). The notion that telecommunications is a potentially competitive industry has now gained strong support, after an almost complete reversal of the conventional wisdom 20 years ago that fixed telecommunications (at least) was a natural monopoly. At the same time, the importance of telecommunications as a crucial enabler of the new digital or electronic economy is now widely recognised - notably at the EU's Lisbon summit in March 2000.

Notwithstanding this revolution in the way policymakers and business executives think about the potential for competition in telecommunications, there remain serious difficulties in the design and implementation of a regulatory and policy framework in which the benefits of competition can be realised. Considerable progress has been made in Europe. Thus the Commission's fifth implementation report on the telecommunications reform package, published in October 1999, reported that over a thousand operators were providing service in member states, but that there was a marked lack of competition in the local access market.

These remarks make it clear that concerns about barriers to entry are by no means over. In order to elucidate the interaction between barriers to entry and the regulatory framework, it is useful to go back to the basis on which investment decisions are likely to be made by potential entrants. In standard investment appraisal procedures, entry requires a positive net present value; in other words, a project's revenues must at least meet its expected costs, including an appropriate return on capital invested. Whether it does so depends upon a range of factors, many of which are acutely sensitive to the regulatory framework. Thus the NRA (National Regulatory Authority) will influence or determine:

- the price at which the entrant can sell its services (indirectly by determining the retail prices charged by the historic operator);
- the price at which interconnection services are sold;
- the price of leased lines;
- the scheme for sharing the cost of USO (Universal Service Obligations);
- the date at which operations can start;
- the cost of capital which measures the returns investors need to undertake the project.

I investigate the first five of these variables in detail in Section 3 below. It is therefore useful to say something here about the factors influencing the cost of capital.

The cost of capital which an entrant is likely to employ in evaluating a decision to enter the telecommunications markets will be driven to some extent by the standard market interdependencies between telecommunications and the rest of the economy. As a monopoly or quasi monopoly, the typical historic operator has exhibited a level of market risk which is less than the average for the country as a whole. As a result, we would expect on this basis a cost of capital lower than average.

This may change, however, for a number of reasons: the increased competitiveness of the market reduces the former monopolist's capacity to control returns, and hence increase its risk; the use of telecommunications networks to carry many fast-developing and innovative services, the demand for which cannot easily be forecast, is a further source of turbulence; entrants may incline to keep their options open and defer entry decisions, which will have the effect of equivalently increasing their cost capital; and initially they will be subject to regulatory risk.

From an entrant's standpoint, regulatory risk arises from concern that an unforeseen change in regulatory arrangements might destroy its business plan and render its investments nugatory. From an investment appraisal point of view, the appropriate way to deal with this is to identify alternative scenarios of 'failure' and 'success', assign probabilities to them, and compute the expected returns to the investment by averaging over the scenarios. Loosely speaking, a higher risk of failure can be shown to be equivalent to a higher cost of capital. For this reason, entrants are understandably concerned about the stability and predictability of the regulatory framework in which they will be involved.

This has the implication that not only the current regulatory arrangements but also the constraints on dramatic changes in them are a major factor in determining entrants' decisions to invest. This accounts for the importance of the appropriate framework of regulation for the sector. The stability of that framework may be helped by having a federal system in which powers exercised at the member state level are constrained by primary European legislation, in the form either of the current directives or the new legislative framework proposed by the Commission in 2000, that come into effect in 2003.

Another crucial regulatory variable - the speed and cost of licensing procedure - influences the rate at which firms can implement their investment plan and bring their products to the market. Licensing delays may allow the historical operator more time to adjust to the new conditions and weaken the impact of entrants.

It is reasonable to suppose that the dependence of investment decisions on regulation will diminish as competition takes hold and the telecommunications industry conforms more closely to the relatively unregulated pattern of most industries. I describe the planned strategy of progressive liberalisation in Section 2. In the medium term, however, and in some cases even in the long term, regulation will still be extremely influential in determining an entrant's profitability. As a result, Section 3 describes the operation of European regulation in four crucial areas: licensing, retail pricing, interconnection and other input pricing, and USO. Section 4 then gives an evaluation of the adequacy of the current regulatory package and of its implementation.

## 2. THE EU TELECOMMUNICATIONS REGULATORY PACKAGE

The first of January, 1998 saw the culmination of the long project to liberalise telecommunications in the European Union. For the ten years or more before that, a series of green papers, directives, recommendations and other interventions had imposed obligations on member states in respect of equipment markets, regulatory structures, value added services and the regulation of infrastructure and service competition where it existed. In 1998 the obligation was imposed on member states to liberalise entry into their telecommunication markets (with the exception of those few countries for whom derogations were granted). The resulting system is in conceptual terms a framework of structural and behavioural regulation appropriate to the development of the European industry. It divides responsibilities between the Commission and NRAs in a way designed to give early adopters of new competitive arrangements the opportunity to press ahead, while giving the Commission powers to force laggards to meet their obligations. It overlays on specific telecommunications law the generic competition law of articles 85 and 86 of the Treaty of Rome.

However adequate the 1998 framework is at a conceptual level, there are serious defects in its implementation. Liberalisation and harmonisation Directives first have to be transposed into national legislation, to take effect in the member states. The (near) completion of the transposition process took nearly two years, but the Commission was able to report in October 1999 that it was largely complete. The Directives, however, give member states considerable latitude in the manner of their implementation. For example, as we note below, the Licensing Directive permits considerable variation on the requirements imposed upon new entrants, and the requirement in the Interconnection Directive that interconnection charge be cost based has permitted a substantial variation in interconnection charges within the EU.

These problems of implementation have permitted the emergence of a substantial gap between theory and practice. To illustrate this proposition, I first set out in very broad terms what we understand to be the strategy underlying the liberalisation of telecommunications in the 1998 package, and then examine in more detail how it has been realised and what have been the effects.

Rather than enumerating the various directives (European Council 1990, 1992; European Parliament and European Council 1997a, 1997b, 1998) we seek to set out the logic of the EU package in terms of key components of behavioural and structural regulation. Achieving the goals of liberalising the industry against the wishes of most incumbent operators and many member states has required substantial regulatory intervention from the Commission. Moreover, the regulatory framework has to be flexible enough to include member states proceeding at quite different rates. In particular, in the early stages of liberalisation, it is necessary to constrain the former monopoly considerably. However, as competitors become better established, arrangements should be in place which make it possible to reduce the level of regulatory intervention.

The key structural requirement is that, in markets where there are no technical restrictions on entry, arising, for example, from spectrum scarcity, *licences* should be granted to operators subject to the minimum of conditions.

As far as behavioural regulation is concerned, three behavioural instruments are required in the early stages of liberalisation, as follows:

- Control of retail prices is necessary where the dominant firm exercises market power at the retail level, and in the absence of retail price controls, customers will be significantly disadvantaged. However, as competition develops at the retail level, possibly supplied by firms relying largely on infrastructure belonging to others, the necessity for retail price controls in effectively competitive markets may disappear. Member states have historically fulfilled this consumer protection function, though under monopoly conditions, the controlled tariffs have been seriously unbalanced.

- In order to maintain any-to-any connectivity in the presence of competitive networks, operators require *interconnection* to one another's networks in order to complete their customers' calls. This requires the operation of a system of inter-operator wholesale or network access prices. Especially in the early stages of competition, entrants will require significant access to the dominant incumbents' network, and this relationship will almost inevitably necessitate regulatory intervention. However, as infrastructure is duplicated (initially the infrastructure necessary for long distance and international conveyance), the need for direct price regulation of certain network facilities diminishes. Interconnection has been central to the development of competition within the single market, and the Commission has been centrally involved. It has also recently lived up to its obligations under the 1992 Leased Line Directive to make these charges cost-related. Excessive leased line prices have an adverse effect upon some entrants.
- Governments have typically imposed a *Universal Service Obligation* on the historic telecommunications operator, based upon two requirements: an obligation to provide service to all parts of the country, and to do so at a uniform price, despite the presence of significant cost differences. Entrants coming into the market without such an obligation have a strong incentive to focus upon low-cost, 'profitable' customers, putting

*Table 3.1 Stages of regulation*

| | Monopoly/ duopoly | Transition | Normalisation |
|---|---|---|---|
| Retail price control | Controls on all services | Gradual relaxation of controls | No controls |
| Access pricing | Not relevant, or arbitrary pricing of small range of services | Services gradually decontrolled<br>Unbundling<br>Use of price caps | Call termination only controlled |
| Universal service obligations | Borne by incumbent | Costed and shared (or ignored if not material) | As in 'transition', with possibility of competitive provision |

the USO operator at a disadvantage. Pressure may therefore build up to equalise the situation, perhaps by calculating the net cost of the USO borne by the dominant operator and then sharing the cost among all operators. In the case of universal service, the concern has been, first that it would be used as a pretext for delaying competition, secondly that high USO contributions imposed on entrants would choke off competitors.

We noted above that regulatory policy in relation to the control of retail and wholesale prices and the allocation of universal service obligations is likely to change throughout the three phases of liberalisation: monopoly (or duopoly), transition and normalisation. Table 3.1 sets out the way in which each of the three regulatory instruments might develop (for example Cave 1997: 691–9). We now examine in greater detail the extent to which the reality has matched the conceptual framework.

## 3. THE IMPLEMENTATION OF THE PACKAGE IN RELATION TO FIXED LINE SERVICES

### 3.1 Licensing

Under the licensing directive, licensing régimes should be light-touch and transparent. These requirements imply that general authorisations should be favoured over individual licences, that potential licensees should know what conditions have to be satisfied, and onerous conditions should be avoided as far as possible; in addition, licences should be issued quickly and fees kept to a minimum.

In the fifth implementation report, published October, 1999, the Commission noted substantial divergences between national licensing régimes 'ranging from light as possible, where operators are free to enter the market without formality … or are required simply to register … or notify … their intention to do so …, to the extremely heavy, where individual licences are the rule and in some cases a government minister is required to sign every licence' (European Commission 1999: 12).

This conclusion rested upon a comparative analysis of the national licensing régime which focussed upon two aspects in particular: first, the level of segmentation of authorisations and the extent to which individual licences are required and, second, the volume of information required about applicants.

As far as segmentation and the use of individual licences are concerned, some member states have a régime in which an authorisation permits a licensee to provide all telecommunications networks and services, excluding services which use scarce frequency resources and therefore require individual licences. This low level of segmentation can be combined with licensing under general authorisations rather than individual licences. At the opposite extreme, other member states distinguish among as many as twelve categories of authorisation, each with its own licensing conditions and procedures, and rely heavily upon the issuing of individual licences which in some case are tailor made in respect of geographical service area and other characteristics. Table 3.2 illustrates the diversity of practice.

Similar differences exist with respect to information requested before market entry. Here the study found that member states with higher levels of segmentation also tended to impose high informational requirements. For example, two member states require information about the operator's marketing plan, three require a financial plan or investment plan, three require a plan of recruitment and nine a schedule for roll-out.

The implementation report identifies that in three member states, procedures for licensing go beyond the deadline laid down in the licensing directive in three countries, and that in Italy, licensing procedures appeared to be protracted, heavy and lacking in transparency. The Commission concluded that in three countries fees and charges appeared to be higher than the administrative costs incurred.

The remedy for such obstacles is fairly straightforward - the achievement of harmonisation by adopting a common set of requirements based upon the

*Table 3.2 Licensing variations in the EU. Table of comparison*

| Use of individual licences | | | |
|---|---|---|---|
| High | | Belgium<br>Germany<br>Luxembourg<br>Spain | Italy<br>United Kingdom |
| Medium | Ireland | | France |
| None/Low | Denmark<br>Finland<br>Norway<br>Sweden<br>Netherlands | | |
| Level of Segmentation | Low | Medium | High |

*Source*: Pontiggia and Vanderbroucke (2000).

procedures of member states operating a light-touch régime, or the introduction of a one-stop shopping régime, in which a licence granted in one member state offers equivalent entitlements throughout the whole of the whole of the EU.

Despite this uneven performance, we do not regard licensing practices as acting, in general, as an obstacle to market entry. Thus in Italy, where both market segmentation and the use of individual licences is high, where procedures are lacking in transparency and information requirements exacting, numerous licences have been issued.

## 3.2 Retail Price Control

At the stages of monopoly and of transition, some control of retail prices is necessary to prevent exploitation of market power by the incumbent. There are a number of ways in which price control can be achieved. The simplest is to impose a regime of cost plus pricing. Under such a regime, the regulator sets prices for the utility in such a way that they cover the utility's cost of production, including a rate of return on capital sufficient to maintain investors' willingness to replace or expand the company's assets (for this reason, cost-plus regulation is also known as 'rate of return' regulation). In some cases, the firm is required to set the price for each service equal to its costs. In others, individual services can be sold at either above or below cost, but the regulator constrains prices overall so that total regulated revenues cover the relevant costs. This regime, or a version of it, was widely practised in the telecommunications sector in the United States until the last decade or so (Sappington 2001).

One revealing way to describe rate of return regulation is as a 'low powered' incentive mechanism - low-powered because the firm benefits little from any efficiency gain. This arises because if cost savings were made, they would almost at once be taken from the firm and given to consumers in the form of lower prices. This naturally raises the question of what would amount to a 'high powered' incentive mechanism. Clearly its distinguishing feature must be that the firm retains, at least temporarily, a substantial proportion of the benefits of any greater efficiency. This can be achieved by decoupling the revenues which a firm can generate from the costs that it incurs.

A very high-powered incentive mechanism would operate by setting a trajectory of prices for the firm's products indefinitely into the future - requiring them, for example, to fall by 2 per cent per year in real terms. In such circumstances, a firm not subject to competition would be able to 'keep' in perpetuity the benefits of any cost savings which it achieved. This is not, however, practical, as setting prices in advance for an indefinite period is likely within a decade or less either to drive the firm into bankruptcy, if they are set too low, or to allow profits to grow to a politically unacceptable level, if they are set too high.

As a result, regulators have increasingly looked for some intermediate variant under which prices are set in advance for a period of four to five years, allowing the firm to benefit from any cost savings made during that period, but recalculated at regular intervals in order to bring them back into line with underlying costs. This regime is known as price capping or RPI-X regulation. Although a few American precursors can be identified, it was first applied on a large scale in the United Kingdom to British Telecom in 1984, and then extended to other British utilities as they were privatised. It is now used widely throughout the world in the communications, energy, transport and water industries, and applied both to privatised utilities and to public sector firms (Armstrong, Cowan and Vickers 1994).

A major component of deregulation is the withdrawal of controls from retail prices as competition develops. This requires an analysis of competition conditions in individual markets, of the kind often undertaken by competitive authorities the world over.

Putting competitive and non-competitive services in the same price cap basket leads to the now well established incentive for the regulated firm to engage in what can be called subsidised predation. Predatory behaviour in an unregulated market typically involves the firm in a sacrifice of short-run profit, as it cuts prices below costs in order either to drive out or permanently weaken a competitor, followed by excess profits in the longer term as it gains its monopoly or recovers. But when a firm is subject to a price control regime which puts competitive and non-competitive services in the same basket, such behaviour is in fact costless, as under the terms of the price cap it can recover any price cuts that it imposes in competitive markets by charging higher prices in non-competitive markets. As a result, the firm's monopoly customers finance its predatory conduct as it occurs.

Choice of the overall rigour, the coverage and the structure of the retail price control are key ways in which the NRA can influence the profitability of entry. Clearly a very harsh retail price control, which drives the dominant firm's prices down very quickly, will have an adverse effect upon the business plans of entrants. Essentially, they are unknown quantities in the market, which typically have to offer, in the early stages of liberalisation, discounts of 10–15 per cent in order to persuade customers to join them. At this stage of their lives, they are also likely to be suffering from a disadvantage *vis à vis* the historic operator as a result of their small scale and high unit costs (this may to some extent be compensated by use of more modern equipment). The regulator is thus placed in something of a dilemma. Consumers would benefit instantly from the lower prices generated by rigorous price control, yet that same price control may also stifle competition.

A second key aspect of the price control is the extent to which it influences the relative prices for various services, particularly the line rental and call prices. Most member states still exhibit an unbalanced tariff in which revenue from line rentals fails to recover the forward looking costs of the access network, the resulting deficit being made up by call prices relative to costs, which are high, particularly for long distance and international calls. If the regulator permits this situation to continue, it will have a major distorting effect on the development of competition. Entrants will shun the local loop and local calls, and pile into the far more profitable long distance market. This process is encouraged by carrier pre-selection, which is now an obligation imposed on European operators enjoying specified levels of market power.

The best way to resolve this dilemma and to avoid both distortions in the retail market and consequential difficulties in the wholesale, is to permit re-balancing of the fastest possible rate which is politically feasible, while simultaneously dealing with difficulties encountered by particular groups of subscribers, such as those with low incomes or making relatively few calls, through targeted subsidisation schemes under an agreed framework for sharing the costs of loss-making customers (see below).

## 3.3 Interconnection Pricing

Access to networks is of fundamental importance for the development of effective competition in the EU telecommunications industry. All infrastructure operators exhibit a growing demand by a variety of potential suppliers to enter the market for network services and to interconnect with established network suppliers. It is clear that the key element that the service is delivered across is network interconnection between compatible and complementary circuits.

An important component of policies to promote effective competition is a regulatory environment guaranteeing that competitors have access to the services of ‘potential bottleneck facilities’ too costly to duplicate. Fair access rules to these facilities and in particular fair access prices will generally improve economic efficiency by easing competition in markets both upstream and downstream of the bottleneck. This is true whether the industries are vertically unbundled/separated or not. More specifically, appropriate access pricing rules are needed whenever a dominant firm controls the supply of one or more inputs that are vital for its competitors. At a more general level, access pricing is part of the anti-trust concern of market foreclosure which is central in the so-called ‘essential facilities doctrine’ developed by the United States. In a broader context, access pricing is related to a variety of competition policy issues that include quantity discounts, cross-subsidies, tie-ins, refuse to deal or to unbundle, exclusive dealing, and predatory pricing.

The price which entrants have to pay for access to the incumbent network is crucial to their commercial success, yet the incumbent has two motives for charging high access prices. The first is a simple desire to maximise monopoly profits; the second, which arises if a network owner is also competing in the supply market, is the desire to raise its rivals' costs and maintain a dominant position in that market.

These considerations have meant that regulators are likely to have to intervene in access pricing either by imposing detailed prices for the use of the elements of the network, or by limiting the overall revenues which the network owner can collect to those which are necessary for the recovery of its costs. Either approach involves a detailed analysis by the regulator of the costs incurred by the network. The first-best solution would involve setting access prices on the basis of marginal cost. This may need to be supplemented by a mark up if such pricing would prevent the incumbent from breaking even (Armstrong 2001).

There is thus the obvious danger that a new entrant may choose to enter the profitable long-distance market even thought it is less efficient at providing long-distance conveyance than the incumbent. This will additionally deny to the incumbent the call revenues that are necessary to cross-subsidise access. One way of eliminating this possibility is by allowing the incumbent to charge new entrants for access to its network at rates which take account of the lack of balance in the tariff structure. The incumbent, for example, could be allowed to make a charge to the entrant for all termination which covers not only the costs of that call termination but also includes an additional element comprising the excess profit which the incumbent *would have made* by providing the call at retail prices which it needs in order to cross-subsidise other services such as access to the network. This approach to access pricing is known as the Efficient Component Pricing Rule (ECPR).

If an interconnection charging regime of this kind were to be introduced, then an entrant would only be able to gain a profitable foothold in the industry if its costs in supplying the services that it provides itself, rather than buys from the incumbent, are less than those of the incumbent. Such a rule would, in consequence, only encourage entry where the entrant is more efficient than the incumbent.

The regulation of interconnection pricing in the EU has not gone down this path. The Interconnection Directive requires that charges for interconnection follow the principles of transparency and cost orientation. The first principle implies the publication of a reference interconnection offer. As a corollary, operators with significant market power are required to keep separate accounts for their wholesale or network activity and for other activities, including retailing.

Cost orientation turned out, however, to be an excessively vague phrase, permitting excessive interconnection charges. In anticipation of the universal availability costing data based upon the Commission's preferred methodology, forward looking long-run incremental costs, the Commission published recommended 'best current practice' interconnection charges, based upon the average of the member states with the lowest charges. The recommendations for 2000 are set out in Table 3.3, together with the actual charges in several member states in November 1999. The data show considerable variation in charges, with some charges substantially above the best practice recommendation.

A further crucial input which entrants have to purchase from the incumbent is leased lines. Despite the 1992 Leased Line Directive, which imposed a cost orientation requirement, leased line prices in Europe continue to be substantially above those charged in the United States. The Commission finally responded to this situation in November 1999 through the publication of a Commission Recommendation, which sets ceiling prices for the rental of leased lines of different capacity over different distances (in view of the very high level of prices in all countries, the Commission did not adopt the 'best practice' terminology used in connection with interconnection charges).

## 3.4 Local Loop Unbundling

The 1999 Implementation Report highlights a lack of competition in local access markets in all member states, even though 375 operators in the EU offer local network services. There are a number of possible reasons for this:

*Table 3.3 Interconnect charges per minute (€-cents)*

| | Local | Single transit | Double transit |
|---|---|---|---|
| Denmark | 0.84 | 1.18 | 1.80 |
| France | 0.63 | 1.33 | 2.01 |
| Germany | 0.88 | 1.49–1.89 | 2.28 |
| Greece | 1.93 | 1.93 | 2.76 |
| Italy | 1.00 | 1.60 | 2.29 |
| Netherlands | 1.00 | 1.41 | 1.70 |
| Spain | 0.99 | 1.59 | 3.07 |
| UK | 0.54 | 0.82 | 1.71 |
| 2000 EC Recommendation | 0.5–0.9 | 0.8–1.5 | 1.5–1.8 |

*Source*: European Commission (2000a).

- the unbalanced nature of many tariffs in members states, leading to a reluctance to invest, particularly in circumstances where carrier pre-selection may deprive the local operator of 'ownership' of the subscriber long-distance international call;
- the failure of fixed radio to provide a viable access alternative;
- the delay in the provision of competition for CATV operators, in member states which are already highly cabled (as a result of the significant incremental investments required), as well as in member states where cable networks are being rolled out.

This has encouraged NRAs to look to local loop unbundling as a means of introducing competition into the market for access, especially the market for high-speed internet access for both residential and subscribers and SMEs. The Commission's 1999 Communications Review indicated that this was an item on the agenda, but opinion quickly hardened around the view that more urgent action was required. A February 2000 working document reported the extent to which unbundled local loops were available in member states (see Table 3.4).

The table interestingly describes a variety of pricing mechanisms: thus in Austria, Germany and (prospectively) Sweden and the United Kingdom, prices for an unbundled loop will be set on the basis of forward looking costs. In Denmark, by contrast, 'retail minus' pricing is employed. The Netherlands has adopted a more nuanced régime in which the price of the loop increases over a five-year period, reflecting the regulator's desire increasingly to encourage competing operators to 'make' rather than 'buy'.

Rather than wait until the implementation of the new communications regulation package in 2003, the European Parliament and Council adopted a Recommendation on Unbundled Access to the Local Loop, which came into operation in 2001 (European Commission 2000c).

Pricing rules should ensure that the incumbent is able to recover its legitimate costs plus a reasonable return, and NRAs have the option of deciding whether unbundled loops should or should not be subject to geographical averaging. There is a particular difficulty associated with the recommendation that the principle of non-discrimination be applied to pricing access to the higher frequency spectrum of the local loop under the line sharing variants. At present, incumbents implicitly charge themselves a zero price for this component when providing their own broadband services. They would clearly not find this a palatable approach to adopt under a non-discrimination rule, and that mode of providing access might introduce significant turbulence into arrangements for the retail price of the local loops. By mid-2001, the debates remained at the theoretical level, as line-sharing had not been introduced in practice.

*Table 3.4 Unbundled local loop prices in EU member states (access to 1 copper pair)*

| | Status of ULL (including monthly rental of unbundled copper pair where available, exclusive of VAT) | Basis for price of ULL |
|---|---|---|
| Austria | 12.4€/month | Price based on current valuation of assets |
| Belgium | Consultation | |
| Denmark | 8.23€/month | Price based on telephone line rental |
| Finland | 5–25€/month | Price based on current valuation of assets |
| France | Under consideration | |
| Germany | 13€/month | Price set by Reg. TP based on FL LRAIC |
| Greece | | |
| Ireland | Consultation | |
| Italy | Proposed by 2000 | |
| Luxembourg | | |
| Netherlands | Less than 15.4€/month | Phased pricing set by OPTA moving from historic costs to current costs in 5 years |
| Portugal | | |
| Spain | Line sharing access can be negotiated | |
| Sweden | Proposed by 2000 | Price proposed to be based on current costs |
| UK | From July 2001. Price likely to be about 13€/month | OFTEL will set price based on FL LRAIC |

*Source*: European Commission (2000b).

## 3.5 Universal Service

The notion that a country's telecommunications operator should have a universal service obligation has a long history, becoming well established in the period of monopoly provision by either a public or a private operator. In telecommunications, universal service is widely recognised as having at least three dimensions:

- The achievement of universal geographical coverage, requiring that a network is rolled out over the whole of the territory in question, so that service is available for the whole population.
- Geographic averaging of tariffs, requiring that customers in the same category (for example domestic or business customers), are charged the same tariffs, irrespective of their individual costs of supply.
- A basic telecommunication service should be made available at an 'affordable' price, so that no household (more realistically, few households) are denied access to the service. This is increasingly replaced by the more nuanced proposition that certain households, characterised by attributes such as low income or by their pattern of use of the telecommunications network should have special 'social' tariffs available to them (Cave, Milne and Scanlon 1994).

The rationale for having a universal service obligation is based on a mixture of political, social and economic considerations. It is desirable on political grounds that citizens in a democracy have access to communication facilities which they require to exercise their political rights, and it is desirable on social grounds that all individuals should have access to communication facilities, to avoid a gulf emerging between 'information-rich' and 'information-poor' groups. Economic arguments derive from 'network externalities' and the link between network expansion and economic growth.

The notion that a universal service obligation for telecommunications should be sustained has survived the introduction of competition in the sector. It had previously been thought that competition and the USO were incompatible, because competitors would focus upon high value customers, defined either by their calling patterns or their (low cost) place of residence, leaving low value customers to the operator with the universal service obligation. As competitors aggressively encroached upon profitable markets, the commercial prospects of the USO operator would gradually unravel, jeopardising the universal service obligation. However, further examination of the issue quickly revealed that it was possible to avoid this outcome if the cost of the universal service obligation were shared on some equitable basis between the operator discharging it and competitors. This triggered a discussion of appropriate means of estimating the cost and appropriate means of sharing it. A number of the governments and regulatory agencies have implemented procedures estimating the cost, and in some cases have instituted arrangements for sharing the costs.

These developments have encouraged a new view of the universal service obligation and its funding as a *sui generis* tax and subsidy regime. Effectively, a limited amount of revenue is raised within the sector through 'taxes', in the form either of a percentage of operators' revenue or of a tax on particular services, such as interconnection, traded at the wholesale level. The revenue thus raised is then distributed to ensure that the universal service obligation is satisfied. This could in principle be done either by subsidising particular groups of customers, to whom, for example, vouchers could be distributed, or it could be achieved by subsidising operators providing services to particular customers. The former model might seem particularly appropriate to cases where the obligation relates to particular categories of customers, but it is less suited to the case where a net cost of the USO arises because of geographical cost differences. As a result, the normal procedure is to fund a designated operator with a universal service obligation.

The seventh and eighth recitals of the Interconnection Directive (European Parliament and European Council 1997b) note that the concept of universal service must evolve to keep pace with advances in technology, market development and changes in user demand. They then go on to note that member states may have more than one firm with universal service obligations and that it may be appropriate in due course to consider whether the obligations should extend to ISDN. The costs of universal service obligations should be calculated on the basis of transparent procedures and where the USO represents an unfair burden on a firm, it is appropriate for it to be shared, provided that the sharing mechanism satisfies the principles of community law, especially those of non-discrimination and proportionality.

The approved procedure of a cost of universal service is adumbrated in the text and in an annex. Where networks are fully developed, the calculation should be of net costs attributable to services provided under cost conditions falling outside normal commercial standards. In areas with expanding networks, the costs calculations should be based on the additional costs of serving those *n* users, which would presumably be net avoidable costs. Where the network is still being developed, the cost calculation should be based on net incremental costs.

As a result of the Directive, a number of studies utilising the net avoided costs approach have already been carried out by NRAs or by the Commission. A key difficulty in undertaking such studies is that, for reasons of practicality, the areas within any country have to be allocated to a limited number of categories characterised by particular cost conditions. Yet, it is one of the principles of USO costing that aggregation or averaging must inevitably reduce the net cost estimate, because it allows cancelling out.

Secondly, it is particularly difficult to attribute to customer groups profits associated with incoming calls to those subscribers, because incoming call data are often unavailable. Thirdly, the computation of net avoidable cost hinges crucially upon what assumption is made about the extent to which a subscriber notionally excluded from the network on cost grounds would continue to make calls. The implicit assumption of most studies is there would be no substitutional replacement. This is the assumption which minimises the estimate of net avoidable costs. Estimates of the net cost of universal service obligations in member states tend to cluster around 2 or 3 per cent telephony revenue - lower in the United Kingdom and higher in less densely populated countries, including France and some Nordic countries. In the event, only one member state has chosen to set up a sharing fund, and that country (France) has been the subject of an investigation by the DGIV, the former Commission's Competition Directorate.

## 4. CONCLUSIONS AND PROSPECTS

The previous section has shown the ways in which regulatory intervention in practice has influenced entrants' business plans, and exacerbated, or helped them to overcome, other barriers to entry to which they might be subject. It is important not to underestimate the handicap which entrants are subject to from other quarters. As well as the disadvantage which they suffer from being – initially – small operators in a network industry characterised by substantial economies of scale, they also face an incumbent which has enjoyed a market share of 100 per cent, for a period of up to a century. At the start of the liberalisation process, that operator had detailed information about every subscriber in the land. In the absence of number portability, entrants must persuade new customers to forego their previous telephone numbers, and incur the associated costs. The incumbent also enjoyed instantaneous brand recognition, although a history of poor performance may reduce the value of this advantage.

In these circumstances, entrants need all the assets which they can get, and some of the most strategic assets on offer at the early stages of liberalisation are in fact regulatory assets. Conversely, obstructive or unsympathetic regulation can make their task a great deal more difficult.

In terms of the five dimensions of regulation described above, there is evidence that the licensing régime has imposed penalties on entrants, to the extent that they encounter delay in the processing of their applications or are required to submit unnecessary information.

Regulation of retail prices may have tended to be rather lax, and to the extent that this has been true, relatively high retail prices charged by the incumbent have created a pricing umbrella under which entrants have been able to shelter.

The clearest regulatory difficulty which entrants have faced has arisen in the field of interconnection. There is ample evidence of a variation among member states in interconnection charges which cannot be explained by plausible variations in costs. As an entrant might typically have to pass over

50 per cent or more of its revenue in interconnection charges, excessive pricing of interconnection has a major impact upon entry prospects. In the past two years, the Commission has had some success in getting interconnection prices down, but there is still substantial variation and *prima facie* evidence of excessive pricing.

Finally, the situation with respect to USO has generally turned out to be relatively favourable to entrants. Only in one member state is there a cost-sharing scheme, and elsewhere the full burden is borne by the incumbent. (Note, however, that an incumbent enjoying a 90 per cent market share would in any case expect to defray 90 per cent of the net cost of USO, so that the benefit which entrants are enjoying is very small.)

The balance sheet of regulatory barriers to entry is thus rather mixed. To date, entry has occurred in those markets where economies of scale are least important and where imbalances in the tariff generally give the opportunity to make high profits. Only in Finland and the United Kingdom is the largest operators' share of the local call market less than 85 per cent.

This suggests that there is room for improvement in regulatory arrangements. The Commission's 1999 Communications Review identifies a number of areas where changes might be made – for example in the harmonisation of licence conditions, in local loop unbundling and in more rigorous scrutiny of interconnection charges. It also identifies a range of new and intractable issues associated with access to networks, which arise as a result of the convergence of telecommunications and broadcasting services. These were embodied in draft directives, which in 2001 were under consideration by the Parliament and the Council (European Commission 2000b).

Considerable progress and liberalisation of telecommunications has been made in the past ten years, and particularly since the start of 1998. What is needed is decisive regulatory action to create the conditions in which genuine competition can flourish. In the existing telecommunications package, and in the changes proposed in the new directives, the conceptual and legislative basis is present. What is required is more diligence on the part of NRAs and greater enforcement powers available at the European level.

## REFERENCES

Armstrong, M. (2001), 'The Theory of Access Pricing and Interconnection', in M. Cave et al. (eds), *Handbook of Telecommunications Economics*, Amsterdam and New York: Elsevier.

Armstrong, M., S. Cowan and J. Vickers (1994), *Regulatory Reform: Economic Analysis of British Experience*, Cambridge, MA: MIT Press.

Cave, M. (1997), 'The evolution of telecommunications regulation in the UK', *European Economic Review*, **41**, 691–9.

Cave, M., C. Milne and M. Scanlon (1994), *Meeting Universal Service Obligations in a Competitive Telecommunications Sector*, Brussels: European Commission.

European Commission (1999), *Fifth Report on the Implementation of the Telecommunications Regulatory Package*, Communication from the Commission to the European Parliament, the Council, the Economic and Social Committee and the Committee of the Regions, Brussels, October, COM(1999)537.

European Commission (2000a), *Commission Recommendation Amending Rec. 98/501/EC of 29 July 1998 on Interconnection in a Liberalised Telecommunications Market (Part 1 - Interconnection Pricing)*, Brussels, 20 March 2000.

European Commission (2000b), *Working Document on Unbundled Access to the Local Loop*, General Directorate for Information Society INFSO A/1, Brussels.

European Commission (2000c), *Commission Recommendation on Unbundled Access to the Local Loop*, Brussels, 25 May 2000, 2000/417/EC.

European Commission (2000d), *Proposal for a Directive for the European Parliament and the Council on a Common Regulatory Framework for Electronic Communications Network and Services*, Brussels, 12 July 2000, COM(2000)393.

European Council (1990), *Directive on the Establishment of the Internal Market for Telecommunications Services through the Implementation of Open Network Provision (ONP)*, Brussels, 28 June 1990, 90/387/EEC (The directive was amended by Directive 97/51/EC, 10 June).

European Council (1992), *Directive on the Application of Open Network Provision to Leased Lines*, Brussels, 5 June 1992, 92/44/EEC.

European Parliament and European Council (1997a), *Directive on a Common Framework for General Authorizations and Individual Licences in the Field of Telecommunications Services*, Brussels, 17 April 1997, 97/13/EC.

European Parliament and European Council (1997b), *Directive of the Interconnection in Telecommunications with Regard to Ensuring Universal Service and Interoperability through Application of the Principles of Open Network Provision*, Brussels, 30 June 1997, 97/33/EC.

European Parliament and European Council (1998), *Directive Amending Directive 97/33/EC with Regard to Operator Number Portability and Carrier Pre-selection*, Brussels, 28 September 1998, 98/61/EC.

Pontiggia, L. and A. Vanderbroucke (2000), 'The impact on competition of differences, in telecommunications licensing régimes', *Communications and Strategies*, **38**, 41–71.

Sappington, D. (2001), 'Price Regulation and Incentives', in M. Cave et al. (eds), *Handbook of Telecommunications Economics*, Amsterdam and New York: Elsevier.

# 4. The relationship between national and European regulation of telecommunications

**Mark Thatcher**

## 1. INTRODUCTION[1]

Until the mid 1980s, the regulation of telecommunications in Europe was almost entirely a national matter. International organisations had few powers. In particular, the EC (European Community) played little role.[2] However, the period from the mid 1980s to the late 1990s saw a remarkable expansion of EC regulation. By the late 1990s, a comprehensive EC regime had been established that covered the entire sector; it prohibited national monopolies and laid down rules governing competition.

Analysis of EC regulation has focused on how and why it grew. It has concentrated on the EC level of decision making, often forming part of general debates on European integration (Sandholtz 1998; Thatcher 2001; Schneider, Dang-Nguyen and Werle 1994; Sandholtz 1992; compare Sandholtz and Stone Sweet 1998). Studies have paid much less attention to national politics. The impacts of EC telecommunications regulation on member states are downplayed or even largely ignored. Yet the importance of EC regulation cannot be assumed. The EC may be following existing national practices and regulation, rather than leading them. Its regulations may have little effect on member states. EC regulation is also implemented at the national level – there is no Euro-regulator.

The present chapter, therefore, analyses the national politics of European telecommunications. It examines the impacts of EC regulation on institutional reform in member states, notably the formal rules governing competition and the organisational structure of telecommunications suppliers. National institutional reform is chosen for two reasons. First, changes in the institutional structure of the sector – such as liberalisation, privatisation and the creation of new rules to govern competition – have been at the heart of political debate in most European countries for several decades, and especially in the 1980 and 1990s (Eliassen and Svojaag 1999; Noam 1992). The role and importance of the EC are studied in relation to other factors for change, offering an idea of the relative importance of EC regulation and of the ways in which it has interacted with other, non-EC pressures. Second, the EC's regulatory framework itself is highly dependent on national institutions. Most EC regulation is implemented at the national level and since it is broad, offers scope for interpretation, delay and variation; its implementation is highly dependent on national organisations. In addition, certain aspects crucial to regulation in practice, such as the ownership of operators or the organisational structure of national regulator, are not specified under EC legislation.

The chapter distinguishes three types of impact: direct/coercive; indirect; legitimising. Direct impacts consist of alterations in national institutions to meet requirements imposed by EC legislation. This coercive effect is the most obvious form of 'Europeanisation' (Radaelli 2000). However, the EC may also have more indirect effects on national institutional reform. It may influence the strategies, coalitions and power of actors within the domestic policy arena, leading them to introduce institutional modifications that are not required by EC law. Finally, the EC may act as a legitimising device - its role is to justify changes desired for non-EC reasons.

In studying the impacts of the EC on national institutional reform in the context of other forces for change, both domestic and non-EC international, it may not be easy to disentangle the role of the EC and that of other factors for change. Nevertheless, timing offers a good test: if national reforms had already been introduced before EC legislation required them, then the EC was following rather than leading member states. Even if national reforms were merely underway before the EC acted, then the leading role of the EC is called into question: its relative importance and relationship with other forces for change need to be considered. Moreover, the force and direction of non-EC forces offer another method of analysing the impacts of the EC.

As a case study, the chapter takes the EC's four largest member states: Britain, France, Germany and Italy. Its central argument is that EC regulation was an additional factor to existing national policies and directions of change. Frequently its direct impacts were limited. Certain provisions had already been introduced by member states or were already underway. National reforms were driven by powerful domestic and non-EC transnational forces for change. Nevertheless, the EC did influence change. Its main effects were to accelerate events, provide extra support for reformers and legitimise change, whilst weakening opponents of institutional modification. Its indirect and legitimising impacts were its most significant effects on national institutional reform.

The traditional framework of telecommunications in Britain, France,

Germany and Italy and the domestic coalitions underpinning it are set out in Section 2, before the development of the EC regulatory regime for telecommunications is traced, with particular attention being drawn to its steady expansion (Section 3). The impacts of that regime for national policy in the four countries concerning the regulation of competition and the organisation of the state are then analysed (Sections 4 and 5), in the United Kingdom, France, Germany and Italy. The final section relates the conclusions from the case study to more general issues about EC regulation.

## 2. THE TRADITIONAL REGULATION OF TELECOMMUNICATIONS IN BRITAIN, FRANCE, GERMANY AND ITALY: CHALLENGES AND OBSTACLES TO CHANGE

Before the 1980s, longstanding institutional frameworks existed in Britain, France, Germany and Italy (Thatcher 1999; Foreman-Peck and Müller 1988; Werle 1990). State-owned PTOs (Public Telecommunications Operators) held monopolies over almost all telecommunications services and networks. In France and Germany, the DGT (Direction Générale des Télécommunications) and the Deutsche Bundespost were units within postal and telecommunications departments; they were therefore linked with postal services, were part of the civil service and, legally, operated under direct Ministerial control. In Britain, the Post Office was a government department until 1969, when it became a public corporation. Italy was an exception in that several PTOs existed, the largest of which, ASST (Azienda di Stato per i Servizi Telefonici), was part of the civil service, but others were public corporations. There were no independent regulators for telecommunications; indeed, the concept of 'regulation' was rarely applied to telecommunications in Western Europe. Instead, PTT (Post, Telegraph and Telecommunications) Ministries[3] combined the functions of national regulators, policymakers and suppliers of services and networks.[4] Their objectives were multiple and usually implicit, but included 'public service', national industrial policy and provision of employment.

A broad coalition of interests lay behind the institutional framework of telecommunications (Noam 1992). Governments were able to use PTOs as policy instruments for their macroeconomic and industrial strategies; thus, for example, they varied PTO investment to meet aggregate demand policies, determined tariffs for telecommunications services according to non-cost political, social and regional policy criteria, supported selected equipment manufacturers through PTO orders and provided employment via PTOs. Residential users, and hence voters, received indirect cross subsidies from businesses: access charges lay below costs and were cross-subsidised by long-distance tariffs, the latter bearing more heavily on firms than households. Postal services were often also supported by telecommunications profits. PTO managements were protected from competition by their monopoly positions, whilst their employees enjoyed civil service rights (notably concerning dismissal and salary increases with length of employment).

The traditional structure of telecommunications faced increasing transnational challenges that began in the 1960s and greatly gathered force over time. Sweeping technological and economic changes, notably digitalisation and new methods of transmission, transformed the sector. New technologies made much existing equipment 'technologically obselete' but required massive investment. They also weakened national monopolies and increased the demands made of PTOs. The boundaries between telecommunications and the competitive computing and audiovisual sectors lessened, further imperilling PTO monopolies. The domestic frontiers of telecommunications were also diminished. Lucrative international services grew very rapidly (especially by multinational firms). At the same time, regulatory reform took place in the United States, in particular the 1984 Bell Settlement. It helped to alter the international climate of ideas towards the virtues of competition, appearing to support beliefs that telecommunications were rapidly ceasing to be a 'natural monopoly'; it also encouraged American firms and policymakers to seek entry to overseas markets. Demand grew and became much more diverse; telecommunications became economically 'strategic'. As users became increasingly reliant on telecommunications supply, they also became more critical of poor supply by PTOs, whilst the stakes for nations in their telecommunications systems rose.

Competition, modernisation, high quality diverse supply to demanding users and international pressures challenged the cosy, stable world of monopoly publicly-owned PTOs in Great Britain, France, Germany and Italy. The coalitions supporting existing arrangements came under strain and existing arrangements were called into question in all four countries. Governments faced dissatisfaction with existing telecommunications services from users, as supply failed to meet demand. They were also confronted with demands by PTOs and users for large-scale capital expenditure to fund modernisation and expansion. PTO managements grew increasingly restive at finding their investment constrained and being used to finance non-telecommunications activities. Increasingly they wished to 're-balance' their tariffs to bring them closer to new cost structures that resulted from the introduction of new technologies. 'Re-balancing' benefited large users, especially businesses, but worsened the lot of many residential subscribers, an unpopular change with voters and governments.

National policymakers began to attempt reforms from the late 1960s onwards. In particular, alterations of the organisational basis of PTOs, away from the civil service and towards public corporations, separated from postal services and enjoying legal identity and a degree of formal autonomy from elected politicians; limited extensions of competition were also discussed, mostly concerning terminal equipment. However, in France, Germany and Italy, attempts at institutional modifications failed or were very modest (Snow 1986; Foreman-Peck and Müller 1988). Removal of PTOs from the civil service and PTT ministries was blocked by powerful and determined coalitions, led by trade unions and employees, but also including elements of the political left, equipment suppliers and parts of the postal service, whilst PTO managements stood out against any erosion of their monopoly. In contrast, the forces supporting reform were less vigorous and organised and often only constituted minority elements within PTO managements and governments. Thus, for example, in France, transformation of the DGT's *statut* into a form of public corporation and separation of telecommunications and postal services obtained considerable political and public support in the mid 1970s, but was blocked by a major postal strike in 1974 (Thatcher 1999). In Germany and Italy changes was discussed without action being taken, as political parties and trade unions prevented action.

The early–mid 1980s saw an exception emerge in Europe: Britain. Already, in 1969, the Post Office had become a public corporation. After a period of failed attempts at institutional reform in the 1970s, there was rapid change following the election in 1979 of the Conservative government led by Margaret Thatcher. BT (British Telecom) was created in 1981, separating telecommunications from postal services. Under the Telecommunications Act 1984, BT was then privatised in 1984 and a semi-independent regulator, Oftel (the Office of Telecommunications) was established to enforce licence conditions. BT's monopoly was largely ended during the 1980s and competition gradually spread. Conservative governments implemented the rapid and comprehensive changes against considerable hostility: they were able to overcome trade union opposition through legislation and re-election in 1983. The reforms were driven by fiscal pressures, the oddities of public accounting in Britain (whereby privatisation receipts count as negative public expenditure), the political interests of the Conservative party and beliefs that only a privately-owned BT facing competition would offer efficient service (Thatcher 1999).

Thus by the late 1980s, France, Germany and Italy faced a legacy of institutional inertia and successful obstruction of reforms. Yet transnational pressures were growing, whilst Britain had broken away from the traditional structure of European regulation.

## 3. THE DEVELOPMENT OF EC REGULATION

Until the mid 1980s, the EC played almost no role in the regulation of telecommunications (Sandholtz 1992: 92–9, Schneider and Werle 1990). After a Green Paper in 1987 (Commission 1987), there was an increasingly rapid flow of EC regulatory measures (notably in the form of Directives) (Thatcher 2001; Bauer 1993). By the mid 1990s, these were sufficiently comprehensive to constitute a fully-fledged supranational regulatory regime covering most aspects of telecommunications accepted by member states. They outlawed many of the traditional features of telecommunications policy in Western Europe.

Most EC regulation concerned competition. One set of provisions prohibited member states from maintaining legal monopolies over supply ('special and exclusive rights'), obliging them to allow competition. Initially, Directives covered limited segments of the telecommunications market (terminals, advanced services, satellites and mobile communications) (Commission 1988, 1990, 1994, 1996a). However, in the mid 1990s, they also ended the rights of member states to maintain monopolies in the core of the sector–voice telephony and the building and operation of telecommunications networks (Council 1995; Commission 1995, 1996b). By 1998, EC law allowed competition throughout the telecommunications sector.[5]

A second set of EC provisions 're-regulated' supply by instituting a host of rules governing the conditions of supply. They comprised provisions in directives ending national monopolies, framework directives[6] and measures dealing with individual services which also contained detailed rules.[7] They were designed to ensure 'fair and effective' competition and to prevent policymakers in member states from using regulatory instruments to prevent or bias competition. They laid down broad principles for the supply of services and networks, including non-discrimination, cost-based tariffs, publication of conditions of supply and access for other suppliers of services and terminal equipment.

EC legislation imposed duties and requirements on 'national regulatory authorities' (NRAs) who were either to implement them or to police their observance by suppliers. It laid down fewer stipulations concerning the structure of the state. The most important was that supply and regulation had to be undertaken by legally separated organisations; hence PTOs could not continue to be regulators. Other provisions concerned the functioning of NRAs; thus, for example, their decisions had to be 'proportional', 'transparent', based on 'objective criteria' and reasoned. However, there was no requirements that NRAs be independent of national governments - indeed, PTT departments were generally counted as NRAs, together with autonomous public bodies with regulatory powers in telecommunications.

## 4. THE IMPACT OF EC REGULATION ON LIBERALISATION AND THE REGULATION OF COMPETITION

The traditional policy framework in the United Kingdom, France, Germany and Italy involved extensive monopolies for national PTOs. Yet EC legislation gave rights to compete and established rules to attempt to ensure that competition was fair and effective. Thus, at first sight, the EC's regulatory regime represented a considerable change for member states. Close analysis, however, indicates a complex pattern of interactions between EC requirements and other factors for change operating within the four countries. Some of the EC's requirements had already been implemented by member states, whilst others were underway. Moreover, the EC was only one pressure for liberalisation and the creation of new regimes based on regulation of competition. Finally, EC legislation did not end the scope for national regulation and differences, which continued within its framework.

In the 1980s and early 1990s, many of the EC measures had already been introduced or were underway in the four countries. In particular, EC directives that competition be allowed in terminal equipment and advanced services (Commission 1988, 1990, 1994, 1996a and 1996b) were largely following national reforms rather than leading them. Thus in Great Britain, BT's monopoly over terminal equipment, 'value-added services' and mobile communications services had been ended in the early 1980s as part of the policy of liberalisation pursued both by the Conservative government and Oftel; competition was extended and new rules were established to ensure that it was 'fair and effective'. Similarly, in France and Germany, PTO monopolies over the supply of customer premises equipment and value-added network services had been restricted during the 1980s, whilst liberalisation in mobile services began in the late 1980s and early 1990s. In the two countries, EC legislation at most merely extended the scope of liberalisation and offered refinements to national rules. Only in Italy, where the development of competition was slow, did EC legislation have a major direct impact as it required major change; even so, there had been discussions of liberalisation of terminal equipment unrelated to EC legislation (for example Foreman-Peck and Manning 1988; Noam 1992).

Liberalisation of terminal equipment and advanced services in the four countries were largely driven by non-EC national and transnational factors. One was pressure by politically-influential large business users who were dependent on high quality advanced telecommunications services. When faced with inadequate supply by incumbent PTOs, they lobbied for competition to be permitted. Notable examples included major financial institutions in Britain and Olivetti and Fiat in Italy (Cawson et al. 1990;

*Financial Times* 15.4.80, 24.4.81 and 1.10.82; Richeri 1985; Foreman-Peck and Manning 1988). Multinationals played an important role, especially in Germany, where calls for liberalisation were led by IBM, supported by the American government (Schmidt 1991; *Financial Times* 31.7.86 and 2.6.86). Excess demand played a central role in the liberalisation of mobile networks in all four countries: the failure of incumbent PTOs to anticipate and meet supply allowed opportunities for firms such as Mannesman to enter and rapidly build successful businesses. Finally, it became increasingly difficult in practice to police and enforce restrictions on CPE and advanced services.

Introducing competition into advanced services and terminal equipment aroused only limited controversy: they represented a limited segment of markets and were not seen as natural monopolies. Such liberalisation offered little threat to incumbent national champion PTOs. Much more difficult was liberalisation of network operation - public voice telephony and the building and operation of networks - which constituted the core of telecommunications and accounted for the bulk of PTO revenues.

When EC legislation on competition in voice telephony and the operation of networks was passed in 1995–96, the regulatory adaptation required in Britain differed from that of France, Germany and Italy. Britain had already introduced competition into network operation before EC legislation. Hence, the degree of national regulatory modification needed to conform to EC law was very limited. BT and the government were strong supporters of EC action to outlaw national monopolies in network operation. They saw it as an opportunity to 'export' the British regulatory model and aid British companies, especially BT, to expand abroad.

In contrast, France, Germany and Italy still maintained monopolies for their historic PTOs in network operation, and indeed during the 1980s had made considerable efforts to protect those monopolies. Moreover, the 're-regulatory' elements of EC legislation were largely new: previously there had been few formal requirements over matters such as interconnection, licensing and universal service because of monopoly provision by a state-owned operator. Therefore, to comply with EC legal requirements to end remaining monopolies, France, Germany and Italy passed major pieces of legislation in the mid 1990s.[8]

Nevertheless, even in France, Germany and Italy, EC requirements for competition in network operation formed part of reform processes already underway within member states (Bancel-Charensol 1996; Werle 1999). During the late 1980s and early 1990s, reducing PTO monopolies became a matter of public discussion, notably through special committees/commissions such as the 1987 Witte Commission, the 1988 Prévot Commission and the 1993 Dandelot investigation (Prévot 1989; Dandelot 1993; Witte 1989). The position of key actors within the national political arena altered. In particular, national governments and PTO managements gradually accepted during the 1990s that competition in voice telephony and telecommunications infrastructure provision was inevitable and indeed even beneficial (Thatcher 1999; Werle 1999).

The changes in the strategies of PTOs and governments were in large measure due to non-EC factors. Policymakers believed that PTOs faced the development of 'bypass': if PTOs did not adapt tariffs and conditions, large users would either use new technologies to re-route their calls to avoid or relocate their telecommunications operations to countries offering more favourable conditions (Longuet 1988). New ideas about natural monopoly and the benefits of competition spread, as did claims that countries which maintained restrictions would be left behind other countries which had liberalised; in particular, Britain was seen as a dangerous competitor, thanks to liberalisation, the presence of the privately-owned BT and its policy of attracting large multinational telecommunications users (Dandelot 1993; Larcher 1993; *Il Sole 24 Ore* 6.6.94, 11.5.96 and 17.12.96). There was growing pressure for liberalisation by business users, especially large multinationals and powerful domestic firms. When monopoly PTOs could not expand supply sufficiently rapidly, they faced particular pressure for liberalisation and the danger of private networks being established - for example, in Germany where Deutsche Telekom had difficulty in coping with the effects of reunification and in Italy, where demand often outstripped supply.

Acceptance of extended competition was also intimately linked to internationalisation, which was vigorously pursued by France Télécom and Deutsche Telekom with the active involvement of their national governments (Elixmann and Hermann 1996). For the operators, overseas development represented a response to increased demand for international services, to alliances being formed by other operators (most notably between BT and the American operator MCI) and to weakening national monopolies.

EC legislation requiring the ending of PTO monopolies in network operation thus introduced changes that actors within national policy debates believed would and should occur for non-EC reasons. Its impacts were to offer an additional pressure for change and an external justification for reforms. The former consisted of accelerating the need for national policymakers to liberalise and of providing a set date for them to do so (notably 1 January 1998 for public voice telephony and infrastructure). Moreover, it appeared to increase the benefits of competition: a single European market offered greater opportunities for cross-national links between European PTOs. Liberalisation was the quid pro quo of privatisation, which was strongly desired by PTO managements and governments (see below).

Legitimising competition was perhaps the most important impact of EC regulation. Ending long-standing PTO monopolies often met strong opposition, led by trade unions representing PTO employees and parts of the political left. During the 1980s, competition in network operation had been rejected by official commissions in France and Germany due to such opposition (Witte 1989; Prévot 1989). EC requirements provided political impetus to overcome inertia and often active resistance to liberalisation. The opponents of reform (particularly trade unions) were organised at the national level and found it more difficult to attack liberalisation legislation domestically as it appeared to follow EC law. By the mid 1990s, competition appeared 'inevitable' and instead, conflicts focussed on privatisation of PTOs. One reason for acceptance of full competition within France, Germany and Italy was EC regulation. Thus, for example, legislation in Germany in 1994 (Postreform III) extending competition was presented as being necessary to meet EC obligations, in the face of powerful lobbying by the DPG trade union; similarly, in Italy, liberalisation in the mid 1990s followed the application of general EC competition law by the Anti-Trust Authority, the requirements of EC telecommunications directives and direct pressure by the European Commission (Werle 1999; Natalicchi 2001; *Il Sole 24 Ore* 6.2.95, 29.3.95, 18.7.95, 7.6.96 and 11.9.96). Even in France, there was remarkably little discussion over the 1996 law that ended France Télécom's monopoly: one major justification was the requirements of EC legislation (DGPT 1994; Dandelot 1993; Chevallier 1996; *Les Echos* 4.4.96; *Le Monde* 6.6.96).

The development of the EC's regulatory framework did not end the importance of the national level. EC Directives were very broad, and were transposed and 'fleshed out' by primary legislation in France, Germany and Italy. In addition, since EC law was largely implemented by NRAs (National Regulatory Authorities),[9] who were responsible, in the first instance, for ensuring that EC law was observed, national regulators had considerable discretion over matters crucial to the development of competition. Thus, for instance, NRAs were responsible for issuing licences to operators and therefore determined licence conditions; although terms had to conform with EC law, notably general principles such as non-discrimination and proportionality, they had significant scope for deciding matters such as the geographical areas that licensees were to serve or standards of service to be imposed. Moreover, for the increasingly important mobile services, only a limited number of licences were available and allocation saw highly political manoeuvres involving large firms and elected politicians.

Thus EC law, in ending the right of member states to maintain monopolies, had several impacts or non-impacts. Certain provisions had already been introduced, most prominently in Britain. In other cases, EC requirements increased pressures for liberalisation at the national level. However, they were additional to other factors pressing in the same direction. They strengthened the hand of reformers and weakened coalitions opposing reforms, but those changes were in large measure designed to respond to non-EC pressures. The EC regulatory regime aided PTOs and governments to adapt to the changing environment of telecommunications and to reduce opposition to change. At the same time, EC law allowed member much power to remain in the hands of national regulators over the nature of regulation and competition.

## 5. EC REGULATION AND STATE STRUCTURES

The 1980s and especially the 1990s saw a comprehensive reshaping of state structures in Britain, France, Germany and Italy. In all four countries, changes involved a two-step process away from the traditional structure of the state as regulator, policymaker and supplier. The first stage in reform was that the PTOs (public telecommunications operators) were separated from postal services and made into autonomous publicly-owned companies (or their equivalents), with their own legal identity, leaving the PTT Ministry as the main sectoral regulator. In Britain, British Telecom was created from the Post Office in 1981,[10] the Deutsche Bundespost was divided in 1989–90 into three corporations, including Telekom which was separated from telecommunications and France Télécom became an *exploitant public*, with its own legal personality, in 1990. The reform process in Italy involved the largest supplier, ASST, being removed from the PTT Ministry in 1992 and then consolidation in 1994–96, through the creation of Telecom Italia, which brought together all the various publicly-owned operators.

Thereafter, the PTOs were wholly or partially privatised. Hence 50.1 per cent of shares were sold in BT in 1984, with the remainder being disposed of by 1993. A minority of shares in Deutsche Telekom and France Télécom were sold in 1996–98, whilst a majority of Telecom Italia shares were sold in 1997. New regulatory authorities were created that were semi-independent from elected politicians: Oftel (the Office of Telecommunications), the ART (Autorité de régulation des télécommunications), the RegTP (Regulierungsbehörde für Telekommunikation und Post) and the AGCOM (Autorità per le Garanzie nelle Communicazioni). They enjoyed considerable formal powers over enforcing licences and ensuring that competition was 'fair', leaving governments with more general functions, notably over licensing and defining the framework of competition.

EC legislation contained few requirements concerning the organisation of the state. Even the most important stipulation in directives – that supply and regulation were to be undertaken by separate organisations – prohibited PTOs from continuing to act as regulators, but did not necessitate PTOs ceasing to be part of the civil service. Other changes, such as privatisation and independent regulators, were not part of EC legislation. Thus the reforms did not represent the transposition of EC legal measures into national law.

Nevertheless, in France, Germany and Italy, the EC played an important role in the reform process in the late 1980s and the 1990s. Transformation of PTOs into corporations in the late 1980s and then privatisation in the 1990s involved lengthy and often bitter struggles. On the one side stood PTO managements and often governments, who supported change. They were opposed by coalitions supporting the status quo. Their core members were PTO trade unions and employees, who wished to protect civil service status for employees, and nationalistic supporters of public ownership (traditionally present in parties of both the political left and right) who argued that states should conserve vital areas of economic life under their direct control and prevent private monopolies from exploiting users.

National coalitions supporting traditional state structures found themselves placed in a defensive position by the EC and struggling against a gradual set of changes that undermined their position and cohesion. The EC's regulatory regime, centred on 'fair and effective competition', undermined traditional justifications for public sector supply such as 'service public', cross-subsidisation and support for domestic manufacturers. It increased pressures on governments and PTOs to alter existing structures: liberalisation engendered processes of entry that appeared to disadvantage suppliers who failed to alter their organisational forms and that increased incentives for governments to distance themselves from supply. In addition, the EC triggered processes of change and contributed to a redistribution of power in struggles over the organisation of the state, weakening opponents of institutional modifications and providing arguments for reformers.

In the first stage of reform, namely transforming PTOs from civil service departments into public corporations, trade unions and employees faced EC requirements prohibiting PTOs from continuing their regulatory functions. The argument was used by PTO managements and governments in France and Germany to justify removing PTOs from the civil service structures and making them legally separate bodies from PTT Ministries. Thus, for instance, in France, the Prévot Commission in 1989 pointed to EC law as one reason to end France Télécom's century-old status as an administration; the issue only became the details of its legal status and how to protect existing rights rather than the principle of change (Prévot 1989). A similar process applied in Germany with the Witte Commission that led to the first Postreform of 1989–90 that saw the creation of Deutsche Telekom (Witte 1989; Schmidt 1991).

In the second stage of change during the 1990s when France Télécom, Deutsche Telekom and Telecom Italia were fully or partially privatised, EC regulation again undermined supporters of the status quo by altering the domestic environment of telecommunications. Ending national monopolies and instituting EC rules on 'fair competition' appeared to threaten suppliers who operated in a non-commercial manner. Moreover, the EC-wide regulatory regime drew attention to other examples of reform in Europe; in particular, Britain supplied an alternative state structure that endangered unreformed PTOs, since BT would be able to enter European markets. Policymakers and PTO managers in France and Italy argued that EC liberalisation made reform urgent and indispensable in order to meet the challenges from the entry of powerful, expansionist operators such as BT and AT&T (see, for example, Larcher 1996; *Le Monde* 7.6.97; *Il Sole 24 Ore* 6.6.94, 29.6.95 and 11.5.96). EC 'imposed' competition offered a particularly useful argument for governments of the left who faced internal hostility to privatisation from their parties and coalitions. Thus in France, Germany and Italy, political parties that had hitherto opposed reforms supported and often introduced them; they claimed that privatisation was essential for their national champion PTOs to be able to compete and form alliance in response to EC regulation. The most striking examples were in France and Italy, where governments of the left depended on supported from Communist or former Communist parties; indeed, partial privatisation of France Télécom after June 1997 ran counter to the election promises of the PS. In Germany, the Social Democrats (whose support was needed to pass constitutional changes) also accepted reforms, citing EC competition as a major reason. In Italy, the EC's role was direct and explicit: IRI, the state umbrella company that owned certain operators was so overburdened by debt that, faced with European state aid law, reorganisation was agreed between the Italian government and the competition Directorate General (DG IV) of the Commission.[11]

The nationalist wing of the coalition supporting traditional institutional structures shrank, as the previous reasons for its support for state ownership of PTOs were gradually removed. Competition and regulation appeared to render public ownership unnecessary to prevent monopoly exploitation of users by private suppliers. Reforms were needed for national champion PTOs to survive and prosper. Trade unions and employees were left isolated, appearing to cling to outdated structures in pursuit of narrow sectional interests, in the face of EC regulation based on competitive markets and successful examples of privatisation that threatened to leave unreformed 'national champion' PTOs vulnerable.

However, although EC regulation aided reformers and increased incentives for institutional modifications, it was an additional influence to other pressures for change. Its role in national politics was to accelerate and facilitate developments driven by non-EC factors. The process of organisation reform of PTOs had begun at the national level during the 1980s, as PTO managements and national governments sought to adapt to new conditions.

Thereafter, the process accelerated in the 1990s, due to both EC regulation and non-EC factors. Rather than representing a decisive break or an external imposition, the EC regulatory regime largely represented a factor congruent with other pressures, as reforms were selected and supported by PTO managements and governments for non-EC reasons.[12]

The alteration in strategies independently of EC regulation can be seen by the fact that the process of modifying state structures had started before most EC legislation. As with competition, Britain represented an extreme case: organisational reforms (notably privatisation of BT and the establishment of Oftel) which took place were introduced in 1984 before EC directives and indeed without reference to Europe. In France and Germany, attempts to move away from civil service status for PTOs were longstanding, dating from the 1960s and 1970s. In France, for example, attempts to transform the DGT/France Télécom into a form of public corporation, had begun in the late 1960s (Thatcher 1999). In the mid/late 1980s, the reform movement was revived in earnest, just as the EC began to develop its regulatory framework. Thus, in France, in 1988 the Rocard government established a special commission to examine alteration of France Télécom's statut (Prévot 1989), which led to legislation in 1990 that transformed the operator into a special form of public corporation. In Germany, the process of reform also got underway through the Witte Commission which was established in 1985 and proposed in 1987 that the Deutsche Bundespost be split into three public corporations, one being Telekom (Thatcher 1995).

Therefore the reforms in the 1990s represented an acceleration and amplification of an existing process, not a new direction. They were supported by both PTO managements and national governments for many reasons that were unrelated to the EC. The former sought restructuring not just to meet EC-imposed competition, but also to escape the constraints of the public sector and to adapt to changing market conditions. They sought increased autonomy from elected politicians from governments and greater freedom to alter their internal management and labour practices. Governments also had their own reasons for institutional reform that were unrelated or only partially related to the EC's regulatory regime in telecommunications. Privatisation offered vital fiscal advantages, as sale receipts allowed governments to reduce debt and meet the Maastricht criteria for public debt; in addition, in Germany and Italy, it avoided use of public funds for essential investment.

The process of reform and the role of the EC did not end national differences. On the contrary, significant cross-national variations in institutional arrangements existed by 2001. Thus, for instance, whereas Telecom Italia was fully privatised, the State maintained a majority share in France Télécom and Deutsche Telekom. The powers and organisation status of regulators also differed - for instance, the Italian regulator AGCOM covered both telecommunications and broadcasting unlike its counterparts in the other three countries. The number and method of appointment of regulators also remained distinct. These institutional features were not covered by EC directives.

Thus, for state structures, EC regulation played a dual role. It increased the incentives for PTOs and governments to reform the structure of the state and change the pattern of relationships, notably through its rules on competition. At the same time, it eased the path of reform: it weakened the coalition supporting traditional organisational forms; it provided arguments and instruments for reformers in PTOs and governments in the pursuit of their strategies of adaptation to altered national and international circumstances, whilst leaving them great discretion through its lack of binding detail and scope for national variations.

## 6. CONCLUSION: THE EC'S REGULATORY REGIME AND NATIONAL REFORM

In analysing the influence of EC regulation on national institutional reforms, a distinction was made between three forms of impact: its direct/coercive effects, whereby member states alter their institutional arrangements to meet EC legal requirements; its indirect effects in leading to reforms that are not required by EC law; its legitimising functions whereby it justifies reforms desired for non-EC reasons. All three impacts can be seen in telecommunications in the 1980s and 1990s.

EC regulation affected institutional reform in telecommunications in France, Germany and Italy. It did so through its legal requirements: the three countries passed legislation to comply with them. This was especially so in the mid 1990s for the extension of competition in public voice telephony and the infrastructure. The EC's regulatory regime also had more indirect effects through the repercussions of liberalisation for existing organisational arrangements, thereby extending its influence well beyond its formal legal requirements. In the late 1980s and in the 1990s, EC liberalisation was one reason for PTO managements and governments seeking to transform PTOs into public corporations and then privatise them, in order to adapt to a new competitive European market.

Yet the EC was only one of several factors responsible for institutional change. EC measures formed part of broader processes of telecommunications reform at the national level. Their impact must be considered in the broader context of pressures for change. Attempts at reorganising telecommunications had begun before the EC even entered the telecommunications field; several processes had started in the 1960s. By the 1980s, when EC regulation began, a number of certain alterations had already been implemented by member states; in these respects, EC legislation was following behind domestic action. The most pronounced example was Britain, where EC decisions required almost no domestic alterations; however, in the other three countries, most early EC requirements had also been introduced. Even in the 1990s, when compliance with EC regulation required significant changes in France, Germany and Italy, non-EC factors were crucial in the desire of policymakers to alter national institutional arrangements. Closer inspection of domestic politics indicates the importance of non-EC influences in the shifting strategies of key actors. In particular, PTO managements and governments increasingly favoured liberalisation and reorganisation and privatisation of PTOs in order to adapt to changing technological and economic conditions in the industry, internationalise, gain fiscal receipts and alter their internal management. Although EC regulation amplified pressures, it was only an additional factor, and often less important than them.

However, reformers were confronted with a powerful domestic coalition that blocked rapid reform. The EC's regulatory regime became part of the national politics of institutional reform. It strengthened the position of reformers in the three countries. Their coalitions were broadened as EC decisions contributed to the alteration of the strategies of PTO managements, governments, political parties and officials in the domestic policy process. EC regulation offered reformers additional arguments to justify changes and played a crucial role in legitimising change. On the other hand, EC regulation weakened the position of opponents of new forms of supply and regulation. Their previous coalitions were reduced, as nationalistic supporters and political parties abandoned them. Trade unions and employees found themselves isolated and confronted by the logic of the EC's regulatory regime which conflicted with their aims and afforded them few arguments in debates on preserving monopolies and civil service supply of telecommunications services.

National modifications were therefore driven by a host of factors, of which the EC was only one. EC decisions required changes, enhanced existing desires for change and aided governments and PTO managements to justify and accelerate reforms that they desired for non-EC reasons. The last was the most important impact of the EC. The central role of the EC's regulatory regime was therefore to reinforce and accelerate moves towards liberalisation and public sector restructuring and to assist reformers in PTOs and national governments in pursuing their strategies of adaptation to changing domestic and international conditions in telecommunications, whilst seeing domestic opponents weakened. Finally, EC regulation did not prevent significant national institutional variations: despite the existence of a comprehensive regime developed over several years, important national differences remained by 2001.

The research forms part of a project on European telecommunica-tions within the ESRC Future Governance Programme, project no. L216 25 2007 and work within the LSE Centre for the Analysis of Risk and Regulation.

## NOTES

1. This chapter arises from a project on European telecommunications within the ESRC Future Governance programme, project no. L216 25 2007 and work within the LSE Centre for the Analysis of Risk and Regulation.
2. References are to the European Community, even after the European Union came into being, since the EU has acted under its EC 'pillar'.
3. Or Ministries incorporating them – for ease of reference, they are referred to as PTT Ministries.
4. Except for Britain after 1969, where the Post Office had its own legal identity.
5. There were some temporary derogations for member states with small or underdeveloped infrastructures; these did not apply to the four countries studied here.
6. Notably Council (1990) – the ONP Directive.
7. See, for instance, directives on leased lines and voice telephony (Council 1992 and 1995), and on licensing and universal service (European Parliament 1997a and b).
8. In France, the 1996 law on liberalisation and competition, no. 96–559; in Germany, the 1996 Telekommunikationsgesetz ('Postreform III'); in Italy, the law no. 249 of 31 July 1997; in Britain, minor modifications were required to meet some EC 're-regulatory' requirements.
9. NRAs were public bodies with regulatory powers within member states; they therefore include both governments and the new semi-independent regulatory bodies established in all four countries.
10. Although the Post Office had become a public corporation in 1969.
11. In the agreement in 1993 between competition Commission Van Miert and the then Foreign Minister, Beniamino Andreatta, the Commission promised not to take legal action concerning state aids if IRI's debts were reduced, which Italy stated would be achieved through some form of privatisation of Telecom Italia; the Commissioner for competition, Karel Van Miert, discussed privatisation with Italian policymakers in 1995–96 (*Il Sole 24 Ore* 3.3.95, 7.6.96 and 11.9.96).
12. For a general discussion of factors responsible for privatisation and changing state structures in Western Europe, see Wright (1994).

## REFERENCES

Bauer, Johannes M. (1993), 'Telecommunications in post-1992 Europe', *International Review of Comparative Public Policy*, **5**, 109–35.

Bancel-Charensol, L. (1996), *La Déréglementation des Télécommunications*, Paris: Economica/ENSPTT.

Cawson, A., P. Holmes, D. Webber, K. Morgan and A. Stevens (1990), *Hostile Brothers*, Oxford: Clarendon Press.

Chevallier, J. (1996), 'La nouvelle réforme des télécommunications: ruptures et continuités', *Revue Française de Droit Administratif*, **12** (5), 909–51.

Commission of the European Communities (1987), *Towards a Dynamic European Economy – Green Paper on the development of the common market for telecommunications services and equipment*, COM(87) 290, 30 June 1987.

Commission of the European Communities (1988), *Commission Directive on Competition in the Markets in Telecommunications Terminal Equipment*,

Commission Directive 88/301/EEC, (OJ L 131, 27.5.88).
Commission of the European Communities (1990), *Commission Directive on Competition in the Markets for Telecommunications Services*, Brussels, 90/388/EEC (OJ L 1922, 24.7.90).
Commission of the European Communities (1994), *Commission Directive Amending Directive 88/301/EEC and Directive 90/388/EEC in Particular with Regard to Satellite Communications*, Brussels, 13 October 1994, 94/46/EC (OJ L268/15).
Commission of the European Communities (1995), *Commission Directive Amending Directive 90/388/EEC with Regard to the Abolition of the Restrictions on the Use of Cable Television Networks for the Provision of Already Liberalised Telecommunications Networks*, Brussels, 18 October 1995, 95/51/EC (OJ L 256/49, 26.10.95).
Commission of the European Communities (1996a), *Commission Directive Amending Directive 90/388/EEC with Regard to Mobile and Personal Communications*, Brussels, 16 January 1996, 96/2/EC (OJ 1996 L20/59).
Commission of the European Communities (1996b), *Commission Directive Amending Directive 90/388/EEC Regarding the Implementation of Full Competition in Telecommunications Markets*, Brussels, 28 February 1996, 96/19/EC (OJ L 74/13, 22.3.96).
Council of the European Communities (1990), *Directive on the Establishment of the Internal Market for Telecommunications Services through the Implementation of Open Network Provision*, Brussels, 28 June 1990, 90/387/EEC (OJ L 192/1, 24.07.90).
Council of the European Communities (1992), *Directive on the Application of Open Network Provision to Leased Lines*, Brussels, 5 June 1992, 92/44/EEC (OJ L 165/27, 19.06.92).
Council of the European Communities (1995), *Directive on the Application of Open Network Provision (ONP) to Voice Telephony*, Brussels, 13 December 1995, 95/62/EC (OJ L321/6, 30.12.95).
DGPT (1994), *Quelle Réglementation pour les Télécommunications Françaises?*, Paris: DGPT.
Dandelot, Marc (1993), *Le secteur des Télécommunications en France: Rapport au Ministre de l'Industrie, des Postes et Télécommunications et du Commerce Extérieur*, Paris: PTT Ministry.
Eliassen, K. and M. Svojaag (eds) (1999), *Liberalising European Telecommunications*, London: Routledge.
Elixmann, D. and H. Hermann, (1996), 'Strategic alliances in the telecommunications service sector: challenges for corporate strategy, *Communications & Stratégies*, **24** 57-88.
European Parliament and European Council (1997a), *Directive on a Common Framework for General Authorizations and Individual Licences in the Field of Telecommunications Services*, Brussels, 17 April 1997, 97/13/EC (OJ L 117/15, 7.5.97).
European Parliament and European Council (1997b), *Directive on Interconnection in Telecommunications with Regard to Ensuring Universal Service and Interoperability through Application of the Principles of Open Network Provision (ONP)*, Brussels, 30 June 1997, 97/33/EC (OJ L 199/32, 26.7.97).
Foreman-Peck, James and Dorothy Manning (1988), 'Telecommunications in Italy', in James Foreman-Peck and Jurgen Müller (ed.), *European Telecommunications Organisation*, Baden-Baden: Nomos.
Foreman-Peck, James and Jurgen Müller (eds) (1988), *European Telecommunications*

*Organisation*, Baden-Baden: Nomos.
Larcher, Gérard, *L'Avenir du Secteur des Télécommunications*, rapport du Sénat no.129, Paris: Sénat, 1993.
Longuet, Gérard (1988), *Télécoms. La Conquête de Nouveaux Espaces*, Paris: Dunod.
Natalicchi, G. (2001), *Wiring Europe*, Maryland: Rowman and Littlechild.
Noam, Eli (1992), *Telecommunications in Europe*, New York: Oxford University Press.
Prévot, Hubert (1989), *Rapport de synthèse*, Paris: PTE Ministry.
Radaelli, Claudio (2000), 'Wither Europeanization? Concept stretching and substantive change', PSA Conference, London.
Richeri, Guiseppe (1985), 'The difficulties involved in the control and organization of telecommunications in Italy', *Media, Culture and Society*, **7**, 49–70.
Sandholtz, Wayne (1992), *High-Tech Europe*, Berkeley, Los Angeles and Oxford: University of California Press.
Sandholtz, Wayne (1998), 'The Emergence of a Supranational Telecommunications Regime', in Wayne Sandholtz, and Alec Stone Sweet (eds), *European Integration and Supranational Governance*, Oxford: Oxford University Press.
Sandholtz, Wayne and Alec Stone Sweet (eds) (1998), *European Integration and Supranational Governance*, Oxford: Oxford University Press.
Schmidt, Suzanne K, (1991), 'Taking the long road to liberalization. Telecommunications reform in the Federal Republic of Germany', *Telecommunications Policy*, **15** (3), 209–22.
Schneider, Volker and Raymond Werle (1990), 'International Regime or Corporate Actor? The European Community in Telecommunications Policy', in K. Dyson and P. Humphreys (eds), *The Political Economy of Telecommunications*, London and New York: Routledge.
Schneider, Volker, Godefroy Dang-Nguyen and Raymund Werle (1994), 'Corporate actor networks in European policy-making: harmonizing telecommunications policy', *Journal of Common Market Studies*, **32** (4), 473–98.
Snow, Marcellus (1986), *Telecommunications Regulation and Deregulation in Industrialized Democracies*, Oxford: Oxford University Press.
Thatcher, Mark (1995), 'Regulatory Reform and Internationalization in Telecommunications', in Jack E.S. Hayward (ed.), *Industrial Enterprise and European Integration*, Oxford: Oxford University Press.
Thatcher, Mark (1997), 'The Development of European Regulatory Frameworks: The Expansion of European Community Policy Making in Telecommunications', in E. Stravridis, E. Mossialos, R Morgan and H. Machin (eds), *New Challenges to the European Union*, Aldershot: Dartmouth Publishing.
Thatcher, Mark (1999), *The Politics of Telecommunications*, Oxford: Oxford University Press.
Thatcher, Mark (2001), 'The Commission and national governments as partners: EC regulatory expansion in telecommunications 1979–2000', *Journal of European Public Policy*, **8** (4), 558–84.
Werle, Raymund (1990), *Telekommunikation in der Bundesrepublik*, Frankfurt and New York: Campus Verlag.
Werle, Raymund (1999), 'Liberalisation of Telecommunications in Germany', in Kjell Eliassen and Marit Sjovaag (eds), *Liberalising European Telecommunications*, London: Routledge.
Witte, E. (1989), *Telekommunikation in der DDR und der Bundesrepublik*, Heidelberg: Decker.

Wright, Vincent (ed.) (1994), *Privatization in Western Europe: Pressures, Problems and Paradoxes*, London: Pinter.

# 5. The persistence of telecommunications policies in national States: Portugal and Spain in the European arena

**Jacint Jordana**

## THE ROLE OF NATIONAL POLICIES IN THE EUROPEAN TELECOMMUNICATIONS SECTOR

The objective of this chapter is to provide an overview of the State's changing role in regulation of the telecommunications sector in Spain and Portugal during the 1990s. Analysing these two cases, we will attempt to determine to what extent EC (European Community) policies influenced telecommunications policy choices at the State level during those years. We will argue that national governments continued to play an important role in the sector while trans-national agreements gradually took effect. They maintained their capacity to shape markets, albeit within the new context of European interdependence.[1]

European States faced with the pressure of operators and producers in favour of market liberalisation and constrained by EC time scales and uniform regulations, maintained control over several key aspects of the new markets. Often, they took up the challenge and used it as a window of opportunity for pushing through domestic institutional changes. By taking a strategic view of the liberalisation process, they established priorities in shaping the development of the main actors in their emerging markets. Countries took advantage of European institutions and their decision-making processes to eliminate several key domestic opponents to change (Schmidt 1998; Thatcher 1999). For this reason, the Member States, not the EC, created specific asymmetric regulations to achieve the kind of competition they thought was best for the new markets. At the same time, they strengthened control mechanisms by setting up national regulatory authorities for monitoring the new market trends.

## THE CASES OF PORTUGAL AND SPAIN: ESTABLISHING A HYPOTHESIS

This chapter illustrates the foregoing argument by analysing the way government telecommunications policies in Spain and Portugal changed during the 1990s. As a departure point, we consider that each Member State established its own path towards liberalisation of the telecommunications sector, despite the co-ordinating role of the European Commission. Of course, states that were more prone to intervening in industry exercised more direct control and strategic guidance of the process than those governments with a more *laissez faire* tradition. However, one can say that most Member States disposed of sufficient means to monitor and control their markets and some governments actively encouraged the emergence of global firms, their national champions (Hulsink and Davies 1997). Liberalisation policy in Spain and Portugal showed one of the greatest similarities among the EC countries. Both countries actively sought to shape their respective internal markets and the actors in them while upgrading their telecommunications infrastructure to European standards. All throughout the decade, the governments in both countries were much more inclined to intervene in the industry than at any moment either before or since. They managed to obtain considerable room for manoeuvre in pursuing these objectives, notwithstanding the new technological challenges facing the industry and growing globalisation trends.

Spain and Portugal's reorganisation of their telecom sectors during the 1990s was atypical in the EC context. The reason for this was that neither country had previously had any kind of specialised public administration for dealing with telecommunications. During the long dictatorships suffered by both countries, political capture, lack of interest, and many other factors considerably limited the government's powers in this field, which remained extraordinarily limited until the late 1970s. Before that, Telefónica, Spain's monopoly telecommunications company, was responsible for defining policies and even determining the country's telecommunications interests. Telefónica was a privately-run company in which the government had held a stake since 1946 (almost 40 per cent of its capital). It enjoyed a considerable degree of autonomy and its practices and priorities were hardly affected by successive governments, not least because the politicians lacked the means to bring the company to heel (Jordana 1998). In Portugal, telecommunications companies were privately run right through from the nineteenth century to the late 1960s. They were then acquired by the State, but the sector remained fragmented with no fewer than three companies: Marconi, CTP and TLP (Companhía Portuguesa Rádio Marconi, Correios e Telecomunicaçoẽs de Portugal and Telefones de Lisboa e Porto) each running its own monopoly. For many years, these companies were strongly linked to ITT's Portuguese manufacturing subsidiary Standard Electrica (Noam 1992). As in Spain, the Portuguese government did not make any serious attempt to control and steer the sector until the 1980s except for the odd measure linked to industrial policy.

However, the state's capacity for prosecuting public policy in the telecommunications field increased dramatically in both countries during the 1980s and was particularly pronounced in the 1990s. There were several reasons for this: the emergence of specialised public administration and the creation of new authorities; the growing importance of telecommunication services for economic development; internal pressures for cutting communication costs and, last but not least, European policies aimed at securing greater liberalisation. In Portugal, new administrative capabilities led the government to reorganise the sector in 1994, creating a new company (Portugal Telecom) which incorporated the three existing telecom firms. The government also succeeded in overcoming internal opposition in doing so, breaking up the historical predominance of business interests. Thereafter, progressive privatisation of Portugal Telecom in the late 1990s was accompanied by a greater presence abroad with maintenance of the monopoly for fixed lines until 2000. In Spain, this increase in the state's ability to run a modern economy allowed the government to gradually disentangle its interests from those of Telefónica (the company was completely privatised in 1997) without weakening its support for the company's globalisation strategy. This 'early' division allowed the government to introduce ever more sophisticated strategies for structuring the domestic telecom markets, fostering new competitive forces and moulding the profile of firms entering the market.

In both countries, the previous absence of state involvement in the industry meant the government started with a clean slate. Thus state intervention was both swifter and more explicit than elsewhere in the EC. However, Spain and Portugal's lack of any appreciable state involvement in telecommunications became a strength at the most critical moments of the liberalisation process. To some extent, freedom from some path-dependent factors was an opportunity window for institutional policy innovation in these South-European countries during the 1990s. Several factors helped both governments in pursuing their respective policies: weak private actors (particularly during the first faltering steps towards liberalisation); powerful monopolistic companies whose presidents were usually government-appointed (hence the general acceptance of state policies aimed at structuring the new telecom markets); a private sector operating tradition in telecom firms which predisposed them to change and restructuring; and relatively strong differentiation of the monopoly operator vis-à-vis the regulatory framework, control and information. Unhampered by existing state mechanisms, the Spanish and Portuguese governments were able to pursue more aggressive strategies than in other EU countries regarding restructuring of their respective telecommunications markets.

Portugal and Spain share many common features which set them apart from other European countries with regard to telecom liberalisation. However, it is also worth considering to what extent small differences in political action, timing and institutional design between both countries might explain substantial differences in terms of market structure and the make-up of companies in the industry. Finally, considering the implications of our analysis for the whole political system, we will discuss if this type of state behaviour in each country represented a departure from or a continuation of traditional political patterns in Southern Europe. A traditional interpretation argues that intense political and economic horse-trading is *de rigeur* for newcomers who want to get a piece of the action (Negrier 1997). However, a new state-led policy mediation process may be emerging as both countries become better-integrated in Europe and their democracies become more firmly established.

## SPAIN'S TURNING POINT: TELEFONICA'S DEVELOPMENT AND NEWCOMERS TO THE INDUSTRY

The United States' case provided a closer parallel to Spanish telecommunications during the twentieth century than did other European countries. The reason is that the creation of CTNE (Compañia Telefónica Nacional de España, latter called Telefónica) was the first case in which AT&T exported its business model abroad (this would later be repeated in many other countries). However, the significant difference was that the Spanish company had no government regulatory agency to respond to, while its foreign technological dependence put it in a very weak position. CTNE was founded in 1923. The company was granted a monopoly over telecommunications the following year given that the firm's main promoter, ITT's founder Sosthenes Behn, had forged strong links with General Primo de Rivera's recently established dictatorship. There is no clear account of what led to the granting of the license to CTNE. However, the alliance with Spanish investors was a key factor, as was Behn's ability to convince politicians and military to build up 'truly national systems operated by the nationals of each country in which we are' with the help of American engineers (Behn, 1925: 2). After getting the license in August 1924, a private contract between ITT and CTNE was signed which designated ITT as the latter's technical and financial advisor and as CTNE's exclusive supplier. Shortly afterwards (1926), ITT founded a subsidiary company for manufacturing electronic equipment in Spain, Standard Eléctrica Española (Carballo 1979). Postal and telegraph services, which were both publicly operated, remained separate from the telephone license.

During the 1920s, the consolidation of the private licensing model in Spain, inspired and controlled by ITT, put an end to the problems of providing Spain with a decent nationwide telephone network. The introduction of planning and rationalisation of Spain's telephone systems provided a big boost to the country's economic development, paving the way for the rapid growth of telephone services. However, ITT imposed extremely tough terms which highlighted the Spanish government's weak bargaining position and the failure of the country's financiers to come up with a more attractive proposition. ITT introduced a model of vertical integration - in which the operator was wholly dependent on the industry supplier - which also happened to be the prevailing telecommunications business model in the United States (Little 1979).

ITT was not interested in renewing its monopoly license after World War II and the Spanish government wanted to increase its control over telephone communications. Accordingly, ITT proposed selling the company and managed to get the Spanish government to buy a controlling share at highly inflated prices. As a result, the controlling interest in CTNE was transferred to the Spanish government. A few months later, a new monopoly licensing agreement was signed with the government. Additionally, an exclusive 20-year agreement to supply equipment to CTNE was struck with the ITT subsidiary, Standard Eléctrica Española, which held manufacturing licenses from the American company (Plaza 1989; Rios and Erroteta 1982).

Twenty years later, a new team took the helm of CTNE in 1967. This change at the top led the company to develop an industrial group of its own, breaking up the supply monopoly Standard Eléctrica Española had maintained for decades. The new strategy aimed to lead the Spanish telecommunications regime a step further towards the model used by most European operators and thus remove excessive technological dependence on ITT subsidiary company (Iturbe 1984).

Efforts by the company to form an industrial group and promote competition between suppliers continued throughout the 1970s. In this respect, the years of democratic transition barely affected Telefónica's strategic aims - which remained largely independent of the main government policies.[2] The company used its profits to pursue the consolidation of its industrial group. However, as Spain's fledgling democracy began to strengthen, criticisms began to be voiced against both the poor quality of Telefónica's services and the government's lack of any kind of telecommunications policy (Gonzalo 1981). The continuing economic crisis at the beginning of the 1980s contributed towards the industry's low returns, demand for Telefónica's services diminished and Standard Eléctrica plunged into a deep crisis (Rios and Erroteta 1982). In spite of this problem, Telefónica's goal of consolidating its industrial group was unaffected by the election of a socialist government in 1983, which decided to continue the same strategy. The socialists introduced greater co-ordination, but there was still no clear governmental policy for developing telecommunications during those years (Fregoso 1988).

There was no effective telecommunications policy in Spain until years later, after the creation of proper agencies and the provision of legal instruments that allowed the development of policies. The posts of General Secretary of Communications and the General Directory of Telecommunications were created in 1985, both being endowed with wide-ranging powers for studying, controlling and co-ordinating the sector. This demonstrated the political will to shape the industry's development (Tirado and Lera, 1985). In December 1987, the Spanish parliament passed the first law regulating the telecommunications sector in over 70 years, the LOT (Ley de Ordenación de las Telecomunicaciones). This move came only a year after Spain's admission to the EC and defined the main lines of public regulation of the sector. The new legislation distinguished between the functions exercised by public administration and the operator, which until then had been fuzzy to say the least. Prior to this, successive governments' *laissez faire* attitudes had allowed Telefónica to effectively dictate public policy.

Towards the end of the 1980s, notwithstanding Telefónica's efforts, it became apparent that the company's attempts to set up an industrial group based on information technologies had flopped. The socialist government at the time failed utterly to achieve this aim, despite having put it high on its list of strategic priorities. As a result, the country lost the opportunity to develop any significant innovative capability in the telecommunications industry (González Rubio 1995). It was under these circumstances at the end of the 1980s and the beginning of the 1990s that the industry began to assert itself. Telefónica gradually distanced itself from its former policy objectives, forging its own corporate identity. It also ditched its industrial group and embarked on strong international expansion, especially in Latin America. Its business in Latin America was based on good knowledge of markets in which Telefónica's longstanding links with local operators stood it in good stead.

A new telecommunications policy began to take shape in Spain at the beginning of the 1990s. The government wanted to gain more time for Telefónica to meet the challenge posed by liberalisation of the sector. Both the government and the company realised that the global trend was towards greater competition and trade. The government, for its part, maintained the monopoly for a while but used the time to pursue its own agenda on prices, employment, disposal of public industrial assets and the provision of universal access to telephone services. The government revamped the country's specialised telecommunications authorities in the years that followed. The General Secretary of Communications was given further powers and the Advisory Council on Telecommunications was established. Industry representatives sitting on the Council were given the opportunity to make suggestions regarding government projects. The Council stimulated also the articulation of a network of actors involved in telecommunications policy, even though it had very little real influence on policy decision-making.

Towards the end of 1992, the LOT was amended by European Directive 90/388/CEE, which was passed into Spanish legislation. The Directive introduced several important features for liberalising the industry. The new LOT limited monopoly services to telephony, telex and telegrams. At around the same time, the government decided to gradually open up various market segments to competition in compliance with the European directive (MOPT 1993). Various Spanish interests groups opposed this strategy, particularly those which sought to play a role in deciding the country's future telecommunications policies and who considered the government strategy too leisurely. Basically, the opposition came mainly from large industrial users, which were eager to reduce their own telecommunications bills, and from corporate interests sectors looking for attractive investment opportunities. Their arguments concentrated on the need to speed up the introduction of competition in the industry and they accused the government of pandering to Telefónica's special interests rather than serving the common weal.

Spain defended the continuing monopoly for basic telephone services before the various EC Councils on telecommunications, arguing that a rapid introduction of a free market economy would hinder building of much-needed telecommunications infrastructure in the country by limiting the capacity of its national operator to invest in less-profitable areas. However, these arguments were not weighty enough to persuade subsequent European Councils. Between May and June 1993, they set a new deadline for liberalising basic telephony (1 January 1998) and established a calendar for resolving other issues. Spain was not really in a position to exercise its veto. In fact, it did not oppose liberalisation *per se* but rather the pace at which it was to be carried out. Spanish representatives finally decided to accept the calendar proposed by the Commission, in exchange for a moratorium - up to five years more - on liberalising basic telephony in Spain. The Spanish government hailed the moratorium agreement as a big achievement. However, many special interest groups did not like the idea of continuing the monopoly for another few years while their foreign competitors learned valuable lessons from operating in free markets. Things came to a head in early 1994 when the Economics Minister stated that he was in favour of faster liberalisation. This sparked off an internal debate in government circles about the way forward, which finally led to the decision to speed up liberalisation of the telecommunications sector. A detailed plan for achieving this aim was then drawn up by the government (Ariño et al. 1996).

The plan was agreed upon by the Council of Ministers (7 October 1994) and gave form to the government's shift in strategy, which implied forfeiting the moratorium granted by the European Council, thus accelerating the liberalisation process (MOTPMA 1994). This included a calendar for the rapid liberalisation of cell phones, network access and renting, satellite communications, local TV and cable telecommunications. Telefónica, for its part, faced the prospect of rapid liberalisation with confidence thanks to the company's rapid growth and success abroad and its customers' tolerance of gradual price reductions. The plan established the aim of universal telephone coverage in Spain by the end of 1996. In short, all the previously unresolved issues were now put on the agenda. At the same time, plans were laid for a new regulatory body capable of ensuring fair competition in the emerging telecommunications market.

## PORTUGAL'S TURNING POINT: THE FORMATION OF PORTUGAL TELECOM

Telecommunications in Portugal were in private hands for most of the twentieth century. It was only from the end of the 1960s onwards that the three traditional telecommunications operators, CTP, TLP and Marconi, more or less became answerable to the public sector. These operators ran sectorial monopolies, managing telecommunications in a highly fragmented fashion. Thus, CTP provided local calls throughout the country except in Lisbon and Oporto and long distance calls to Europe and North Africa. TLP provided local calls in Lisbon and Oporto while Marconi had a monopoly on cable and satellite communications with the rest of the world.

Standard Eléctrica Portugal, a subsidiary of ITT, was set up in Portugal in 1932 with the aim of producing telephone equipment for the country. The company was to become the main manufacturer of communication equipment in Portugal. As time went by, ITT forged close links with Portuguese telecom operators to the point where the company trained most of the country's telecommunications engineers. Standard Eléctrica covered 50 per cent of Portuguese equipment needs, its only competition being Centrel, a Portuguese company which acquired the assets of British Plessey when the latter company pulled out in the 1970s, later producing equipment under license from Siemens. This situation remained virtually unchanged over many years. However, there was a big scandal in 1985 when the government invited tenders from all the major international telecom manufacturers for a large purchase. There were accusations of government corruption, with the

Portuguese operators defending the interests of ITT-Standard Eléctrica (Noam 1992). Once the crisis had blown over, the Portuguese government took strong measures to encourage investment in telecommunications, pushing through rapid modernisation despite the industry's traditional lack of initiative.

As mentioned earlier, Portuguese telecommunications were in government hands during the 1970s, despite the lack of a well-defined regulatory framework and the high degree of self-regulation prevalent in public companies. The first step towards systematic regulation of the sector was the establishment of a public body, the ICP (Instituto das Comunicacoês de Portugal) in 1981. This was a highly innovative move at the time, the ICP being one of the first telecom regulatory agencies in Europe. However, it was only with the enactment of new legislation in 1989 that the ICP really began to get to grips with its task. The ICP was made independent from the ministry in order to separate its regulatory functions from the activities of public operators (which, in the final analysis, were government-directed). The ICP's functions were fairly wide-ranging, covering everything from the granting of licenses to controlling equipment and allocating wavelengths. Apart from its purely regulatory functions, it also advised the government on the industry and co-ordinated Portugal's participation in international telecommunications treaties. Insofar as the government was responsible for appointing the managers of the new regulatory agency, one can say the ICP was not a fully independent body. It had a certain amount of administrative and financial independence (licenses and charges for the use of the airwaves provided it with income) but it had to inform the Minister for Communications of its proposals. This meant its margin for manoeuvre in internal government debates was anything but clear-cut (Noam 1992)

The first real definition of a telecommunications policy occurred during the Social-Democratic party's term of office. The government was a conservative one and held office from 1985 to 1995. Portugal's entry in the European Union in 1986 (that is at the same time as Spain) put the government under pressure to modernise and change some aspects of the country's telecom sector. It was not that the EU imposed changes on Portugal but rather that the government took the opportunity to shake up an industry which had remained virtually unchanged for decades, despite the overthrow of the dictatorship in the 1970s. In May 1986, four months after Portugal's accession to the EC, the Secretary of State for Transport and Communications set up a Special Commission to study the telecom sector in Portugal. The Special Commission (Comissaõ para o Estudo do Desenvolvimento Institucional e Tecnológico das Comunicaçoẽs) reported its findings a year later. The report provided radically new proposals on future Portuguese telecommunications policy. Its main recommendations included: (1) putting the ICP to work; (2) setting up a holding company to concentrate public stakes in the various telecom firms operating in Portugal;

(3) separating postal and telecommunications services; (4) preparing the way for injections of private capital in telecom companies; and (5) liberalising the price of non-basic telecom services.

These recommendations formed the basis of a Telecommunications Act which was enacted in September 1989, coinciding with the operational deployment of the ICP. The Act represented a big step forward in Portuguese telecommunications policy since it was the first piece of legislation whose scope embraced the whole telecom industry. The new law defined public responsibilities regarding telecommunications, guaranteeing access to certain services and opening up competition with regard to other value-added ones. The Act also established the basic principles for regulating competition and anticipated the European Council Directive 'Open Network Provision', which imposed similar measures on EC member countries (Council 1990).

Portuguese policy during the mid 1990s tried to ensure that the country's telecommunications remained in national hands while preparing the way for eventual implementation of a liberalising EC regulatory framework (Sousa, 1996). In this respect, it mirrored Spanish aims. Portuguese politicians realised they had little scope for stemming the tide of telecom liberalisation in Europe, however they grasped the fact that they had much more freedom in laying out the industry's development path in Portugal itself. They therefore began to take an active role in structuring the market.

The first step was the separation of postal and telecommunications services which until then were part of CTP. CTP's telecommunications division was hived off to form TP (Telecom Portugal). Later, acting on the recommendations of the Special Commission mentioned above, the government established a holding company, CN (Comunicaçoẽs Nacionais) in order to run the business side of the industry and prepare for privatisation. As well as taking the three traditional telecom operators under its wing, CN also incorporated postal services (which had been split off from telecoms) and TDP (Teledifusora de Portugal), a publicly-owned company responsible for TV broadcasting. TP had unsuccessfully opposed this government strategy since 1990, insisting on the need to merge all the public companies in a single telecom operator. The appointment of TP's new President in 1993 changed matters since he exercised considerable influence in the ruling Social Democratic Party. This made it possible to convince the government of the need for a single public telecom operator. However, the other two publicly-owned companies opposed this strategy, realising they would lose their corporate identity. They argued that the merger would give rise to an unmanageable firm and create untold problems. Marconi put up the strongest opposition to the government's plans given that it was expanding rapidly in the international telecom market (operating in over 15 countries) and that only 51 per cent of its share capital was publicly-owned.

Despite the pressures and criticisms concerning the big merger proposal in many business and political circles, a small core of politicians were behind the strategy. Their efforts were finally crowned with success with the setting up of PT (Portugal Telecom) in May 1994 (taking in TP, TLP and TDP) under the supervision of CN, which had supported the idea of business concentration. Bringing Marconi into the picture proved more difficult, but the CN also transferred the publicly-owned shares in Marconi to PT in 1995. At the same time as PT began privatisation, the company made an offer to Marconi's small private investors. The proposal involved a straight swap of Marconi shares for PT ones. The upshot was that PT rapidly gained control of over 90 per cent of Marconi's share capital. Thus, by 1995 at a time of wholesale liberalisation of telecom markets, Portugal paradoxically achieved what other countries had had for decades: a single public telecommunications operator running a monopoly.

The whole process of business concentration was rushed through with very little public debate. Two main arguments were used to persuade those opposing the merger. The first one concerned the need for a large national operator able to withstand fierce competition from foreign operators after market liberalisation. The EC directives stipulated that this liberalisation would take place in Portugal between 1998 and 2003. The Social Democratic government decided to wait until 2003, because of the time needed for this purpose. The second argument was to achieve sufficient size to act effectively in foreign markets, particularly in Brazil where a common language and longstanding trade relations gave Portugal a competitive advantage. Both arguments were thus of a business nature and identified national interest with the idea that Portuguese shareholders would control the new company. In contrast, very little attention was paid to the effects which this would have on reducing competition and hence in pushing up prices under a future liberalised market regime.

## THE GREAT TRANSFORMATION: STATE POLICIES AND THE CREATION OF THE NEW MARKET

### Establishing a Pre-competitive Market: the Spanish Way

Spanish telecommunications policymaking and implementation began to gather pace in early 1994. The calendar for liberalisation announced by the socialist government in October of 1994 was rapidly put into effect. The first move was the granting of digital mobile phone licences (GSM). Similar initiatives followed and new legislative proposals were put forward in 1995, including one on cable telecommunications. The privatisation of Telefónica was also on the agenda, as was the creation of a duopoly before full liberalisation. The duopoly involved granting a second license to a new basic telephony operator. Successive Spanish governments introduced a host of changes between 1995 and 1998 to determine the main corporate players in the new telecommunica-tions market. Their basic strategy was to use the transition towards liberalisation to influence both the scope of competition and the rate at which it took root. Put baldly, the government had two aims: to favour the Spanish telecom industry and to smooth Telefónica's path towards multinational status. In pursuing these objectives, the Spanish government armed itself with policy instruments capable of controlling the future liberalised market and minimising dependence on large world operators.

The government's policy aims were both shared and driven by other actors in the Spanish telecommunications arena in 1995 and 1996, particularly big Spanish firms and banks (Jordana et al. 1997). However, policy implementation was to prove complicated and the outcome was not a foregone conclusion. The business opportunities for those in the industry would be strongly affected by government decisions on key regulatory and corporate issues. Although the European Commission kept a watchful eye on the Spanish government's stratagems, it largely let matters ride, confining its efforts to controlling competition from large multinationals on a European scale and monitoring the application of directives and compliance with deadlines.

The first large competitive telecommunications market was established with the award of two GSM cellphone licenses. One license was directly awarded to Telefónica and the other to a consortium established for the purpose (which won the public competition). The development marked the take-off of Spain's cellphone market. However, the playing field was anything but level. The private consortium, Airtel, had to pay a very high fee (85 thousand million Pesetas) whereas Telefónica paid nothing. This fee was hotly debated afterwards. Two years later, the European Commission considered it a flagrant breach of the laws governing open competition and, after long negotiations with the Spanish government, forced the latter to compensate Airtel and to retroactively change the terms of the license (Sancho 2000).

Another issue, which came to the fore after the government's policy shift, concerned cable telecommunications. This was particularly important because it covered a sector that did not form part of Telefónica's monopoly. The new law followed the market model established by the cellphone licenses a few months earlier. A duopoly was created in each licensing zone. Given that Telefónica was automatically granted a license in each zone, the second operator was given a head start. Thus, Telefónica was barred from competing during an initial period to allow the second operator time to establish itself. The new law covered cable telecommunications in general, allowing the installation of fibre optics for every conceivable combination of telephony and data transmission (Domingo 1999). The business hopes of the private licensees were pinned on building their infrastructure before liberalisation took effect, thus giving them a strong market position when free competition came into effect.

The idea of nurturing a second telecommunications operator began to take root in some government and industrial circles in 1994. The plan was to use telecommunications infrastructure owned by various public utilities to provide the core facilities. The goal was to establish a transitory duopoly up until liberalisation, allowing the new company time to prepare itself for open competition. Obviously, Telefónica was none too keen on the idea. However, the company's ties with government were weakening, 15 per cent of the company's stock being floated during the Socialist Party's last year in office.

The incoming Partido Popular[3] speeded up implementation of the previous government's telecommunications policies. Although the new administration introduced some changes in this respect, the broad thrust of government policy remained the same. The PP's policy on telecommunications between 1996 and 1998 centred on what might be called 'building up the market' by: completely privatising Telefónica; founding the regulatory agency; introducing asymmetric regulations; and granting new licenses prior to full liberalisation. In June 1996, a Royal Decree awarded Retevisión a license as new global operator in the sector; created the CMT (Comisión del Mercado de las Telecomunicaciones) as a semi-autonomous regulatory agency; and also introduced some asymmetric regulations concerning Telefónica (Sanz 1999). Although the PP quickly appointed its own supporters to Telefónica's Board of Directors, this did not stop the company putting pressure on the government to reduce the impact of these measures on its business strategy. Telefónica made no bones about its stance, stating in its Annual Report, 'One should note Telefónica strongly favours rapid adoption of European-style liberalisation for two reasons: first, to provide Telefónica with a similar framework to that enjoyed by other European and world operators, and second, to avoid asymmetric regulations being applied during the transitory duopoly period' (Telefónica 1998: 11). The company's consolidation as a multinational, as well as the value of its stock during the privatisation period helped Telefónica win special treatment in the run up to full liberalisation. The privatisation of Telefónica was completed in 1997, with the state selling off its remaining stock. However, the government retained a 'golden share' which gave it power to veto some company decisions for a period of ten years.

On winning office in 1996, the new government reconsidered the previous government's decision to forego the five-year period of grace granted by the EC for implementing full liberalisation. The government found itself in a difficult spot. The European Commission was keeping a close watch on Spain and could not help but notice that Telefónica was taking maximum advantage of free markets abroad – participating also in international aliances like Unisource - while sheltering behind protectionist barriers at home. The government, for its part, wanted to shape the corporate structure of the telecommunications market before liberalisation was completed. To achieve this aim, the government not only used transitional arrangements but also restricted the awarding of new operating licenses. The government haggled with the European Commission, finally securing an eleven-month postponement of full telecom liberalisation *vis-à-vis* other EC members. Thus, liberalisation in Spain was to begin in December of 1998, with the government previously offering a third license for fixed telephony and cell phones. The Commission was to approve the incorporation of Telefónica in the European Unisource consortium within this timescale. This meant the government had roughly two years in which to influence which telecommunications operators would be major players in Spain following liberalisation. The government had two objectives in this respect: first and foremost, to stimulate competition at all levels rather than simply in the most attractive market niches; and second, to establish a hard core of Spanish companies capable of competing over the long term.

The awarding of a second license for telephone services in June of 1996 to Retevisión constituted the first great breach in the existing monopoly. Telefónica did everything in its power to make things difficult (for example failing to co-operate in providing cellphone access for third parties). Where possible, the government used its limited resources to foster the second operator's growth. During this period, the government also prepared laws and regulations for full competition (the new Ley General de Telecomunicaciones was approved in April 1998) and it continued to provide some limited support for Telefónica (for example raising charges for local calls, for which the firm still held the monopoly).

The CMT, the new regulatory agency, had been active since 1997 and gradually built up experience during these years, taking several regulatory decisions and defining its guidelines for intervention. The Ministry, however, continued its direct control of interconnection tariffs up until full liberalisation. The regulatory measures taken by the CMT at the time were moderately asymmetric. It should be noted that the CMT supported Retevisión's successful bid as Spain's second large operator. This was how the President of the CMT, J.M. Vasquez Quintana saw the body's role: 'We seek asymmetric but fair regulation because competition on equal terms is impossible when a newly-established operator faces a company which has the lion's share of the market'.[4] In the case of Retevisión, the government retained its stake after partial privatisation in March 1997, thus helping the firm's development. The government continued to provide firm support on issues like retaining one's telephone number even when using another operator and interconnection rights. This stance led to frequent complaints by Telefónica. In this connection, one should note remarks made by J. Villalonga, Telefónica's President concerning the Ministry and the CMT: 'It behoves them to arbitrate rather than play the wizard's apprentice. Most arbitrators usually succumb to the temptation of devising weird and wonderful rules which then have disastrous consequences'.[5] The government's support for Retevisión was maintained for a period beyond December 1998 on issues like the monopoly covering television signals. The Ministry even continued to control Telefónica's rates after liberalisation (not only through price caps but also by authorising the whole tariff structure). When the government invited bids for the third cell phone license in June 1998, it obliged both Telefónica and Airtel to share their infrastructure to make room for the new operator. Retevisión won this third license, allowing the company to consolidate its position as Spain's second operator shortly before full liberalisation took effect.

To summarise, when full liberalisation came in December 1998, both Retevisión and Telefónica were operating in Spain in a range of market segments. In addition, Airtel was a well-established mobile phone operator and the Lince group, the winner of the third fixed telephone licence, began offering public service the very same day liberalisation took effect. Spanish corporations were well-established among the consortia. Operators of all sizes rushed to apply for licenses once liberalisation came into force in December 1998. It was in this context that the CMT assumed greater leadership, quickly developing its observation methods and fine-tuning its measures (CMT 1999 and 2000). The distribution of functions between the regulatory agency and the government also became more complex, and several adjustments to the new institutional framework were adopted in 1999 and 2000. Whereas the government continued to take the main decisions in drawing the road map for the industry's strategic development; the CMT was much more concerned with monitoring the market and applying regulations on a day-to-day basis. While it is true the government no longer had the power to make the kinds of decisions that typified the transition period, it nevertheless retained its influence over several key aspects of the market. Besides price regulation, it was the administration's control over scarce resources like new cellphone licenses, bandwidth or telephone numbering that made this possible.

## Shaping a Late National Champion: the Portuguese Way

One of the big issues dominating telecommunications policy in Portugal from 1995 onwards was the decision to privatise Portugal Telecom, the public operator. This decision was gradually taken during the second half of the

1990s by successive Portuguese governments, without external pressures. The privatisation was begun by the Social Democratic government in its last year of office. The process was continued by the Socialist government which came to power in 1995. Thus, one can say that Portuguese telecommunications policy suffered no brusque changes despite a change of the party in power. Rather, the policy followed the general lines laid down at the end of the 1980s with a few minor changes here and there but in which market liberalisation gathering steam from 1997 onwards.

The Portuguese government signed a contract with PT for 30 years in May 1995, granting the company use of the network (which remained publicly-owned) in return for guaranteeing universal service. The quid pro quo was that PT would guarantee access to the network by other operators in accordance with EC legislation on fair competition. The timing of this move was highly significant, coming as it did just before PT's first partial privatisation (28 per cent of PT's share capital). Both the government contract and the privatisation provoked the ire of those companies operating in markets where there was already competition (for example data transmission and cell phones). Prominent among these companies was Telecel (backed by private Portuguese investment groups) and Air Touch which had both held second licenses in a new cellphone duopoly. These two companies had shown considerable growth and were concerned that a privatised PT would adopt a much more aggressive business strategy to stifle competition without the government being able to do much about it. They also argued that the government's policy favoured foreign companies (which were better-placed to withstand competition from PT) to the detriment of Portugal's new home-grown firms (Sousa 1996).

The government's reasons for pushing through privatisation went beyond following international trends. Both the CTT and PT had run up large pension fund deficits, having used the money to finance their telecommunications infrastructure in previous years. The restrictions on the public deficit imposed as part of the general economic and policy convergence requirements for acceptance into the Euro during the late 1990s meant the government had very little room for manoeuvre (Jeronimo 1998). Privatisation provided a source of income to help finance public spending. However, privatisation sparked off considerable controversy because the country's constitution had to be amended to make this possible. Additionally, the government dissolved CN after the first partial privatisation and directly managed successive share issues in order to strengthen its hand in dealing with political and business lobbies (Sousa 1996).

The success of the first privatisation in 1995 led the incoming socialist government to embark on a second share issue in 1996 (a further 21 per cent of the share capital was sold off), leaving the government with a 51 per cent stake in PT. This measure undoubtedly played a part in the government's policy of not pushing ahead with regulatory changes and further liberalisation. Up until at least 1997, the government's parlous finances meant that it had a vested interest in squeezing as much money out of privatisation as possible. The European Commission drew up a new timetable for telecom liberalisation in Portugal after negotiating with the Portuguese government in 1997, which aimed to avoid the Commission veto to PT's involvement in an international alliance (Concert). Under the new deal, the socialist government only took partial advantage of the moratorium established by the European Council, reversing the decision taken by the previous Portuguese government. As a consequence, January 2000 was set as the date for liberalising basic telecom services. A new framework Telecommunications Act was passed in August 1997 which incorporated European Directives on competition in the industry. Between 1997 and 2000, the government wavered between fostering competition and encouraging new businesses on the one hand, and consolidating PT's position on the other. Not surprisingly, this vacillation produced very little change in the overall situation, because of the difficulties of reconciling both policy objectives. Nevertheless, PT's argument that it needed sufficient breathing space to prepare for an onslaught of new competitors meant that limits were set to the pace of liberalisation. As a result, the transition to an open telecommunications market was relatively slow (Donegan 2000).

It should be noted that the socialist government appointed a Cabinet minister (the Minister for Social Infrastructure) as President of PT from October 1995 and 1996. He headed the same Ministry responsible for overseeing PT's activities. This made the position of PT regarding privatisation abundantly clear. There would be no further delay in introducing a competitive framework but new entrants would not be granted any special favours. Speaking at the end of 1998, PT's President Francisco M. Nabo put the matter bluntly, in a way which echoed similar statements by Telefónica's President: 'Only a clear and stable regulatory framework can guarantee growth on equal terms for all the parties. As I always say, competition means competition for everybody. We neither want nor need protection. But that does not mean we are willing to see our competitors being given an unfair advantage'.[6]

The government took an important decision in beefing up the ICP to cope with the entry of private companies. The ICP was given a new remit for fostering the general development of telecommunications, the idea being to establish it as a body which was more independent of PT (Junqueiro 1997). A third cellphone license was granted, this time to Optimus, in August 1998. This company was based on a consortium comprising mainly Portuguese partners, with France Telecom as technology partner. Strong competition in the cellphone market led to a sharp fall in call rates, which in turn led to rapid growth in service provision towards the end of the 1990s.[7] Various Portuguese business groups proposed setting up a second fixed telephone operator before full market liberalisation. The idea was considered by the government but not put into effect. Government officials felt that such a move would make the national market easy meat for large European companies without any corresponding advantages for Portugal.

PT quickly strengthened its business position from then until 2000. Meanwhile, it enjoyed government protection (the State was still PT's main shareholder), allowing it to tackle market changes in a relatively leisurely fashion.[8] The company continued to be the only provider of basic telecom services. It had sufficient time to carry out thorough business integration without having to deal with immediate competition. This allowed PT to embark on new business activities such as the provision of advanced cable services and to consolidate existing ones (for example its foreign business). PT's managers were aware that they would need to offset future losses in the domestic market with a greater overseas presence, even though turning the firm into a big multinational was not one of their aims.[9]

The complete privatisation of PT was finished at the end of 2000 when the government decided to dispose of its remaining 11 per cent of the company's share capital (which gave it the power to appoint the Board of Directors). At the beginning of 2001, the Portuguese State retained just 500 'golden shares' which gave it the final say on certain strategic matters. The question of effective regulatory powers remained unresolved given that the government continued appointing the PT's President until full privatisation of the firm as well as choosing ICP's Directors who reported to the Ministry of Social Infrastructure. ICP might respond to such criticisms by arguing that its experience as a regulatory body (one of the first in Europe) gives it unrivalled knowledge of the market. In fact, the body has so far managed to arbitrate between operators even when it is forced to intervene in the market. ICP's aim since the end of the 1990s has been to speed up liberalisation of the telecommunications market, which has involved issues like transferring telephone numbers and opening up local telephony.

## RE-EXAMINING THE EUROPEAN DIMENSION OF THE NEW REGULATORY SYSTEM: A FRAMEWORK FOR RENEWED STATE INTERVENTION?

During the 1980s, new relationships between the state and privately run monopolistic operators emerged with the advent of new public bodies designed to cope with telecommunications in Portugal and Spain. Old relationships were characterised by a double bond between state and operator.

One concerned ownership (the aim being to increase efficiency and hence profits). The other was the concession of monopolies (responding to economies of scale in the provision of public services). Both bonds tended to be mutually reinforcing and the system tended to be fairly self-regulating. However, both EC policy since the 1980s and other external factors forced the governments of Spain and Portugal to improve their control mechanisms. This was necessary if they were to be in a position to independently verify the information furnished by operators. Accordingly, both governments introduced new policy instruments. This process led to monopoly operators being stripped of their longstanding powers of self-regulation. As a result, these firms began direct lobbying of their respective governments in pursuit of their corporate aims. Former monopolist companies possessed sufficient information, resources and options to influence government liberalisation policy.

In Spain's case, the bond of ownership was broken in 1997 with the privatisation of Telefónica, but the monopoly concession bond remained - albeit partially modified - until December 1998. Telefónica's strategy at this juncture was to make sure the regulations being drafted favoured its competitors as little as possible. The arguments used by the company to defend this position revolved around the need to maintain its international expansion and to thwart the opportunism of its rivals. However, Telefónica also favoured rapid market liberalisation in order to stop strong competitors springing up during protracted transitional arrangements. For its part, the Spanish state had been building up its regulatory capabilities since 1996 and had created new actors in the industry. The government was thus in a position to identify and define its own interests and strategy, which no longer fully coincided with Telefónica's. The high stakes involved led to heated exchanges at both political and business levels. This changed the whole model of public sector regulation and led to a new relationship between state and players in the industry. As a result, the state found itself in a position to mould Telefónica's market behaviour (albeit not without discord) and to apply the European Commission's regulatory framework as it deemed fit.

The process followed a similar course in Portugal but the pace was different. The government there decided to reinforce its regulatory powers (the second link) by establishing a semi-autonomous agency. This provided institutional continuity in liberalising the telecom sector virtually from the outset but this was even more apparent during the final stages of the process. Privatisation of the public operator was a long-drawn-out affair covering five distinct stages. Nevertheless, when comparing company privatisation in Portugal with Spain's, one should bear in mind that the Portuguese government began with 100 per cent of PT's share capital whereas the Spanish executive only held one-third of Telefónica's shares. Thus in this case, the first link did not disappear until the end of the process given that the Portuguese government retained significant control of the company up until 2000. Nevertheless, maintaining public control over PT during the whole transitional period also meant a stronger government commitment to safeguarding the operator's net value and may explain why a second general operator was ruled out until full liberalisation took effect.

After the pitfall of ICT industrial policies in the 1980s, the business outlook for 'national champions' and their willingness to forge strategic alliances and conquer markets abroad was the government basic strategy in the 1990s for both countries. This policy orientation helped overcome the state's reticence concerning the benefits of liberalisation. Indeed, these developments could well explain the increasing impetus behind the Europeanisation of telecommunications policies during this period (Jeronimo, 1998; Hulsink and Davies 1997). In both countries, governments took an active role in these issues in order to prepare their 'champions' for global competition and to retain control of their national markets. They were particularly sensitive to corporate rigging of markets, taking advantage of the opportunities for intervention which the transition period provided. Accordingly, state policies concentrated on: influencing national markets; defining the number of cellphone operators; preparing their 'national champions' for the approaching competition; establishing duopolies before full liberalisation; and blocking the entry of more aggressive corporations in the future liberalised market. The European Commission tried to impede anti-competition strategems by governments or dominant operators, but often found itself unable to put a stop to such practices.

Throughout the 1990s Spanish political debate on the subject frequently centred on just one topic: the pace and strength of measures intended to secure a competitive telecommunications market. The whole debate really concerned how much time Spanish companies needed to build up strong positions in preparation for the new competitive regime. However, all concerned politely refrained to generate public debates on this issue. As we have seen, this strategy was used to defend Telefónica's domestic and international expansion until around 1994. In 1995 and particularly from 1996 onwards (that is when the PP took office) government strategy revolved around establishing a strong second national operator.

Privatisation in Portugal may have been more hotly debated than in Spain, but also the aim of establishing a 'national champion' required much more effort by successive Portuguese administrations. Portugal's need to merge existing public operators in a single company during the early 1990s was not a problem with which Spain had to contend. This inevitably hindered Portugal's strategy of establishing a company which could compete in a global telecom economy. From 1995 onwards, Portugal no longer had enough time to set up a second national operator before liberalisation if it was to both strengthen PT's position at home and make the firm competitive abroad (objectives which the Spanish government largely achieved for Telefónica during the early 1990s). On the other hand, it was hard for Portugal to argue the case for further extension of the liberalisation moratorium until 2001 or 2002 when the country had already modernised its telecom infrastructure. It would also have hurt the country's international image precisely at a time when Portugal occupied the EU Presidency.

In both South European countries, it seems clear that the state took an extremely active role in determining the structure of the industry during the market transition arrangements. Its role was very wide-ranging, involving everything from arbitration between large financial and telecommunications groups to promoting corporate initiatives. In the process, it became abundantly clear that states, far from losing their power to take decisions, found themselves in a unique position to shape the future of the industry. There came a point when the Spanish and Portuguese governments stopped squabbling with the European Commission over basic regulation of the telecommunications industry and the adoption of free market principles. Instead, they accepted these ground rules and employed other means such as licensing arrangements to pursue their national interests. In other words, they began to use the EC-created policy instruments to make nationally-based policy choices.

The foregoing discussion allows one to reflect on the dynamics of multi-level government and the telecommunications sector in Europe during the 1990s (Fuchs 1994). At first sight, one might think that decision-making in the telecommunications policy domain was simply concentrated at the European level to the detriment of the powers previously exercised by the governments of Member States. However, it seems more likely that the liberalisation process led to greater specialisation at both levels. Both the EC and national governments simply resorted to the instruments at their disposal to pursue their own ends. Doing this, however, the new context conducted to a limitation of the traditional state-led policy mediation in these countries, because of the nature of the instruments adopted.

Perhaps not surprisingly, this approach enabled national governments to continue exercising some powers that they had theoretically relinquished, but also to accept a new policymaking framework. Among other things, EC regulations established a broad common framework in which incumbent monopolies were excluded. This helps explain how the relationship between many Member States and the European Commission developed from one of mutual suspicion at the beginning of the 1990s to one of relative co-operation by the end of the decade. This new relationship led to the definition of roles in a completely different economic, institutional and regulatory context. This explains why national telecommunications markets in Europe at the beginning of the twenty-first century retain strong identifying features even though they are well-integrated in the world market. Nevertheless, one should bear in mind that markets change and that the present situation may not last as long as as the earlier PTO regime.

## NOTES

1. See for example a similar thesis in the Levi-Faur (1999) study on the Dutch case.
2. In 1975 the dictator Francisco Franco, died, and after a transition period, a new democratic constitution was approved in 1978.
3. The Partido Popular - a broadly conservative political party - won the Spanish national elections in March 1996.
4. *Expansión*, 27 November 1997.
5. *Cinco Días*, 29 January 1998.
6. 'Fair Competition Without Privileges' (interview), *Telcom*, II (1998).
7. 'Will PT put foot wrong?', *Public Network Europe*, February 2001, pp. 33-6.
8. 'A step too far in the right direction?', *Public Network Europe,* January 1999, pp. 43-6.
9. F. Nabo, 'Fair Competition Without Privileges' (interview), *Telcom*, II (1998).

## REFERENCES

Ariño, Gaspar, J.M. de la Cuétara and Lucía Aguilera (1996), *Las Telecomunicaciones por Cable. Su regulación presente y futura*, Madrid: Marcial Pons – UAM.

Behn, Sosthenes (1925), 'Our Objective', *International Telephone Review*, **1** (1), 2-3.

Carballo, Roberto (1979), 'El capital extranjero y la Dictadura: la I.T.T. en España', *Cuadernos Económicos del ICE*, **10**, 579-600.

Comisión del Mercado de Telecomunicaciones, CMT (1999), *Informe Anual 1998*, Madrid: CMT.

Comisión del Mercado de Telecomunicaciones, CMT (2000), *Informe Anual 1999*, Madrid: CMT.

Council of the European Communities (1990), *Council Directive on the Establishment of the Internal Market for Telecommunications Services through the Implementation of Open Network Provision*, Brussels, 28 June 1990, 90/387/EEC.

Domingo, Teresa (1999), 'Telecomunicaciones y Audiovisual en la España de los Años Noventa. Sectores en convergencia, ¿Políticas en convergencia?', in J. Jordana and D. Sancho (eds), *Las Políticas de Telecomunicaciones en España*, Madrid: Tecnos, pp. 35-78.

Donegan, Michelle (2000), 'Aspirations and limitations', *Telecommunications* (International edn), **34**, 31-4.

Fregoso, Rosa (1988), 'The PEIN in Spain: telecommunications and government policy', *Journal of Communication*, **38**, 85-95.

Fuchs, Gerhard (1994), 'Policy-making in a system of multi-level governance - the Commission of the European Community and the restructuring of the telecommunications sector', *Journal of European Public Policy*, **1** (2), 177-94.

González Rubio, David (1995), 'El sector de la Informática. Ilusiones frustadas', *Telos*, 44.

Gonzalo, Angel Luis (1981), 'Las telecomunicaciones en España', *Mundo Electrónico*, 110.

Hulsink, Williem and Andrew Davies (1997), 'The emergence of national champions in global telecommunications', *Telematics and Informatics*, **14** (4), 349–56.

Iturbe, Begoña (1984), 'La industria de las telecomunicaciones en España. El grupo industrial de la CTNE', *Revista T*, **2**.

Jeronimo, Venilde (1998), *On the Same Wavelength: the Politics of Telecommunications Reform in Southern Europe*, PhD Thesis, Claremont: Claremont Graduate School.

Jordana, Jacint, Teresa Domingo, Santi Macià, Eugenia Salvador and David Sancho (1997), *Opiniones y actitudes sobre las políticas de telecomunicaciones en España*, Barcelona: Departament de Ciencies Polítiques i Socials, Universitat Pompeu Fabra.

Jordana, Jacint (1998), 'La política de telecomunicaciones en España: del Monopolio a la Transición al Mercado', in R. Gomà and J. Subirats (eds), *Políticas Públicas en España*, Barcelona: Ariel, pp. 270–93.

Junqueiro, Raul (1997), 'Las telecomunicaciones portuguesas. Transformaciones e incertidumbres en el procesos de desregulación', *Telos*, **48**, 23–9.

Levi-Faur, David (1999), 'Governing Dutch telecommunications reform: state-business interactions in the transformation of national policy regimes to (European) embedded policy regimes', *Journal of European Public Policy*, **6** (1), 102–22

Little, Douglas J. (1979), 'Twenty years of turmoil: ITT, the State Department, and Spain, 1924–1944', *Business History Review*, **53** (4), 390–408.

Ministerio de Obras Públicas y Transportes, MOPT (1993), *Plan de Convergencia europea en telecomunicaciones*, Madrid: Instituto de Estudios del Transporte y las Comunicaciones (5 April 1993).

Ministerio de Obras Públicas, Transportes y Medio Ambiente, MOPTMA (1994), *Acuerdo sobre la política de telecomunicaciones durante el período transitorio hasta 1998*, Madrid: Instituto de Estudios del Transporte y las Comunicaciones (27 September 1994)

Négrier, Emmanuel (1997), 'Public policy, organized interest and patrimonialism in Southern Europe: the case of telecommunications', *South European Society and Politics*, **2** (1), 36–65.

Noam, Eli (1992), *Telecommunications in Europe*, New York: Oxford University Press.

Plaza, Crisanto (1989), 'La Compañía Telefónica', *Papeles de Economia Española*, **38**, 390-408.

Ríos, César Alonso and Peru Erroteta (1982), *Auge y caída del imperio ITT en España*, Madrid: Editora Popular.

Sancho, David (2000), 'Politics and institutional networks in Spanish telecommunications policy', *South European Society and Politics*, **5** (1), 25–52.

Sanz, Ana (1999), 'Debate Político y Marco Regulador de las Telecomunicaciones en España', in J. Jordana and D. Sancho (eds), *Las Políticas de Telecomunicaciones en España*, Madrid: Tecnos, pp. 79–130.

Schmidt, Susanne K. (1998), 'Commission activism: subsuming telecommunications and electricity under European competition law', *Journal of European Public Policy*, **5** (1), 169–84.

Sousa, Helena (1996), 'Telecommunications reforms in Portugal and the European Union', *Telecommunications Policy*, **20** (9), 653–67.

Thatcher, Mark (1999), *The Politics of Telecommunications*, Oxford: Oxford University Press.

Telefónica (1998), *Informe Anual 1997*, Madrid: Telefónica.
Tirado, Carlos and Lera Emilio, (1985), 'The Spanish telecom sector in the international turbulence', *Bulletin de l'IDATE*, **21**.

# 6. Normative foundations of electronic communications policy in the European Union

**Johannes M. Bauer**

## 1. INTRODUCTION

European telecommunications policy has gone through a major metamorphosis since the beginning of the 1980s. During these two decades, the traditional monopoly-based public service model was gradually replaced by a pro-competitive approach. Several factors contributed to this substantial transformation of European telecommunications policy. Technological changes, inherent inefficiencies, and a growing scepticism about the ability of the public sector to supply telecommunications services efficiently exposed the weaknesses of the public service model. Community institutions, less tied to national policy compacts, became the main promoters of market-based reform. Slowly, policymakers at the national and European levels adopted the notion that competition, rather than monopoly, would maximise the benefits of the ICT for society. After more than a decade of policies designed to facilitate the transition to competition, in 1999 the European Commission initiated a thorough review of the legal and regulatory model. This review intended to define the contours of a successor regulatory regime that could be put into place after the transition to a more open market environment had been completed.

Telecommunications liberalisation was initially seen as part of the common market project. Beginning in the mid 1990s it was increasingly seen as a precondition for the development of a vibrant European 'information society'. A first formulation of a European approach to the Information Society was expressed in the Delors Paper of 1993 (European Commission 1993). At the centre of this paper was a concern for employment and international competitiveness of European businesses. However, the subsequent Bangemann Report (European Commission 1994) marked a shift towards a more neo-liberal framework, pleading for a withdrawal of the government and the increased involvement of the private sector as the main driver of the

European Information Society (Servaes and Burgelman 2000). Subsequent initiatives by the EU have attempted to translate these broad visions into practical policy initiatives arguably with mixed success. In part, this may be due to the vagueness and malleability of the notion of an 'information society'. This opaqueness has led Garnham (2000) to emphasise its nature as an ideological construct rather than an operational description of the transformations induced by ICTs. Regardless, the idea of an 'information society' became an overarching vision integrating and legitimizing fundamental changes in European policies towards electronic communications.

At a more practical level there was growing perception that the various ICT sectors (telecommunications, broadcasting, cable television and computing) would eventually converge into one dynamic mega-industry, thus requiring a more integrated legal and regulatory framework. An initial set of policy responses was drafted in the context of the Convergence Green Paper (European Commission 1997). The discussion surrounding the Green Paper had already indicated a split between proponents of a laissez-faire approach and those concerned about the protection of a more broadly defined public interest, especially in the realm of content regulation. Recognizing the potential difficulty of finding a common position in this sensitive area, the 1999 Review was restricted to communications infrastructure and associated services. After its initial report (European Commission 1999e) and a subsequent consultation phase with stakeholders (European Commission 2000h), the EU is currently defining the details of the envisioned harmonised framework. In December 2000, the Commission issued a set of five draft Directives as well as complementary communications and recommendations (European Commission 2000a, 2000b, 2000c, 2000d, 2000e and 2000f; European Union 2000). In March 2001, the European Parliament amended three of the draft directives in a first reading and on 4 April 2001 the Council of Ministers found political agreement on these three directives. According to the current timetable, the key measures become effective in 2003.

There is wide agreement that the technological and economic changes affecting ICT industries require a modified policy approach. Whereas public ownership or government regulation of monopolistic service providers were appropriate responses to a naturally monopolistic industry, interconnection, open access and unbundling are sensible responses in an open market environment. Tacitly this position assumes that the same theoretical model applied to the old and the new telecommunications would yield different recommendations. This position overlooks that the process of institutional reform since the 1980s concurred with a change in the conceptual model applied to shape public policy and, simultaneously, in the vision of where the industry is heading and what the best policies for the sector would be. Therefore, in order to comprehend the current revisions more fully, the analytical approach, the policy vision and policy implementation all need to be understood in a dynamic and interactive relationship. The vision of a particular type of 'information society' shapes the perception of the policy problem at stake and the solution deemed as most adequate for a problem. At the same time, the adopted vision excludes a discussion of issues and policy options that are not part of this concept of the information society. Often, these normative roots of policymaking are not transparent in the public discourse. To stimulate a continued rational dialogue it would be desirable to bring these explicit and tacit normative foundations to the fore.

This chapter attempts a critical analysis of the normative concepts guiding the emerging European policies towards electronic communications. To keep the chapter manageable, it will primarily focus on the 1999 Communications Review (European Commission 1999e) and the ongoing implementation of its main outcomes. Issues related to content regulation in the broadcasting and new electronic media are beyond the scope of that review and this chapter. As the prescriptive vision guiding a set of policies is generally not fully explicated, the chapter employs an interpretative approach by reconstructing the normative roots of the emerging policies from the substance of the main policy documents. Section 2 briefly discusses the role of normative concepts in policymaking. Section 3 provides a sketch of the evolution of European telecommunications policy. Section 4 discusses the main contours of the new framework, Section 5 discusses its key normative roots and Section 6 summarises key points.

## 2. NORMATIVE CONCEPTS AND POLICY FORMATION

Public policies and private actions to influence public policies are inevitably derived from normative reference concepts. Whereas this chapter cannot explore the theoretical issues in great detail, it is necessary to review key arguments. Normative concepts have several roots and are in a complex dynamic relation to actual courses of action and their interpretations by stakeholders. Normative concepts shape the goals motivating public and private policy and the choice of a policy approach and instruments. Furthermore, they yield frameworks to legitimise certain courses of action either *ex ante* or *ex post*. Moreover, normative lenses filter the perception of issues that are considered worthy of a public policy response. With the advent of science and social science, these reference concepts are frequently related to scientific models. However, normative frames are also derived from values, beliefs and other *a priori* concepts (see Table 6.1). In both realms some aspects of these normative foundations will be made explicit but some remain hidden.

The importance of research in the process of policy formation merits special

*Table 6.1 Normative foundations of electronic communications policy*

| | Explicit | Tacit |
|---|---|---|
| Theory-based | Policy recommendation based on empirical analysis (for example, pricing of interconnection at incremental cost) | Tacit assumptions underlying social scientific models (for example, autonomy of individual preferences); conjectures and visions in areas of lacking knowledge |
| Value-based | Explicit values underpinning public policies (for example, preferences for universal service as expressed in specific policies) | Hidden value judgments included in statements or actions (for example, belief in superiority of private sector investment decisions |

attention. A great deal of scientific work attempts to be 'positive' in the sense that it strives to generate reproducible, empirically testable results that can serve as the basis for predictions (Friedman 1953). However, scientific models are also based on open and tacit assumptions that are neither explained by the model nor supported by empirical evidence (Hodgson 1988). For example, the notions of rational decision making or methodological individualism pervade large segments of the social sciences and thus 'bias' the perspective of its outcomes. Moreover, scientific knowledge is almost always incomplete and afflicted with uncertainty. Often, in the applications of incomplete theories to policy issues, these gaps are patched with visions and other a priori constructs. For example, incomplete knowledge about the impacts of the Internet on the economy may be filled by visions of a 'new' or 'digital economy' and its 'policy imperatives'. These visions, in turn, are translated into prescriptions for policy action.

Many scholars base their work on the assumption that positive scientific inquiry can be separated from its use in the policy process. For example, in the influential Tinbergen–Theil approach to economic policy, a division of labour was postulated between policymakers, who are responsible for defining the policy objectives (ends), and social scientists, who devise the most effective way (means or instruments) of reaching these goals. For this purpose, (positive) knowledge about the functioning of the economy had to be inverted and reinterpreted in a prescriptive fashion (Tinbergen 1952; Theil 1964). This approach immediately raises the question of how public policy goals are being determined. Arrow (1951) pointed out that under fairly general assumptions it was impossible to derive aggregate preferences from the preferences of individuals. To fill the void several scholars proposed social welfare functions, each based on different notions of the policy process and assumptions as to the position of individuals.[1] While these approaches have sharpened our view as to the consequences of different welfare functions for optimal policy solutions, they still lack a model as to how these preferences evolve.

Modern political economy has shed light on policy formation in the context of multiple stakeholders and uncertainty. Interactions among these stakeholders typically take place in an environment of limited, asymmetrically distributed information and bounded rationality. Stakeholders behave opportunistically, pursuing their own interests according to their differing value systems and preferences (Brock 1994; Dixit 1996; Stiglitz 1994). Consequently, information and communication policy – like other areas of public policy – is necessarily based on simplified models of the problems that policies aim to address. Ideally, these models would capture the main features of the situation and are the basis for the choice of a specific policy approach (Cuilenburg and Verhoest 1998). Different actors will often take part in the policy debate with competing models of the issues at stake, from which divergent policy recommendations will be drawn. The choice between policy models generally cannot be based on scientific merits such as superior predictive power (Hodgson 1988; Ferré 1998).

Rather, a choice will emerge from a complex process of persuasion and search for legitimacy (Majone 1989). Power relations, resources of players, the institutional framework of policy, as well as the history of decisions will affect policy approaches (Dutton 1999). Furthermore, any choice of a particular explanatory and normative framework shapes policy options and tends to exclude a search for alternative solutions. For example, the adoption of a competitive market framework has fundamentally altered the meaning and pursuit of universal service goals in the EU. As policy decisions typically unfold gradually over time, the medium and long-run trajectory of policymaking has strong aspects of path dependence. Whereas it would be interesting to study this process in which an explanatory model is adopted, such an endeavour would exceed the scope of this chapter.[2] Suffice it to say that in the light of modern research policies can be seen as the outcome of a complex evolutionary interaction in which scientific models, values, and power are intricately interwoven.

## 3. FROM PUBLIC SERVICE TO LAISSEZ FAIRE

Until its full liberalisation in January 1998, telecommunications service providers in most European nations, most of them fully or partially state-owned, were protected from competition in their core markets. In some countries (for example, Germany) telecommunications services had been provided by the public sector from the very beginning. In other countries (for example, Sweden and Austria) telephone service was initially provided by private entrepreneurs but later nationalised or gradually absorbed into the public sector. Among the factors that contributed to the establishment of public monopoly structures were national security arguments and a widely shared view that infrastructure services were best provided by the government. Later, various forms of market failure were accepted as a rationale for government ownership and control. Although governmental involvement in telecommunications was generally strong, a variety of approaches emerged. Initially, most PTTs (Posts, Telephone and Telegraph) organisations were fully integrated into the administrative apparatus of the public sector. During the last two decades, many PTTs were reorganised as corporations according to public or private law and given more autonomy in their business decisions. In Italy and Spain the PTTs were historically operated as mixed enterprises, partly owned by the state and partly by private investors (Noam 1992).

The public service models had some unique features. Under the system of public ownership no strict separation between the operation of telecommunications networks and their regulation - as is typical for North America - was deemed necessary. It was a widely held tenet that public ownership was sufficient to secure PTT action in the public interest. Nevertheless, competing notions of how state-owned PTTs should foster the public interest coexisted. In a more narrow perspective, the state was seen as a 'stopgap' for tasks that the private sector could not provide (Snow 1988). A broader, widely held view saw the PTTs as instruments of government policy and therefore required contributions to macroeconomic and microeconomic policy goals (Thiemeyer 1983). From this mission contributions to full employment, anti-cyclical investment policy and universal service obligations were derived. The public service concept reflected a strong belief in a mixed economy, in which the public sector plays an active and beneficial role, complementing the private sector. Public sector intervention was not only sought to correct market failure but also to achieve legitimate non-market policy goals. However, the complexity of goals and the rivalry of public sector institutions for control often led to conflicting demands and weak accountability leading Aharoni (1986) to describe state-owned enterprises as an 'agent without a principal'. In practice, this approach has generated a diverse record with examples of successful reliance on the public service model but also many instances that demonstrate its weaknesses and failures.[3]

Under the public service model, public interest goals were generally not expressed in quantitative and operational terms but determined in a continuous relation between policymakers and management. Most PTTs were able to establish minimal community access through a network of public payphones, often located in post offices. However, they were less vigorous in meeting individual household and business demand, often allowing the build-up of significant backlogs. Public sector management principles were generally not conducive to operational efficiency. This weakness was aggravated when the pursuit of socio-economic goals served as an excuse for poor operational performance and later to delay the introduction of competition. The joint pressure from technological change, diversified needs of large users and vanishing trust in the public sector destabilised and eventually overturned the public service model.

During the late 1970s, European policymakers gradually placed a higher emphasis on the importance of telecommunications and information technologies for economic growth. Although it would take a little more than a decade and a half before the notion of an emerging 'information society' permeated most of European telecommunications policy, a new consensus emerged that the traditional monopoly model needed reform. The European Community institutions became an important player in this transformation of national monopolies into open markets. Among the three major European actors, only the Commission of the European Communities, essentially the executive branch of the European government, acts independently of national interests for common European goals. In key areas it became the promoter of liberalisation policies that were more difficult to establish at the national level. In contrast, the Council of Ministers and the European Parliament are designed to reflect national interests, which often results in less radical policies than those favoured by the Commission (Schneider and Werle 1990; Simpson 2000). This effect has become more visible since, in 1993, the Treaty of Maastricht strengthened the participation rights of the Parliament with the introduction of the co-decision procedure.

Compared to the United States and Japan (and with the exception of the United Kingdom), the EU started the process of telecommunications liberalisation relatively late. In 1987, the Commission published its first blueprint for liberalisation in the Green Paper on the Development of the Common Market for Telecommunications Services and Equipment. In the wake of the Green Paper, the Commission and later the Council adopted numerous policies to gradually liberalise telecommunications services. Council or Commission Directives obligate the Member States to implement their principles within a given timeframe. National governments are given discretion in choosing a method of implementation, although they typically amend national laws to comply with EU Directives. If a Member State fails to implement a Directive within the given timeframe, its provisions become effective regardless and constitute executable rights for individuals and organisations.

The major initiatives towards liberalisation of the telecommunications markets are discussed in great detail elsewhere (Kiessling and Blondeel 1998; European Commission 1999a, 1999d and 2000g). The main trajectories of reform included the successive liberalisation of terminal equipment (1988), non-basic services (1990), mobile and personal communications service (1996), and of voice telephony (1998). In parallel, the markets for the provision of infrastructure networks were liberalised starting in the mid 1990s, with full liberalisation in 1998. To overcome problems resulting from lack of competition for certain essential facilities, the ONP (Open Network Provision) framework was established with the intent of securing open access to networks and services (1990–present). Common rules for the licensing of service providers, standardisation initiatives through the ETSI (European Telecommunications Standards Institute), and a separation of regulation and operation were further important features in the integration, harmonisation and liberalisation of the European markets. It was also clarified that the competition rules of the Treaty of Rome, which require the abolishment of exclusive monopoly rights, would apply fully to the telecommunications sector.

From the beginning, this series of measures was intended to facilitate the transition from a monopoly to a competitive regime. As a consequence, many measures of asymmetric regulation, which put more stringent conditions on incumbent service providers, were adopted. Moreover, the legal reforms contained many instances of ex ante regulation. Last but not least, they continued to be based on legacy legal frameworks, which had created technology-specific rules for telephony, cable television, broadcasting, and data communications networks. In 1999, the European Commission launched a thorough review of the experience with regulatory reform in telecommunications with the goal of defining the basic building blocks of a future regulatory framework. The reforms of the 1980s and 1990s were primarily designed to manage the transition to competition and therefore focused in the creation of a competitive open market environment and the rights of new entrants. The proposed new policy framework should seek to 'reinforce competition in all market segments' and to allow the development of 'new, dynamic, and largely unpredictable markets with many more players'. In this context, regulation should be 'progressively limited to areas where policy objectives cannot be achieved by competition only' (European Commission 1999e: iv).

The new framework built on the evaluation of the existing legal and regulatory framework, reported in the *Fifth Report on the Telecom Regulatory Package* (European Commission 1999a). The Commission found that the combination of sector-specific legislation and application of the competition rules of the Treaty of Rome had worked well. However, while the process of creating an internal market for telecommunications services was well under way, the provision of pan-European services was still hampered by the relatively fragmented national frameworks, in particular the licensing regimes and the interconnection regimes. This was complicated by the fact that considerable divergence existed between Member States' implementation of the principles of the current regulatory package.

Whereas new entrants added a new dynamic to the European telecommunications markets, disparities in the division of regulatory powers between ministries, regulatory agencies, national competition authorities and other agencies continued to create market entry barriers. Moreover, there existed wide differences between national licensing regimes, forcing new market entrants to cope with different procedures, periods of validity of licenses, fees, classification of operators in addition to a multiplicity of languages. It was further found that the cost accounting, which is the basis of interconnection tariffs as well as the provision of leased lines and voice telephony, suffered from weaknesses, exposing new entrants to vertical price squeezes and reducing their ability to compete effectively. The process of price rebalancing was not yet completed and, at the time of the review, only one universal service fund was in operation. However, several Member States were considering the establishment of such a funding tool.

In addition to this review, the EU conducted several consultations whose results also influenced the proposed new framework. Of particular importance was the consultation on the Convergence Green Paper (European Commission 1997, 1999c). This process had revealed the conviction that a separate regulation of information transport networks and of content was appropriate. The transport network infrastructure and associated services should be regulated in a more horizontal fashion, irrespective of the services carried. The Commission received further comments in the consultation on the Radio Spectrum Green Paper (European Commission 1998). In 1999, the Commission also issued a report on the development of the market for Digital Television in the European Union (European Commission 1999b). Lastly, the Review included the main findings from the consultation on a European Regulatory Authority, which had not produced decisive support in favour of such a new agency. So far, the reform process has resulted in five draft directives by the European Commission. The framework directive, which details the horizontal approach and defines the tasks of national regulatory authorities, the interconnection and access directive, and the authorisations directive were discussed in a first reading in the European Parliament and amended in March 2001. Early in April the Council adopted a political agreement on these three directives. Despite the likelihood of further changes, the main contours of the new approach are now visible and largely uncontested.

## 4. THE EMERGING POLICY MODEL

The new framework is designed to facilitate the process of convergence, create conditions for sustainable competition, and consolidate and considerably simplify the existing legal framework of European communications. Once approved, the number of directives will be reduced significantly (Table 6.2). Acknowledging convergence between different information and telecommunications networks and services as a main driver of the further evolution of information and communications industries, the framework aims at creating a technologically neutral environment in which competitive forces can freely unfold for the benefit of consumers and the overall European economy. To this end, the new framework uses the new generic terms electronic communications networks, electronic communications services, and associated facilities (that is, those facilities to which access is necessary for the competitive provision of electronic communication services on equal terms) and establishes a set of harmonised horizontal rules (Figure 6.1). The framework does not apply to the politically more contested issues of content regulation or to higher-level services such as e-commerce. Thus, the politically sensitive nature of these areas is recognised and admitted that they may be governed by more diverse sets of national and European measures.

The overarching policy objectives of the new framework emanate from the earlier European initiatives and from the review process. They are formulated in the framework directive as guidelines for regulation at the level of member States (European Commission 2000d, article 7). NRAs (National Regulatory Authorities) shall, first, promote an open and competitive European market for electronic communication services. To this end, they shall ensure maximum choice options for consumers, eliminate restrictions of competition, encourage efficient investment into infrastructure, and ensure an efficient allocation of radio spectrum. Second, national regulatory authorities shall contribute to the development of the internal market, among others, removing remaining obstacles to the provision of network and services at a European level, and ensuring that in similar circumstances there is no discrimination between undertakings providing electronic communications networks and services. Lastly, measures shall benefit the European citizen by ensuring affordable access to a universal service and access to Information Society services. As well, national regulators shall ensure a high level of data protection and privacy, increased market transparency, and services addressing the needs of special social groups, in particular disabled and the elderly.

*Table 6.2 Consolidation of EU legal framework*

| New legal framework | Consolidates the following directives of the existing legal framework |
|---|---|
| Competition Directive (to be adopted after the specific directives are approved) | Services Directive (90/388/EC)<br>Satellite (94/46/EC)<br>Cable (95/51/EC)<br>Mobile (96/2/EC)<br>Full Competition (96/19/EC)<br>Cable Ownership (99/64/EC) |
| Framework Directive | ONP Framework Directive (90/387/EEC) amended by (97/51/EC) |
| Authorisations Directive | Licensing Directive (97/13/EC)<br>GSM Directive (87/372/EEC)<br>ERMES Directive (90/544/EC)<br>DECT Directive (91/287/EEC)<br>S-PCS Decision (710/97/EC)<br>UMTS Decision (128/99/EC)<br>European Emergency Number Decision (91/396/EEC)<br>International Access Code Decision (92/264/EEC) |
| Access and Interconnection Directive | ONP Leased Lines Directive (92/44/EEC amended by 97/51/EC)<br>TV Standards Directive (95/47/EC)<br>Interconnection Directive (97/33/EC amended by 98/61/EC) |
| Universal Service and User Rights Directive | Interconnection Directive (97/33/EC amended by 98/61/EC)<br>Voice Telephony Directive (98/10/EC) |
| Data Protection and Privacy Directive | Telecoms Data Protection Directive (97/66/EC) |
| Local Loop Unbundling Regulation | Newly adopted in December 2000 |
| Radio Spectrum Policy Decision | Newly adopted in July 2000 |

*Source*: European Commission 1999: 17, and European Commission Press Release IP/00/749, 12 July 2000.

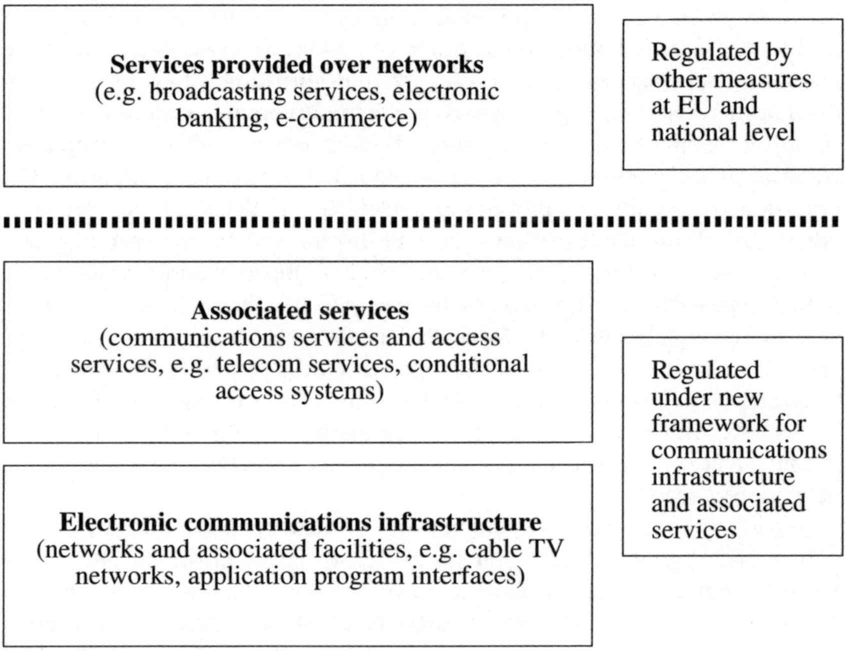


*Figure 6.1 Technological neutrality and horizontal approach*

The proposed directives are a major step towards a further harmonisation of the electronic communications sector in the EU. In addition to consolidating and simplifying the provisions of earlier legal measures, the new framework also introduces new important features or strengthens existing aspects. Convergence between telecommunications, broadcasting, as well as ICT and competition are seen as the main drivers of further change. The envisioned framework responds to these perceived trends by eliminating, as far as possible, differential treatments between electronic communications technologies. Furthermore, it seeks to shrink the realm of *ex ante* regulation in favour of *ex post* antitrust supervision. This is achieved by limiting regulation to situations in which service providers have significant market power and by requiring the periodic review and elimination of rules that are not necessary to cope with such market power. Moreover, it seeks to foster Europe-wide electronic communications markets through simplified market access rules and more stringent co-ordination through new advisory bodies.

The draft framework directive defines a common set of rules for all electronic communications, covering all satellite and terrestrial, fixed and wireless networks and services. That is, it covers circuit and packet switched fixed networks including the Internet, mobile terrestrial networks, satellite networks, radio and television broadcasting networks, and CATV. The scope of the provisions is limited to electronic communications services, which are defined as 'services provided for remuneration consisting wholly or mainly in the transmission or routing of signals on electronic communications networks' (European Commission 2000d, article 2). Services providing or exercising editorial control over content are thus excluded, as is terminal equipment. The draft directive establishes procedural guidelines and delineates the duties of NRAs based on the principles of non-discrimination, transparency and accountability. Besides committing the NRAs to the above-mentioned set of policy objectives, the directive establishes specific duties in several areas. One of the new features includes the requirement to allocate and assign spectrum efficiently as well as the right of NRAs to permit the trading of frequency assignments subject to certain safeguards. Besides clarifying the obligations with respect to rights of way management and co-location, the document also provides for mechanisms to allow facilities sharing among network providers.

According to the proposed framework, ex ante regulatory measures can only be adopted if an NRA finds significant market power in one of the markets identified on an annual basis by the Commission (European Commission 2000d, article 14 and annex 1). In all other cases, NRAs need to seek and receive permission from the Commission before they can introduce ex ante regulations. Market power is determined by examining both market structure and conduct of firms. With respect to the first test, current EU policy identifies 25 per cent market share as a critical threshold for the potential existence of market power. Furthermore mobile and value added services are essentially exempted from these provisions. The new Market Analysis Guidelines (European Commission 2001a) define significant market power in accordance with the Treaty of Rome as interpreted by the European Court of Justice, which significantly raises the critical threshold for dominance to a 50 per cent market share. In addition, NRAs will have to define the relevant product and service markets as well as the relevant geographical market (except in cases of trans-national markets, which will be identified by the Commission), for example by applying the 'hypothetical monopoly test' (European Commission 2001a: 7). The directive distinguishes between single and joint dominance, collective dominance (that is, anti-competitive behaviour in oligopoly markets), and leveraging of market power from a dominant market segment into a closely related market.

Undertakings are deemed to hold significant market power if they enjoy a 'position of economic strength allowing them to behave in an appreciable extent independent of competitors, customers and ultimately consumers' (European Commission 2001a: 18). The net effect of this revised approach is difficult to assess. In fixed networks, it will reduce the realm in which ex ante regulatory measures will be deemed compatible with EU law and consequently weaken those NRAs, which had relied upon a more stringent approach to regulation. On the other hand, the approach may bring hitherto largely exempted segments, like the mobile industry, into the fold of ex ante regulation. This has potentially far-reaching implications in the ongoing debate on infrastructure sharing to mitigate the high costs of third generation licenses (European Commission 2001b). The European Parliament has in its first reading proposed to exempt markets with emerging competition from ex ante regulation, which might provide relief for the mobile industry. The Council has also endorsed the Commission's position of declaring dominance the trigger for possible ex ante regulation.

The new framework confirms the existing approaches towards universal service. Contrary to earlier expectations, the scope of services to be provided on a universal basis was not broadened to include more advanced Internet access services. The new draft universal service directive continues to limit universal service funding to the provision of a fixed access line usable for voice, fax and Internet access services, directory listing and inquiry services, payphone services and services for the disabled. NRAs are allowed to designate one or more operators to guarantee part or all of the universal service obligations in part or all of the national service territory (European Commission 2000d, articles 3–8). Universal service programmes can be funded via universal service funds – ideally based on some value-added tax model – or from general tax funds. Recovery via supplements on interconnection charges is no longer permitted in the proposed directive.

The proposed framework also aims at enhancing user rights and data protection. Article 16 of the draft directive requires NRAs to regulate the retail prices of any organisation with significant market power. It gives regulatory agencies reserve powers in case service providers fail to supply an acceptable quality of service. It also allows the introduction of regulatory measures to enhance market transparency, including the requirement to provide per call tariff information. As lack of market information has been a source of continued market power in fixed and wireless networks this initiative is welcome. In the area of data protection, the new framework does not introduce new measures but adapts the existing directives to reflect the horizontal and technologically neutral design. Thus it retains the stringent principles with respect to data processing and individual participation laid out in previous European data protection measures.[4]

The framework directive also proposes institutional reforms. Whereas an earlier consultation process had not found convincing arguments in favour of a European Regulatory Agency, the Commission saw a need for improved co-ordination between the EU and national levels. For this purpose, two new forums are established. The Communications Committee is composed of representatives of the Member States and shall assist the Commission. This committee shall facilitate the exchange of information between the Member States and between the Member States and the Commission. In addition, an advisory group, the HLCG (High-Level Communications Group) is proposed, which consists of representatives of the NRAs. (The European Parliament proposed to change the name to Advisory Communications Group.)

## 5. DISCUSSION

The proposed framework solidifies the transition to a market-based environment for electronic communications. Its leading normative foundation is the vision of a fully competitive, largely self-regulating marketplace in which consumer choices and not government policy determine outcomes. The role of ex ante regulation is limited to situations in which there is strong evidence of significant market power. In all other cases there is a basic trust in the efficiency of unfettered market forces safeguarded by ex post competition rules. The European discussions on electronic communications policies are often highly technical and have historically not been conducted in the public sphere. It is thus tempting to characterise the emerging framework as the outcome of a capture of European policymakers by stakeholders with a vested interest in a neo-liberal environment in electronic communications, especially corporations and large customers. These actors regularly supply the vast majority of comments in the customary consultation processes. For example, of the 229 parties who submitted comments during the consultation phase of the 1999 Review, 156 (more than 68 per cent) represented the interests of operators, hardware and software vendors, and large users, and 41 responses came from national regulatory agencies and government units. The remainder of 32 submissions originated from research organisations and universities (2), special interest groups such as the European Disability Forum (20), and individual respondents (10).

However, the process in which policies evolve is much more complex, with many rifts and possible conflicts of interest fragmenting the stakeholders. For example, within industry, strong conflicts of interest exist between incumbents and new entrants. NRAs differ widely with respect to funding and human resources and have developed unique styles of governance, some more aggressive and proactive and others more reactive. Moreover, there are significant differences of opinion between the different directorates of the European Commission. The Directorates General for Competition (former DG IV) as well as Enterprise and Information Society (former DG XIII) have historically favoured a pro-competitive approach. In contrast officials in the Directorate General for Education and Culture (former DG X) have attempted to protect a higher degree of national autonomy, at least in determining content-related issues. Likewise, differences as to the relative role of European and national policy exist between the Commission, the Council of Ministers, and the European Parliament. The latter have repeatedly modified Commission proposals to secure a relatively higher degree of national autonomy and flexibility. It is remarkable that, compared to the more mature US regulatory system, participation of special interest groups other than industry is rather limited.

As a result, the emerging framework is shaped by many compromises. This is evident in the decision to exempt all content-related issues (and to a certain degree broadcasting issues) from the current discussion. It can be doubted whether such a separation is sustainable in a digital communications industry where the boundaries between networks and content are increasingly obfuscated. Thus, by limiting the current round of discussion to network infrastructure issues the EU may have inadvertently limited future options in the areas of content policy. Another area in which the compromise between stakeholders is visible is the envisioned role of national and European policymakers. Compared to the existing regulatory environment, the scope of national autonomy is reduced in some areas but expanded in others. It is limited in as far as the Commission seeks a strong influence on the markets in which NRAs can impose ex ante regulation. Moreover, it asks effectively for a right of pre-emption of NRA actions where there is a conflict between the European and national interpretation of a policy. On the other hand, the new framework gives NRAs choice menus of policy options that will likely increase the diversity of national frameworks.[5] Strong resistance exists against stronger EU institutions in the Council, as reflected in the modifications expressed in the political agreement of April 2001. Among the most contested issues is the ability of the Commission to overrule NRAs. Thus, in this conflict the second reading in the European Parliament will have a decisive influence in determining the future balance of power between EU and national organisations.

Overall it is, however, striking how deeply the notion of the superiority of unleashed market forces has permeated the positions of the various stakeholders. Participants in the discussion apparently did not question the fundamental premise that a competitive market organisation was feasible and would lead to the desired outcomes. The framework adopts the classic notion that efficiency and other goals of information and communication policy can be separated and the latter pursued with means and funds external to the industry. Regulation and public policy are conceptualised as antagonistic to free enterprise and market forces and should thus be as light-handed as possible. At a very fundamental level, this basic attitude overlooks the fact that competition is inherently undetermined and can unfold starting from many distributional states.[6] From such a perspective, distributional goals (such as universal service) do not conflict with efficiency goals but will need to be determined before the concept of efficiency can be meaningfully defined. At least in crucial parts, the framework tacitly adopts a dynamic, Schumpeterian rather than a neo-classical equilibrium-oriented notion of competition (Bauer 1997). Thus, it is willing to accept market concentration as long as it does not coincide with anti-competitive behaviour. While this approach seems appropriate for a dynamic industry it can be expected that its operationalisation will be very difficult and highly contested. In particular, the significant market power test will have to be conducted on a going-forward basis, leaving wide room for litigation. Thus, the linchpin for ex ante regulatory intervention may turn out to be poorly construed.[7] Overall, whether by deliberate choice or oversight, the proposed framework is highly influenced by a neo-liberal ideology, which rests in a basic trust in unregulated market forces and attributes a minimal role only to state agencies.

The basic premises of the approach are seemingly corroborated by the practical experience with liberalisation so far. After all, the transformation to a more open market-based environment has significantly improved the performance of the European telecommunications industry and created a much broader range of choice options for consumers. Between 1994 and 2000 the typical residential consumer has benefited from a price decreased for fixed voice services by 20.4 per cent. Business customers experienced an even higher decline of 38.2 per cent in the average price for national voice services. In both market segments, the EU has outpaced the US and the OECD overall (Cherry and Bauer 2001). At the same time, the availability of fixed and mobile services increased steadily (European Commission 2000g). Some of the observed changes need to be attributed to fast-paced changes in technology, which probably would have affected the industry even if the regulatory regime had not been changed. There is, however, clear evidence that the opening of markets for competition had a strong contribution to these developments (Boylaud and Nicoletti 2000). What cannot be told conclusively from the data is whether similar changes can be expected on a forward-looking basis. The observed improvements probably reflect the elimination of past inefficiencies and may be less indicative of the potential for further improvements. Indeed, in some countries that had introduced competition earlier than most EU Member States (for example, the United States or Sweden) efficiency improvements have started to taper off. In part, this effect may be due to an increased share of marketing expenses, diseconomies of scale in advanced computer networks, and of the duplication of infrastructures. Thus, it will have to be seen whether the expectations placed in the new framework will indeed materialise.

Overall, the proposed framework is relatively coherent within a neo-liberal tradition. However, the neo-liberal bias has prevented stakeholders from addressing important issues and limited the search for policy alternatives. For example, there is evidence that, contrary to the neo-liberal paradigm, strong (not capricious) regulation actually improves the performance of the industry and facilitates the achievement of non-price goals (Melody 1999). The proposed framework does not prohibit Member States from pursuing more ambitious goals such as broader universal service funding. However, by forcing Member States, in times of tight budget constraints, to rely on general tax funds for more ambitious universal service funding, the EU unduly limits their ability to seek such non-price goals. In a similar vein, the limitation of ex ante regulatory measures to instances of significant market power risks that important issues will not receive attention. For example, the present draft directives link interconnection obligations to the presence of market power. Where such dominance is absent, they impose only a duty to negotiate but no general interconnection obligations (like the United States Telecommunications Act of 1996). This overlooks that in a competitive environment competitors may have strategic incentives to avoid interconnection, thus increasing the risk of network fragmentation and reducing the overall benefits of a ubiquitous network (Mansell 1993).

It would be interesting to more systematically explore how the consensus around the neo-liberal model emerged from an extended process of persuasion and structuration of the issues. This process unfolded during the past two decades, with earlier decisions shaping and limiting later policy options. Thus, the recent modifications are in part the outcome of a path-dependent policy process originating in the late 1970s and early 1980s. In this process, blueprints from other regions, especially the United States, interacted with local policy attitudes and preferences to generate a unique approach with many similarities at a macro level yet many differences at a micro level (Schneider 2001). The emerging neo-liberal bias blocks the view to recognise some of the severe limits of markets in network industries, where market power may remain pervasive throughout (Trebing 1994). It has also limited the recognition of potential alternative models for formulating a coherent framework for electronic communications policy. During the past decades, researchers in disciplines such as communications, law, or computer science have proposed interesting alternative frameworks but have, so far, only had limited practical influence (Lenert 1998; Lessig 1999; Longstaff 1999; Noam 1999). This is particularly worrying as the current framework is based on the traditional approach to telecommunications policy, in which networks and content could be segmented rather clearly. In the emerging datacentric world, policy issues may require solutions including both network and content layers. It may be true, as Zerdick et al. (1999) remark, that seen from the perspective of an Internet economy, the emerging European regulatory approach reveals many gaps and may be an expression of regulatory helplessness in the face of complexity.

A key integrative vision for the new framework was the notion of a European Information Society. However, our discussion supports the view of Servaes and Burgelman (2000) that many of the social initiatives, emphasising, among other things, the opportunities for lifelong education, access to information, or the enhancement of democracy are only the 'sugar coating' on an unbridled strategy of electronic communications liberalisation. In contrast to previous normative foundations of European policy, the new framework does equate the public interest with consumer choice and the outcome of free market forces. A content analysis of the 1999 Review reveals that the term 'access' is used 189 times in various contexts such as access to the market for new entrants, access to bottleneck facilities for competitors, access for consumers to networks and services. A second core concept is 'competition', which is mentioned 106 times. The 'public interest' or 'general interest' is only mentioned 18 times but not defined in an operational way. On the one hand, this indicates the difficulties of finding a clear and agreeable notion of public interest. On the other hand it reflects the fundamental shift away from the view that the public interest requires strong regulation to modify undesirable outcomes of unfettered market outcomes. It can be expected that a practice of public interest policymaking, within the narrower constraints of the proposed framework, will eventually emerge in a complex process involving the national and European policy levels.

## 6. CONCLUSIONS

During the past decade, European and national policies have transformed the European telecommunications industry from an era dominated by public monopolies to an open market environment. The more competitive environment has contributed to significantly improvements in the performance of the industry. Telecommunications prices have decreased, service penetration has increased, and choice options for residential and business customers have proliferated. Emphasising these synergies between liberalisation, performance and choice, the EU is drafting a blueprint centred on the notions of convergence, competition and consolidation of the existing rules. The proposed new regulatory framework seeks to create an integrated and more homogenous framework for communications infrastructure and associated services (telecommunications services, conditional access services). At this point, policies affecting services provided over these networks as well as content are left for further debate at the EU and national levels.

The new European regulatory vision is firmly rooted in a belief in competition as an organising principle of the 'information society'. It is based on the pragmatic assumption that issues affecting the communications infrastructure can be separated from issues related to the provision of services and content. This basic premise may collapse in the emerging datacentric environment, in which networks and content are intricately interwoven. Moreover, as the initial beneficial effects of competition will taper off eventually, the limits of competition in providing ubiquitous access to advanced networks, access to information resources, and the skills needed to productively use abundant information, will likely become more visible. These issues cannot be addressed from a purely economic perspective and will require an inclusive political dialogue, which is currently missing. In this dialogue it will be necessary to address the multiple linkages between the organisation of electronic communications networks and the public sphere as well as the impacts of communications in creating communities and shared meaning. In the European environment of diverse national interests, finding such a consensus will be difficult.

It seems that, until 1998, the European Commission was concerned about Member States' reluctance to introduce pro-competitive regulation. With the establishment of NRAs, new players have entered the policy arena and begun to claim their jurisdiction. The new framework seems to reflect a new concern that these agencies might begin to regulate too strongly. Nevertheless, a more flexible approach, giving Member States the freedom to deviate from EU mandated policy may be a meaningful solution to explore the advantages and disadvantages of different policy solutions. Contrary to widespread fears, such an approach would likely not jeopardise the further evolution of competition. After all, competition and innovation flourish in differentiated and not homogenous environments. Experiments in Member States would advance the understanding of the role of information technology in the economy and the implications of different electronic communications policies.

## NOTES

1. See Acocella (1998: 71) for an overview.
2. Schneider (2001) presents an interesting evolutionary analysis of the transition of telecommunications policy in major industrialised nations from its origins in the nineteenth century to the present. Habermas's theory of agency, Giddens's theory of structuration, or notions of the framing of policy discourse all offer promising roads for further inquiry.
3. See Mayer-Schönberger (1999) for a concise review of these initiatives.
4. Often, failure and success follow each other. For example, the French publicly switched telephone network was of rather poor quality until the mid 1970s. However, in an ambitious modernisation strategy, France Telecom leapfrogged a generation of technology and built a fully digital network by the 1980s. The upgraded network allowed the development of the Minitel system as a public platform for many business applications. The Minitel also

illustrates the disadvantages of commitment to large infrastructure project as is has likely slowed the migration of French users to the next generation of network platform, the Internet.

5. For example, in the area of interconnection NRAs can impose one or more of the following: access to and use of specific network facilities, price controls, transparency, non-discrimination, and accounting separation.
6. This is expressed very elegantly in the two theorems of welfare economics (Arrow 1951). In a nutshell, these theorems state that under certain conditions competition will lead to an efficient, Pareto optimal, outcome and that such an outcome can be reached from many distributional starting points. Thus, one could argue that competition is inherently undetermined and can unfold starting from many distributional states. From such a perspective, distributional goals (such as universal service) do not conflict with efficiency goals but will need to be determined before the concept of efficiency can be filled with meaning.
7. Substantiating a case is complicated by the fact that the burden of proof presumably will be borne by the regulatory agencies (or plaintiffs).

## REFERENCES


Acocella, Nicola (1998), *The Foundations of Economic Policy: Values and Techniques*, Cambridge, UK: Cambridge University Press.

Aharoni, Yair (1986), *The Evolution and Management of State-Owned Enterprises*, Cambridge, US: Ballinger.

Arrow, Kenneth J. (1951), *Social Choice and Individual Values*, New York: John Wiley.

Bauer, J.M. (1997), 'Market power, technical change and efficiency in telecommunications: Schumpeter reconsidered', *Journal of Economic Issues*, **31**(2), 557–65.

Boyland, O. and G. Nicoletti (2000), 'Regulation, Market Structure, and Performance in Telecommunications', Economics Department Working Paper 237, Organisation for Economic Co-operation and Development.

Brock, Gerald W. (1994), *Telecommunications Policy for the Information Age: From Monopoly to Competition*, Cambridge, US: Harvard Business School Press.

Cherry, B.A. and J.M. Bauer (2001), 'Institutional arrangements and rate rebalancing: empirical evidence from the United States and Europe', unpublished manuscript, Department of Telecommunication, Michigan State University, East Lansing, US.

Cuilenburg, J. and P. Verhoest (1998), 'Free and equal access: in search of policy models for converging communication systems', *Telecommunications Policy*, **22** (3), 171–81.

Dixit, Avinash K. (1996), *The Making of Economic Policy: A Transaction Cost Politics Perspective*, Cambridge, US and London, UK: MIT Press.

Dutton, William H. (1999), *Society on the Line: Information Politics in the Information Age*, Oxford: Oxford University Press.

European Commission (1993), *Growth, Competitiveness, Employment: The Challenges and Ways Forward into the 21st Century*, Brussels: Commission of the European Communities.

European Commission (1994), *Europe and the Global Information Society: Recommendations to the European Council and the European Commission*, Brussels, Commission of the European Communities.

European Commission (1997), *Green Paper on the Convergence of the Telecommunications, Media and Information Technology Sectors, and the*

*Implications for Regulation*, Brussels, Commission of the European Communities, COM(97) 623.

European Commission (1998), *Green Paper on Radio Spectrum Policy in the Context of European Community Policies such as Telecommunications, Broadcasting, Transport, and R&D*, Brussels, 9 December 1998, COM(98) 596.

European Commission (1999a), *Fifth Report on the Implementation of the Telecommunications Regulatory Package*, Communication from the Commission to the European Parliament, the Council, the Economic and Social Committee and the Committee of the Regions, Brussels, October 1999, COM(99) 537.

European Commission (1999b), *Report on the Development of the Market for Digital Television in the EU, in the context of the TV Standards Directive 95/47/EC*, Communication from the Commission, Brussels, 10 November 1999, COM(99) 540.

European Commission (1999c), *Results of the Public Consultation on the Green Paper on the Convergence of the Telecommunications, Media and Information Technology Sectors*, Commission of the European Communities, Brussels, 10 March 1999, COM(99) 108.

European Commission (1999d), *Status Report on European Union Electronic Communications Policy*, Directorate General Information Society, Brussels, 22 December, INFSO/A/1.

European Commission (1999e), *Towards a New Framework for Electronic Communications Infrastructure and Associated Services. The 1999 Communications Review*, Communication from the Commission to the European Parliament, the Council, the Economic and Social Committee and the Committee of the Regions, Brussels, Commission of the European Communities, COM(99) 539.

European Commission (2000a), *Proposal for a Decision on a Regulatory Framework for Radio Spectrum Policy in the European Community*, Brussels.

European Commission (2000b), *Proposal for a Directive of the European Parliament and of the Council Concerning the Processing of Personal Data and the Protection of Privacy in the Electronic Communications Sector*, Brussels, 12 July 2000, COM(2000) 385 final.

European Commission (2000c), *Proposal for a Directive of the European Parliament and of the Council on Access to, and Interconnection of, Electronic Communications Networks and Associated Facilities*, Brussels, 12 July 2000, COM(2000) 384 final.

European Commission (2000d), *Proposal for a Directive of the European Parliament and of the Council on a Common Regulatory Framework for Electronic Communications Networks and Services*, Brussels, 12 July 2000, COM(2000) 393 final.

European Commission (2000e), *Proposal for a Directive of the European Parliament and of the Council on the Authorisation of Electronic Communications Networks and Services*, Brussels, 12 July 2001, COM(2000) 386 final.

European Commission (2000f), *Proposal for a Directive of the European Parliament and of the Council on Universal Service and Users' Rights Relating to Electronic Communications Networks and Services*, Brussels, 12 July 2001, COM(2000) 392 final.

European Commission (2000g), *Sixth Report on the Implementation of the Telecommunications Regulatory Package*, Communication from the Commission to the European Parliament, the Council, the Economic and Social Committee and the Committee of the Regions, Brussels, Commission of the European Communities, Brussels, 7 December 2000, COM(2000) 814.

European Commission (2000h), *The Results of the Public Consultation on the 1999*

*Communications Review and Orientation for the new Regulatory Framework*, Communication from the Commission, Brussels, 26 April 2000, COM(2000) 239 final.

European Commission (2001a), *Commission Working Document on Proposed New Regulatory Framework for Electronic Communications Networks and Services: Draft Guidelines on Market Analysis and the Calculation of Significant Market Power*, Brussels, 28 March 2001, COM(2001) 175.

European Commission (2001b), *The Introduction of Third Generation Mobile Communications in the European Union: State of Play and the Way Forward*, Communication from the Commission to the Council, the European Parliament, the Economic and Social Council and Social Committee and the Committee of the Regions, Brussels, 20 March 2001, COM(2001) 141 final.

European Union (2000), *Regulation of the European Parliament and of the Council on Unbundled Access to the Local Loop*, Brussels, 5 December 2000, 2000/0185 (COD).

Ferré, Frederick (1998), *Knowing and Value: Toward a Constructive Postmodern Epistemology*, Albany: State University of New York Press.

Friedman, Milton (1953), *Essays in Positive Economics*, Chicago: University of Chicago Press.

Garnham, Nicholas (2000), 'The Role of the Public Sphere in the Information Society', in Christopher T. Marsden (ed.), *Regulating the Global Information Society*, London and New York: Routledge, pp. 43–56.

Hodgson, Geoffrey M. (1988), *Economics and Institutions: A Manifesto for a Modern Institutional Economics*, Philadelphia: University of Pennsylvania Press.

Kiessling, T. and Y. Blondeel (1998), 'The EU regulatory framework in telecommunications: a critical analysis', *Telecommunications Policy*, **22** (7), 571–92.

Lenert, E.M. (1998), 'A communication theory perspective on telecommunications policy', *Journal of Communication*, **48** (4), 3–23.

Lessig, Lawrence (1999), *Code and other Laws of Cyberspace*, New York: Basic Books.

Longstaff, Patricia H. (1999), 'Regulating Communications in the 21st Century: New Common Ground', in Benjamin M. Compaine and William H. Read (eds), *The Information Resources Policy Handbook*, Cambridge, MA: MIT Press, pp. 453–89.

Majone, Giandomenico (1989), *Evidence, Argument and Persuasion in the Policy Process*, New Haven: Yale University Press.

Mansell, Robin E. (1993), *The New Telecommunications*, London: Sage Publications.

Mayer-Schönberger, Viktor (1999), 'Operator, Please Give Me Information: The European Union Directive on Data Protection in Telecommunications', in Sharon Eisner Gillett and Ingo Vogelsang (eds), *Competition, Regulation and Convergence: Current Trends in Telecommunications Policy Research*, Mahwah, US: Lawrence Erlbaum, pp. 121–36.

Melody, W.H. (1999), 'Telecom reform: progress and prospects', *Telecommunications Policy*, **23** (1), 7–34.

Noam, Eli M. (1992), *Telecommunications in Europe*, New York: Oxford University Press.

Noam, Eli M. (1999), 'Information and Communication Policy Research: More Important, More Neglected', in Benjamin M. Compaine and William H. Read (eds), *The Information Resources Policy Handbook*, Cambridge, MA: MIT Press, pp. 423–29.

Schneider, V. (2001), *Die Transformation der Telekommunikation. Vom Staatmonopol zum globalen Markt (1800-2000)*, Frankfurt am Main: Campus.

Schneider, V. and R. Werle (1990), 'International Regime or Corporate Actor? The European Community in Telecommunications Policy', in K. Dyson and P. Humphreys (eds), *The Political Economy of Communications: International and European Dimensions*, London: Routledge, pp. 77–106.

Servaes, J. and J.-C. Burgelman (2000), 'In search of a European model for the Information Society', *Telematics and Informatics*, **17** (1–2), 1–7.

Simpson, S. (2000), 'Intra-institutional rivalry and policy entrepreneurship in the European Union', *New Media and Society*, **2** (4), 445–66.

Snow, M.S. (1988), 'The State as stopgap: social economy and sustainability of monopoly in the telecommunications sector', *Review of Social Economy*, **46** (1), 1–23.

Stiglitz, Joseph E. (1994), *Whither Socialism*? Cambridge: MIT Press.

Theil, Henry (1964), *Optimal Decisions Rules for Government and Industry*, Amsterdam: North Holland.

Thiemeyer, T. (1983), 'Deregulation in the perspective of the German Gemeinwirtschaftslehre', *Journal of Institutional and Theoretical Economics*, **139** (3), 405–18.

Tinbergen, Jan (1952), *On the Theory of Economic Policy*, Amsterdam: North-Holland.

Trebing, H.M. (1994), 'The networks as infrastructure: the reestablishment of market power', *Journal of Economic Issues*, **28** (2), 379–89.

Zerdick, Axel et al. (1999), *Die Internet Ökonomie: Strategien für die digitale Wirtschaft*, Berlin: Springer.

# PART II

# Creating New Policies for a European Information Society

# 7. Internet @ Europe: overcoming institutional fragmentation and policy failure

**Raymund Werle**

## INTRODUCTION

The Internet has had a hard time in Europe. Only in the second half of the 1990s, after a long period of ignorance and resistance, did Europeans gradually start to accept and use the network of networks. In this chapter I analyse the Internet's career in Europe.[1] After providing a short sketch of the evolution of the Internet in the United States and an overview over the present state of its diffusion and utilization in Europe and the United States, I examine why it took so long before European policymakers realized thc Internet's potential for innovation and economic growth. The central institutional obstacles to the Internet will be identified and policy failures evolving from this backdrop will be illustrated. I will then show that it required radical institutional change to open a window of opportunity for the Internet and unleash its dynamic potential. The last section – followed by a short conclusion – illustrates the contours of a new European Internet policy emerging from a changing institutional setting and a new user-oriented strategy to promote the Internet as the electronic backbone of a European information society.

## EVOLUTION OF THE INTERNET AND ITS PRESENT STATE IN EUROPE

As is well known, the Internet started as ARPANET – a network that served research and, to a minor degree, military purposes when it was launched by the United States Department of Defense's ARPA (Advanced Research Projects Agency). The pioneering TCP/IP (Transmission Control Protocol/Internet Protocol) protocol stack, which facilitates the interconnection of heterogeneous networks in a way that allows them to be used as if they were one single network, was implemented in the ARPANET at the end of 1982. In the same year, technical recommendations specifying the protocol details of crucial services, including electronic mail, were approved by informal governance committees of the ARPANET. TCP/IP was a United States military standard, but it was not classified and could be implemented free of charge by anybody who wanted to use it. In this sense TCP/IP was an open standard.[2]

In 1985, the NSF (National Science Foundation) - a United Sates public agency - became involved in research and education networking. The NSF initiated the NSFNET, a backbone network designed to provide both access to remote supercomputers and a test bed for experiments in data transmission and switching. Early on, the NSF officials responsible for the NSFNET also had in mind to create an encompassing multi-purpose research and education network. Rather than opting for one of the existing proprietary standards for computer networks such as SNA or DECet, the NSF chose TCP/IP to be implemented in the NSFNET. In doing so, the NSF created a niche in which TCP/IP was sheltered from market competition and could develop into a mature protocol stack that attracted the development of complementary software for a variety of applications. University networks and other local area networks linking research organizations to one another could be connected to the NSFNET on the condition that they use TCP/IP as the interface standard.

With the advent of the WWW (World Wide Web) in the early 1990s, the research and education network exploded and started transforming itself into the commercially viable global Internet. Also in this case the non-proprietary, open nature of the basic protocol - the HTTP (Hypertext Transfer Protocol) - proved to be instrumental for the rapid diffusion of the WWW. In 1995 the NSF ceased operating the NSFNET. Today the Internet is owned and operated by private corporations, non-profit organizations and other collective entities. Internet service providers, telephone companies, cable television companies, computer hardware and software vendors, media companies and all kinds of firms that enter into electronic commerce use the Internet as a communications infrastructure and business channel.

In summary, the network of networks appears to be well described by the label 'the accidental superhighway', which was employed by *The Economist* magazine in July 1995. In its early stages the Internet was promoted and funded, but not designed, by the United States government. In this sense, the Internet is a product of US science (and technology) policy. However, at no point in time did some kind of master-plan exist to guide the Internet's evolution, even though there were critical decisions taken by public agencies that powerfully shaped the course of that evolution – such as the NSF decision to implement the TCP/IP protocol in the NSFNET, and the subsequent decision to privatize the NSFNET backbone.

At the time *The Economist* coined the phrase of 'the accidental superhighway' the Internet was not a well-known phenomenon in Europe. Today, some seven years later, the network of networks is well established in the member states of the European Union. From 1996 to 2001, the number of hosts in the so-called ccTLDs (country code Top-Level Domains) grew from 1.9 million in January 1996 to 5.0 million in January 1998, to 9.5 million in January 2000 and to some 13.7 million in January 2001 at constantly very high growth rates.[3] However, the absolute number of hosts (Figure 7.1) as well as the density of hosts per country (Figure 7.2) varies considerably in different parts of Europe. The number of hosts per 1000 inhabitants is much lower in Southern than in Northern Europe.

We find a similar picture if we look at the percentage of people with Internet access in Figure 7.3, which contains the most recent data. Again the Scandinavian member states of the EU and the Netherlands have the highest penetration rates. In an encompassing report for the European Commission, the telecommunications consultants Fischer and Lorenz argue that 'cultural differences, language barriers, income levels and the general lack of IT infrastructure (such as PCs)' account for the imbalances in Europe. The consultants also emphasize that 'Europe is generally behind North America in

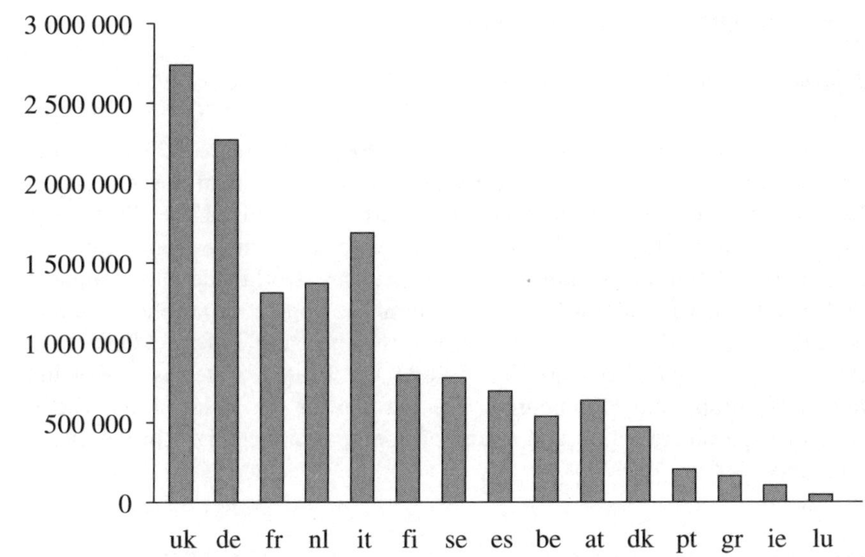


*Source*: Internet Software Consortium.

*Figure 7.1 Internet host count - January 2001*

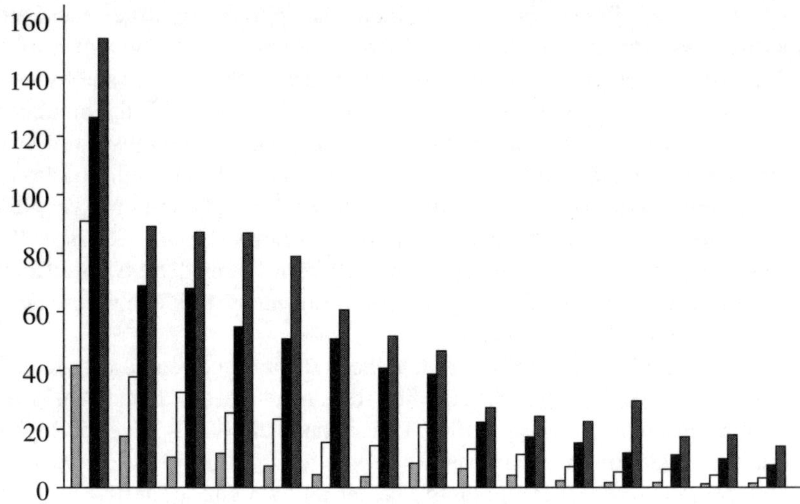


| | fi | se | dk | nl | at | lu | be | uk | de | ie | fr | it | es | pt | gr |
|---|---|---|---|---|---|---|---|---|---|---|---|---|---|---|---|
| 1996 | 41 | 17 | 10 | 11 | 7 | 4 | 3 | 8 | 6 | 4 | 2 | 1 | 1 | 1 | 1 |
| 1998 | 90 | 37 | 32 | 25 | 23 | 15 | 14 | 21 | 13 | 11 | 7 | 5 | 6 | 4 | 3 |
| 2000 | 125 | 68 | 67 | 54 | 50 | 50 | 40 | 38 | 22 | 17 | 15 | 12 | 11 | 10 | 8 |
| 2001 | 152 | 88 | 86 | 86 | 78 | 60 | 51 | 46 | 27 | 24 | 22 | 29 | 17 | 18 | 14 |

*Source*: Internet Software Consortium/own calculations.

*Figure 7.2 Development of hosts per 1000 inhabitants: 1996-2001*

Internet development' (Fischer and Lorenz 2000: 6-8). Figure 7.3 shows that, compared with 28 per cent of the Europeans, 48 per cent of the Americans have Internet access. At the time the report was finalized the differences between Europe and the United States were even more significant. In November 1999 the total number of Internet users worldwide was estimated at 201 million: 101 million (or 35 per cent of the population) in the USA and 43 million (or 12 per cent) in Europe (Fischer and Lorenz 2000: 28).[4] Apparently the gap between Europe and the United States is narrowing although Europe still lags behind. The reasons for this delay date back to inadequate strategic action and a lack of appropriate incentives in the 1980s and early 1990s.

## OBSTACLES TO THE DIFFUSION OF THE INTERNET IN EUROPE

Trying to detect why the Internet has had difficulties in Europe, we can rule

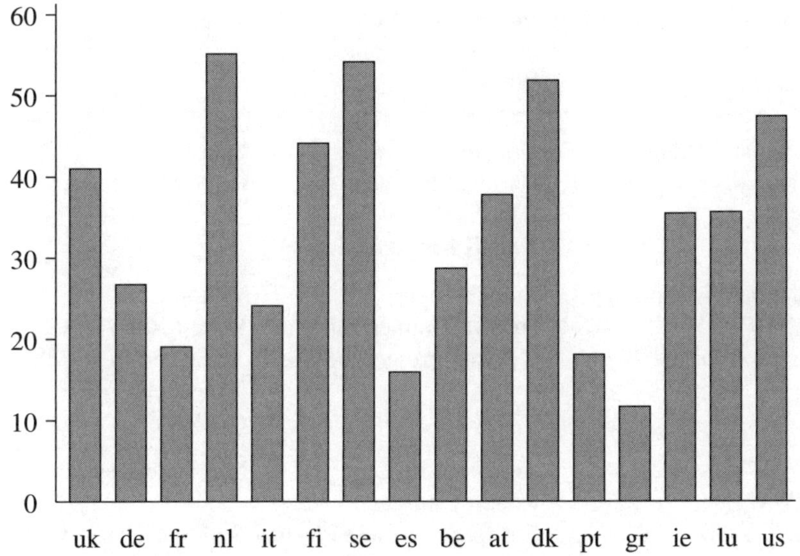


*Source*: EUROBAROMETER, NTIA for US (US data August 2000).

*Figure 7.3 Internet penetration in European homes (%) - October 2000*

out the suggestion that it was a lack of inventiveness that accounts for these difficulties.

**No Lack of European Inventiveness**

Among the pioneering technical inventions, which facilitated the evolution of the Internet, were packet switching, the TCP/IP protocol stack and what we today call the World Wide Web. All these innovations were invented or co-invented in Europe (Table 7.1). 'Packet switching' describes a switching and transmission technology which splits complete messages into small packets. These packets can be transmitted along different lines of a network (in a store-and-forward mode), and they are re-assembled into the original message by the receiving host when they reach their final destination. In the middle of the 1960s packet switching was invented simultaneously by Paul Baran at the RAND corporation in the United States and Donald Davies at the NPL (National Physical Laboratory) in England.[5] While Baran's ideas became one of the technical foundations of the Internet's forerunner ARPANET, Davies' proposals to base a new network on packet switching was rejected by the British General Post Office, which at the time also operated the public telephone network. Davies' own organization, the NPL, did not have the

*Table 7.1 Pioneering inventions in computer networking*

| | Europe | USA |
|---|---|---|
| Packet switching<br>(First half of the 1960s) | Donald Davies<br>National Physical Laboratory, United Kingdom | Paul Baran<br>RAND Corporation |
| Datagram Technology (TCP/IP)<br>(First half of the 1970s) | Louis Pouzin/<br>Hubert Zimmerman<br>Cyclade Project, France | Vinton Cerf/<br>Robert Kahn<br>Advanced Research Projects Agency (ARPA) |
| World Wide Web (WWW)<br>(Early 1990s) | Tim Berners-Lee/<br>Robert Cailliau<br>European Particle Physics Laboratory (CERN) | Marc Andreessen<br>National Centre for Supercomputer Applications (NCSA)<br>Later: NETSCAPE Corporation |

resources and the authority to build such a network. A smaller restricted network (called Mark I) sponsored by the NPL was started in 1967 but developed slowly. It came to be used by researchers at the NPL but did not have the impact that the ARPANET had in the USA (Abbate 1999: 7–41).

TCP/IP, the protocol stack which constitutes the technical basis of the network of networks because it facilitates the interconnection of technically heterogeneous networks, was developed by Robert Kahn and Vinton Cerf at ARPA. It was presented to the public for the first time in 1973. The protocol, among other functions, sets up connections between hosts and provides reliable transmission of data packets in diverse environments as far as design and basic protocols of networks are concerned. The packets transmitted are called datagrams. They can be compared with envelopes which transport all kinds of binary data (including voice or video) across a network. Each datagram contains the address of its destination – whether it is a traditional host or a personal computer desktop. This allows for what the experts call connectionless transmission. Datagrams are handed over from one host to another, and they do not require a channel to be set up from the sender to the final receiver before the transmission process starts. Thus, using datagrams, interconnecting different networks is not very demanding. Long before datagram transmission technology was employed in the ARPANET, it was used in an experimental network project in France called Cyclades. Funded by the French government and invented by Louis Pouzin and Hubert Zimmerman, Cyclades had been explicitly designed to facilitate internet-working. TCP/IP reflects the design of Cyclades. Pouzin and Zimmerman struggled to convince France Telecom, the French public (monopoly) telecommunications carrier, to employ datagram transmission in the public data network (Abbate 1999: 123–7). However, France Telecom and most other European telephone administrations (PTTs) opted for another, a connection-oriented, technology, which emerged in 1974 and was later adopted as an international standard (X.25) by the ITU (International Telecommunication Union). The X.25 networks are homogeneous and more centralized than TCP/IP networks. Their architecture parallels that of the public switched telephone networks (Schmidt and Werle 1998). X.25 technology cannot be used to interconnect networks with different basic protocols.

Finally we turn to the World Wide Web, which provides another, well-known, Internet-related example of European inventiveness. Initially, one drawback of using the Internet was the difficulty of locating and retrieving online information. At the beginning of the 1990s a service called the Gopher system was developed at the University of Minnesota. However, Gopher, like other hierarchical systems of information representation, was very soon outperformed by the WWW. Its foundation was laid by Tim Berners-Lee and Robert Cailliau at CERN, the European Particle Physics Laboratory, in 1990 (Berners-Lee and Fischetti 1999). Since the early 1980s CERN used TCP/IP as the common protocol for its various networks. Berners-Lee created a hypertext system, HTML (Hypertext Markup Language), which could handle different data formats and which would run on TCP/IP (using the HTTP). An addressing scheme was employed, called URL (Uniform Resource Locator) for locating files on the Internet. CERN made the software available on the Internet but did not regard it as lying within its responsibility to promote further development of this technology towards commercial viability. In 1993 the basic ideas were taken up by the NCSA (National Center for Supercomputer Applications) at the University of Illinois, which obviously had no problem integrating WWW-related activities into its work programme although they had nothing in common with supercomputer applications. Marc Andreessen and his colleagues developed a web browser called Mosaic. In 1994, Andreessen left NCSA to set up his own company Netscape. In the same year Tim Berners-Lee left CERN to join the MIT (Massachusetts Institute of Technology) and become director of the World Wide Web Consortium, which was affiliated to the MIT (Dertouzos 1998: 3–54). By 2001, the Consortium, which develops and adopts web standards, had over 500 member organizations including all relevant players in the computer, telecommunications and Internet industry.

## Telecommunications Monopolies

The examples of packet switching, TCP/IP (datagram) protocols and the World Wide Web demonstrate that Europe did not lag behind the US in terms of inventiveness. Yet, the first two examples in particular indicate that the institutional opportunity structure of European telecommunications was unfavourable to these kinds of innovations at the time they were invented. Organizations enjoying a monopoly status either were not interested in packet switching – as in the case of the British General Post Office – or were committed to X.25 rather than datagram-based packet switching – as in the case of France Telecom. Both organizations may have had good reasons for their choices, but their monopoly position left no room for other organizations to take up the innovations and develop them into attractive software products.

The public monopolies dominated the 'market' for telecommunications services in most European countries at the time the Internet started to gain a standing as a research and education network in the United States. Here competition prevailed in the telecommunications industry. Concerning data communication services, for instance, several competing providers of so-called value-added networks such as Telenet, Tymnet, CompuServe and GE-Information Services served companies and later in the 1980s also the general public providing dialup and leased-line connections. After the divestiture of AT&T in the early 1980s, the Bell Operating Companies, striving for new commercial opportunities, also entered the market for data services. Many of them also got involved in funding and building regional research and education networks in collaboration with universities and state and local authorities (Mandelbaum and Mandelbaum 1996). Although it was promoted by federal government agencies the Internet was not uncontested either. Several research and education networks based either on proprietary or on open standards, but not on TCP/IP, competed with or complemented the Internet. One of these networks was BITNET – a co-operative university network which was based on IBM technology (VNET). In the first half of the 1980s more universities were connected to the BITNET than to the Internet. This network directs our attention to another example of European constraints on networks outside the PTT domains.

BITNET's European sister was EARN – the European Academic and Research Network. The IBM Corporation launched and sponsored EARN in the early 1980s. The network was welcomed by the research community. In the mid 1980s more than 500 computers in the research organizations of 19 countries were linked to EARN. This was only possible after the European telecommunications monopolies – for the first time in history – had accepted data transmission across national borders along private lines. The EARN board of directors had to struggle hard to secure the permission for this. This included problems with governments, among them the German government, which only gave the green light on the condition that EARN evolve a system based on open systems standards as defined by the official international standardization organizations (OSI standards, see below). The German position reflected a widespread governmental concern, shared by the European Commission, that EARN might be part of IBM's strategy to expand market dominance, to which some substance was lent by the fact that initially only IBM mainframes and Digital Equipment's Vax computers could be linked via EARN. The open systems standards requirement for EARN was conceded by the board of directors, but in the event it never came to be implemented.

The German government, like other governments, reacted to EARN through initiating a national science network. This was in line with government programmes to support the German computer industry and the national champion Siemens. The European Union also reacted. In 1986 it set up RARE (Réseaux Associés pour la Récherche Européenne) to promote coordination of national operators of science networks and fund network-related research and development projects with the ultimate goal of stimulating the development of a European data network. One strategic component – controlled by RARE with the European Commission acting as project coordinator – was COSINE (Cooperation for Open Systems Interconnection Networking in Europe). COSINE's aim was to create an international packet-switched network for researchers based on the X.25 standard.[6]

## Failed Standards Policy

Technical standards played a strategic role in the area of science networks, public data networks and in the European computer industry. The central focus was on the already mentioned OSI standards. OSI, the Open Systems Interconnection Reference Model, was adopted as an international standard in 1984. OSI's seven-layer protocol architecture was meant to provide a reference system for defining inter-networking protocols and coordinating the standardization of data communications systems. It was the product of an engineering programme that was organized mainly in Europe. The engineering activities were complemented and backed by the emerging Open Systems Movement, whose members were industry consortia, voluntary standards-development organizations and government agencies that were committed to OSI with regard to realizing the vision of universal non-discriminatory access to communications via a global network. The design, standardization and public procurement of information and communication technology should pave the way for a truly open non-proprietary network (Schmidt and Werle 1998).

For some participants in the movement the principle of non-discriminatory open standards had a rationale beyond that of an open global network. European computer vendors, European governments and, in particular, the European Commission saw the OSI programme also as an instrument of industrial policy to protect the European manufacturers against United States competition – especially since many North-American vendors were already well entrenched as the dominant vendors of proprietary network solutions for business. OSI was specifically intended to arrest the widespread deployment of IBM's SNA network standard in Europe (Werle 1997).

In the second half of the 1980s, the United States government also officially declared that it would switch to OSI with regard to its procurement policy. The Department of Commerce and the NBS (National Bureau of Standards) promoted OSI, but they also accepted other standards as long as OSI products were not available. In the American Internet community TCP/IP was obviously preferred to OSI. Criticism tended to be levelled against the poor technical performance of specific standards. Strong opposition was focused on X.25, the already mentioned international standard for connection-oriented packet-switched networks. Being essentially a pre-OSI standard, X.25 was incorporated into OSI, but it could not be used to interconnect heterogeneous networks. Internet enthusiasts never adopted an explicitly favourable stance towards OSI. In the eyes of many observers the battle between the partisans of TCP/IP and OSI network protocols degenerated into a 'religious war' (Drake 1993). In this war the European commitment to OSI did not tolerate any 'deviant' activity (Malamud 1993). Computer scientists could not expect to receive public funding for TCP/IP-related research. The United States government, in contrast, took a more pragmatic stance, in particular after it became apparent that many of the hopes focusing on OSI were to be disappointed because it was taking extremely long until OSI products appeared on the market – too late for OSI to be regarded as a serious competitor to TCP/IP.

The European Commission and many European governments did not promote the Internet and TCP/IP until the increasing commercial viability of this network of networks made acceptance of this innovation inevitable. Until this official change of mind, TCP/IP had only been used in private networks with the exception of the so-called European Backbone (EBONE) – a hybrid network with regard to standards and funding. Launched in 1992 with many promoters in Northern Europe and in the Netherlands, EBONE was a multi-protocol network, which included TCP/IP and was partly funded by RARE. The early openness of the Scandinavian countries and the Netherlands towards TCP/IP accounts for the leading position of these countries with regard to Internet penetration and use (see Figures 7.2 and 7.3).

In summary, the European standards policy towards OSI on the part of the

European Commission and of many governments turned out to be a failure. The tendency to keep up a strong commitment to OSI without considering the prospects of TCP/IP account to some degree for the fact that Europe is significantly behind the United States in Internet diffusion and utilization.

**Fragmented Industrial Policy**

European standards policy evolved in an institutional setting that was shaped by a weak and declining computer hardware industry, a stagnating software industry, monopolistic structures in telecommunications services and a comparatively strong telecommunications manufacturing industry that to some degree relied on sheltered national home markets. Technology policy and standards policy was industrial policy – and it was nationally fragmented. European policy fragmentation and concomitant barriers to trade also account indirectly for the problems European policymakers had accepting – let alone promoting – the Internet.

One of the most spectacular examples of fragmented and parochial technology policy in Europe can be found in an area where telecommunications, data processing and TV broadcasting overlapped. It focused on what was called 'interactive videotex' in the terminology of the ITU (International Telecommunication Union). In the late 1970s and the early 1980s, almost simultaneously, telecommunications operators in the United Kingdom, France and Germany, as well as in the United States, Canada, Japan and a few other countries, planned and heavily promoted an information service for the public with a potential for professional application. Some functions were similar to the Internet – though at the time, of course, not as sophisticated. The system was called Prestel in the United Kingdom, Bildschirmtext in Germany and Télétel/Minitel in France.

In contrast with the efforts in the other countries, the French undertaking not only achieved the status of an industrial *grand projet* with an extremely high degree of concerted political and industrial action but also turned out to be a success at the national level. Télétel, however, never developed into a transnational or global system. The other European systems did not even take off within their national confines. Each country followed the strategy of exporting the system to other countries while keeping the national market closed. For the actors involved, future market shares in a global market were tied to getting their standard accepted as the single world standard for interactive videotex. But they never achieved consensus, neither internationally nor at the regional European level (Schmidt and Werle 1998: 147–84). In an open European market without telecommunications monopolies, interactive videotex might have developed into a successful European service with national variants on a common technical platform. In terms of the market, Télétel demonstrated early on that European consumers were prepared to buy information and transaction services on screen. Before the Internet started to gain ground in France the Télétel system had more than six million private and business subscribers and had created many new jobs, directly and indirectly.

## BREAKING INSTITUTIONAL BARRIERS

The last section illustrated that it was not a lack of inventiveness, but rather the institutional 'lock in' in monopolistic structures and the fragmented national industrial policy, combined with policy failure in an area of standardization where a European consensus was achieved, that to a high degree accounts for the delayed and slow development of the Internet in Europe. Some of the institutional barriers to the Internet have been removed but, as will be examined now, some obstacles have remained.

The inherited telecommunications regime is suspected of having posed a serious obstacle to the diffusion of the Internet. Only since 1998 are the markets for telecommunications services and networks open to competition in most of the Member States of the European Union. It took a long time to deregulate and liberalize telecommunications if we consider that the first crucial step towards liberalization and deregulation was taken with the European Commission's 1987 Green Paper on telecommunications. It marked the starting point of a long series of directives, communications and reports, all of which brought about the largest liberalized telecommunications market in the world. As a result, in countries such as Germany the rates have gone down dramatically, in particular for long-distance and international telephony.

On the side of the European Commission, telecommunications policy was initiated and driven by the goal of liberalization and market integration according to the Internal Market Programme (1982) and the Single European Act (1986), though industrial policy concerns also played a role. From this perspective a common market without any internal barriers to trade would be instrumental as a home base for European conglomerates to improve their respective positions in the export markets (Schneider and Werle 1990). Early on, telecommunications was regarded as being part of the information technology industry. Therefore early technology-focused programmes such as ESPRIT (European Strategic Programme for Research and Development in Information Technology, 1984) and RACE (Research and Development in Advanced Communications Technologies in Europe, 1987) embraced both communication and information technology. They aimed at promoting trans-European and cross-sectoral collaboration. Both programmes had a strong bias towards large private corporations (the Big Twelve) and the operators of public telecommunications networks. RACE had a strong infrastructural component. The ultimate goal of the RACE projects funded by the EU was to facilitate integrated broadband communication. In this context, the promotion of ISDN (Integrated Services Digital Network) and of European standards played an important role. From the point of view of Internet diffusion in Europe, the plan to modernize and expand the telecom infrastructure appears to be a helpful step. However, in the 1980s the European technology programmes in effect created a technology push without an equivalent user-oriented demand pull.

In the early 1990s, therefore, the Commission tried to gear its policy to a comprehensive model, which we can call the *old Information Society Approach.* Building on the Commission's 1993 White Paper on growth and competitiveness (the Delors paper), the so-called Bangemann Report (European Commission 1994) specifies this approach deemed necessary to guide Europe's transition to an information society. The report mimics components of the 1993 United States NII (National Information Infrastructure) initiative but carefully avoids referring to the Internet, which is only mentioned in passing, whereas the American initiative is modelled on the Internet and its governance structure (CSTB 1994; Kahin 1997). Another difference is that the action plan of the Clinton/Gore administration left more activities to private initiative and the market than it did in the past, while the Bangemann report calls for public 'assistance' in ten exemplary areas (including a network for universities and research centres) where uncoordinated market forces alone might fail to reach a critical mass of users. The information society's need for an efficient and internationally competitive telecommunications infrastructure had already been emphasized in the Commission's White Paper, which tends to regard provision of infrastructure as the responsibility of the public sector because markets might not provide them in the politically desired manner. This has found an expression in the TEN (Trans-European Networks) programme (McGowan 1993), which originally included an ambitious investment plan but later was cut back to a number of voluntary agreements among Member States of the EU. An important element of TEN is the provision of telecommunications infrastructure in peripheral regions of the EU to which markets might not actually deliver what is needed. Other elements focus on Advanced Communications Technologies and Services (ACTS) in continuation of RACE (Fuchs and Werle 1993). They include ISDN and integrated broadband communication, in particular ATM (Asynchronous Transfer Mode) technology.

The old Information Society Approach was affected by the dawn of telecommunications liberalization. The incumbent network operators were preparing for market competition and hesitated to commit themselves to infrastructure programmes whose commercial viability was insecure. Moreover, while the approach included an attempt to align the projects to market demand and involve users, this often only occurred after the projects were launched. This is why observers from the United States applauded this approach as 'a step in the right direction' but at the same time criticized it as being not well attuned to changing user demands (McKnight and Neumann 1995: 145–6). More often than not the critical remarks explicitly referred European policy makers to the Internet, which for a long time - perhaps too long a time - remained in the background as a kind of hidden agenda.

However, if we inquire into the merits of the old Information Society Approach, two points must be stressed. The first is that the European Commission and the Council started to promote this concept earlier than most European governments, which triggered similar programmes in the member states (Chatrie and Wraight 2000). Germany, for instance, followed two years after the Bangemann Report with the policy plan 'Info 2000: Deutschlands Weg in die Informationsgesellschaft' (Germany's Way to the Information Society). The second point is that the Commission managed to convince corporations and governments to abandon national egotism and parochial policy and to establish a supranational telecommunications regime (Sandholtz 1998).

## TOWARDS EUROPEAN INTERNET POLICY

The European Summit in Lisbon in March 2000 endorsed the Commission's '*e*Europe' proposal which aims at 'bringing every citizen, home and school, every business and administration into the digital age and online' (European Commission 1999). At last with this endorsement - exactly three years after an Internet Advisory Group stressed the Internet's 'truly enormous influence on all citizens of the Union and on the implementation of the Single Market' and advised the Commission and the Council to get involved in these developments 'very significantly'[7] - a period came to an end which was characterized by considerable passive ignorance and initially even active resistance towards the Internet and the underlying TCP/IP protocol technology. Early European attention to the Internet appeared to be drawn by risks rather than opportunities. In a communication of 1996 the Commission deals with 'Illegal and harmful content on the Internet' (European Commission 1996a). A complementary Green Paper 'On the Protection of Minors and Human Dignity in Audiovisual and Information Services' issued in the same year examines the challenges that society faces in the light of the Internet (European Commission 1996b).

The Commission's reaction to the problems is critical but balanced insofar as not only the risks but also the opportunities of the Internet are stressed. However, although the Internet Advisory Group recommended participating rather than fence sitting in the process of Internet diffusion, European policymakers remained relatively passive. The Commission, for instance, initially played a marginal role in the process of reorganization of Internet naming and addressing – a central issue with regard to techno-economic *governance* of the network of networks. When, in 1997, the US Department of Commerce issued a Request for Comments concerning the future role of governmental and non-governmental organizations in this area after privatization of the Internet, the Commission's response unveiled a lack of detailed knowledge about naming and addressing procedures. Thus, the Commission only emphasized the need to establish an internationally recognized transparent system and to ensure adequate European representation.[8] Eventually the private non-profit ICANN (Internet Corporation for Assigned Names and Numbers), which guides and oversees registration, was set up perfectly in line with the United States' government initiative to exclude international organizations such as the ITU from governing the Internet and leave it to private sector self-regulation. The Commission could live with the latter but heavily criticized the exclusion of intergovernmental bodies with the effect that a Governmental Advisory Committee (GAC) to the ICANN board of directors was established (Leib 2002).[9] This minor success of European interest policy in the process of reorganization of Internet techno-economic governance indicates that the Commission was not very well prepared to become involved in Internet-related issues. The Commission's relative indifference towards the institutionalization of the naming and addressing procedure corresponds with a delayed emergence of private registration firms (registrars) in the EU. The registrars, which need an ICANN accreditation, assign names and numbers competitively. If we look into ICANN's list of accredited registrars we find only 34 in Europe, compared to 89 in United States' firms (Table 7.2).

In the context of the debate on Internet governance, the EU realized the growing significance of this network. Digital technologies were seen as the key factor for growth and employment and in 1998, in a Communication of the Commission, the Internet was acknowledged - if somewhat reluctantly - to be the principal infrastructure for electronic communications (European Commission 1998). In particular, issues related to *electronic commerce* have evoked the Commission's and the Council's engagement. In December 1999, the Commission launched its *e*Europe initiative, in which the Internet is qualified as the backbone of the European information society (European Commission 1999). It was endorsed by the European Summit only four months later.

The recent effort to establish a .eu Internet Top-Level Domain (TLD)

*Table 7.2 Internet domain name registrars*

| Region | Number of registrars |
|---|---|
| USA | 89 |
| Germany | 9 |
| France | 6 |
| United Kingdom | 12 |
| Other EU member states | 7 |
| Worldwide | 170 |

*Source*: ICANN website (4.4.01). Only generic Top Level Domains (.com; .net; .org).

complementary to the national TLDs is more than just a symbolic action.[10] It signals Europe's presence in a network whose technical specifications, functions and services have to a considerable degree been shaped by the users and by small firms – a striking difference to the traditional telecommunications networks. From this angle the EU-effort relates to other *activities geared at increasing user involvement,* such as the IST (Information Society Technologies) programme, which provides funds for research, development and demonstration projects towards a 'User-friendly information society'.[11]

A series of regulatory actions aimed at enabling or accelerating electronic commerce fits into this picture. They include digital signature, encryption, intellectual property and privacy issues. None of these problems is trivial, and it is also an open question whether EU-regulation, self-regulation, public–private co-regulation or no regulation at all turns out to be the most appropriate. Adequate answers require a broader participation of those involved in the provision and use of the Internet. The number of actors who are either interested or have a stake in the Internet is growing at a fast rate in Europe. We can observe that in the EU policy arena, which has become more open to Internet-specific issues, an Internet policy domain is evolving which will provide appropriate collective responses to the 'regulatory needs' of electronic commerce and other Internet areas. In the United States such an *Internet policy domain* has already achieved an autonomous status *vis-à-vis* the telecommunications or the media domain. The set of corporate or collective actors in the Internet domain includes technology vendors, network operators, service providers, business interest organizations, consortia and forums of technical and organizational coordination, in addition to civil rights groups, funding organizations, government agencies and parliamentary committees, to say nothing of the diverse mailing and discussion groups with a genuine Internet base (Werle 2000). Similar trends can be detected in Europe. One indication is the emerging European network of an association representing the ISPs (Internet service providers) (Figure 7.4). Ten national ISPAs (Internet Service Providers Associations) with a constituency of up to 221 members (in Germany) are members of the EuroISPA. Compared to other associations, EuroISPA is still a small organization. Considering, however, that some other associations also represent ISPs, both nationally and at the European level, this development provides evidence of a multifarious process of interest formation and the constitution of an Internet policy domain.

In the American Internet policy domain, the belief is widely shared that the Internet constitutes the pivotal infrastructure of the information society. Therefore accommodating the institutional environment in a way that promises the greatest benefit of this network is a common desire. Organizations rooted in the United States Internet domain struggle to keep away regulatory impositions stemming from the telecommunications or the media domain. Similar problems are encountered by the actors in the European Internet domain. The problems are aggravated by the domain's somewhat transient state. The question remains open as to whether the European domain has already achieved self-sufficiency.[12] Its stability and leverage will grow first and foremost to the extent that barriers to *access to the Internet* are removed. Widespread access will also mark a crucial step towards a European information society.

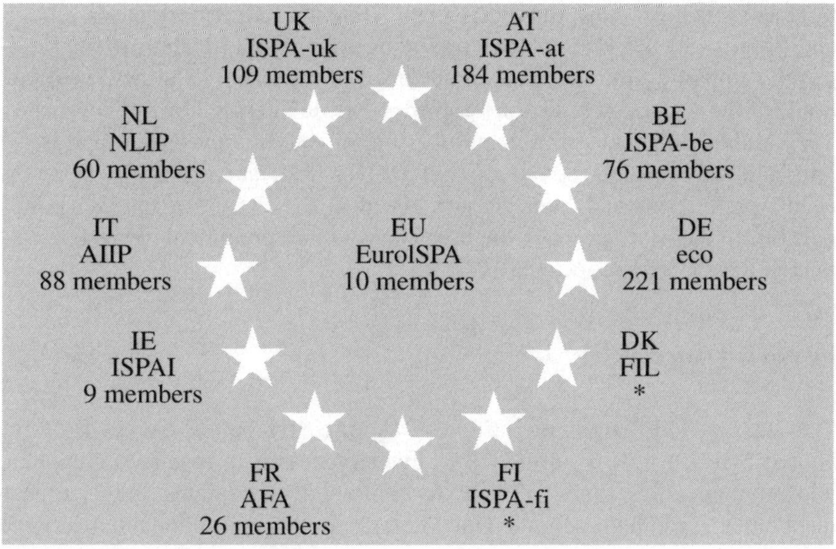


*Note*: * No membership data available.

*Figure 7.4 European and national Internet service providers associations*

There can be no doubt that the high cost of Internet usage including data transmission is still a significant barrier to access. The European Commission's '*e*Europe' Progress Report stresses the negative correlation of Internet access cost and penetration (COM (2000) 130). Consequently, in an '*e*Europe' Action Plan issued by the Commission in June 2000 several actions are proposed to provide cheaper (and faster) Internet access (European Council and European Commission 2000). Most effective in terms of cost reduction has been the deregulation and liberalization of telecommunications in Europe. Ongoing monitoring of this process through the EU Commission helps spur on liberalization. It appears likely that in the near future Internet access providers are going to offer flat rates instead of charging for time, as has been one of the prevalent features of the traditional business model of the telephone network operators.

If, in order to catch up with the United States, Internet usage is to be increased within a relatively short period of time and if a 'digital divide' within the European society is to be avoided, the EU will have to address other barriers to entry to the Internet such as computer illiteracy and lack of public access to the network in peripheral regions. In the USA, where a comparatively extensive understanding of the universal service concept prevails, we find, for instance, 'E-rate' and other federal programmes which, in combination with a series of public and private initiatives at the state and the local level, promote Internet access. They aim at connecting all schools and libraries to the Internet and providing training and technical support – thereby imparting the required competence for the use of the new medium. Some of the American efforts are copied, others are debated by the Europeans. They embody elements of a *new Information Society Approach* which is not only passively open to the Internet but evolves from and actively takes up the needs, preferences and interests articulated in the European Internet policy domain. In the new approach the user plays a more prominent and active role than in the earlier European efforts.

## CONCLUSION

The Internet's diffusion in Europe is significantly below the level of the United States. But it is not a lack of inventiveness with regard to computer, telecommunications and software technology that explains the European difficulties to catch up with the United States. Rather institutional barriers and policy failure account for the fact that Europeans lost valuable time to convert inventions into marketable products and gain experience with the development and use of components of the Internet. In the second half of the 1980s and in the early 1990s when the TCP/IP protocol stack established itself in the landscape of computer networks in the United States, European computer scientists and software engineers were confronted with virtually unsurmountable resistance if they tried to mobilize funds for Internet-related development projects in the public as well as in the private sector of most countries. In this period public agencies and private corporations in the member states of the European Union - usually unwilling to coordinate industrial policy and strategy with each other - were united concerning their goal to counterattack the United States predominance in information technology including computer networks. Guided by the European Commission they saddled the wrong horse committing themselves to technology and products based on OSI standards. Only recently more favourable conditions for the Internet have evolved, triggered by:

- a growing sense of the Internet's infrastructural significance,
- institutional changes in particular in the European telecommunications industry, and
- a reorientation of European technology policy towards user involvement and the requirements of competitive markets, as a result of a painful learning process.

However, given the well known technological and organizational lock-in effects with network technologies (Shapiro and Varian 1999), the legacy of the past which accounts for the time lag and accordingly the competitive disadvantage of European corporations in the area of computer networks and network services will not be overcome in the near future.

## NOTES

1. For research assistance I am indebted to Ulrich Müller, Dörte Nielandt and Dejan Perc.
2. This also indicates the in most parts civilian nature of the ARPANET. 'The Internet grew out of the Department of Defense's need to interconnect its various research networks' (Norberg and O'Neill 1996: 193, 194; see also Leib and Werle 1998). ARPA has been an agency 'that is really charged with civilian technological innovation but hides its mission behind the smoke screen of national defense interests' (Kitschelt 1991: 489).
3. Country codes are standardized by the ISO (International Standardization Organization). Examples of national domains are .nl for the Dutch, .de for the German or .it for the Italian Top-Level Domain. By far the largest number of hosts (about 44 million) is registered in the global .com domain. But also the global .net domain includes 32 million host registrations. The .us, .gov, .edu, .mil domains can be regarded as national United States domains. They comprise about 12.8 million hosts (all figures as of January 2001).
4. In the late 1990s, according to different sources, the Internet penetration rate was highest in the United States (estimations vary from 34 per cent to 42 per cent) and in the Scandinavian member states of the EU, in particular in Sweden (estimations vary from 42 per cent to 52 per cent). In Germany and the United Kingdom between 11 per cent and 17 per cent were estimated to have access whereas the penetration rate in Spain varied between 5 per cent and 7 per cent. The EU average was estimated between 8.5 per cent and 12 per cent.

5. 'Davies initially developed his ideas without any knowledge of Baran's work' (Norberg and O'Neill 1996: 161). One of the goals – but neither the only nor the most important goal – of RAND's research and development activities in the first half of the 1960s was 'devising a communications system that could survive an enemy attack' (Norberg and O'Neill, 1996: 160).
6. The very first European activity to set up an EIN (European Informatics Network) dates back to the early 1970s. EIN was designed to promote computer science and provide a test bed for networking techniques rather than offering communications services.
7. http://www.cordis.lu/esprit/src/i2eurepo.htm
8. http://www.ntia.doc.gov/ntiahome/domainname/email/late.htm
9. However, the US government insisted that the role of governmental and intergovernmental organizations should be strictly limited to advisory functions (http://www.ntia.doc.gov/ntiahome/domainname/6_5_98dns.htm).
10. ICANN agreed in principal to delegate jurisdiction on this domain to the EU.
11. The IST programme (1998–2002) is part of the Fifth Framework Programme. It has an initial budget of 3.6 billion EURO (see http://www.cordis.lu/ist/home.html).
12. In a report on impact and priorities of the '*e*Europe' initiative the European Commission stressed that 'the Internet sector is now big enough to exert an influence on the entire economy' (European Commission 2001).

## REFERENCES

Abbate, Janet Ellen (1999), *Inventing the Internet*, Cambridge, MA: MIT Press.

Berners-Lee, Tim and Mark Fischetti (1999), *Weaving the Web. The Original Design and Ultimate Destiny of the World Wide Web by its Inventor*, San Francisco: Harper.

CSTB (Computer Science and Telecommunications Board), US National Research Council (1994), *Realizing the Information Future. The Internet and Beyond*, Washington, DC: National Academy Press.

Chatrie, Isabelle and Paul Wraight (2000), *Public Strategies for the Information Society in the Member States of the European Union*, an ESIS report, Brussels: DG Information Society, Sept. 2000 (http://europa.eu.int/ISPO/esis/).

Dertouzos, Michael L. (1998), *What Will Be: How the New World of Information Will Change Our Lives*, San Francisco: Harper Edge.

Drake, William J. (1993), 'The Internet religious war', *Telecommunications Policy*, **17** (9), 643–8.

European Commission (1994) *Europe and the Global Information Society: Recommendations to the European Council*, Brussels COM (94) 347.

European Commission (1996a), *Illegal and Harmful Content on the Internet*, Communication to the European Parliament, the Council, the Economic and Social Committee and the Committee of the Regions, Brussels, COM (96) 487.

European Commission (1996b), *Green Paper on the Protection of Minors and Human Dignity in Audiovisual and Information Services*, Brussels, October 1996, COM (96) 483

European Commission (1998), *International policy issues related to Internet governance*, Brussels, COM (98) 111 final.

European Commission (1999), *eEurope. An Information Society for All*, Brussels, COM (1999) 687 final.

European Commission (2000), *'eEUROPE–an Information Society for All'. Progress Report for the Special European Council on Employment, Economic Reforms and Social Cohesion*, 24 March 2000, Brussels, COM (2000) 130.

European Commission (2001), *eEurope 2002. Impact and Priorities*, Brussels, 13 March 2001, COM (2001) 140 final.

European Council and European Commission (2000), *'eEurope 2002'. Action plan. An Information Society for All*, Brussels, 14 June 2000.

Fischer and Lorenz (2000), *Internet and the Future Policy Framework for Telecommunications. Study on the development of new telecommunications services, in particular those exploiting Internet, and their impact (economic and otherwise) on the European Union regulatory and policy framework for telecommunications*, a report for the European Commission, Copenhagen 2000.

Fuchs, Gerhard and Raymund Werle (1993), 'Liberalization and integration. Pathways to a trans-european network in telecommunications', *Utilities Policy,* **3** (3), 187–200.

Kahin, Brian (1997), 'The U.S. National Information Infrastructure Initiative: The Market, the Net, and the Virtual Project', in Brian Kahin and Ernest J. Wilson III (eds), *National Information Infrastructure Initiatives. Vision and Policy Design*, Cambridge, MA: MIT Press, pp. 150–89.

Kitschelt, Herbert (1991), 'Industrial governance structures. Innovation strategies, and the case of Japan: sectoral or cross-national comparative analysis?', *International Organization*, **45**, 453–93.

Leib, Volker (2002), 'ICANN - EU can't: Internet governance and Europe's role in the formation of the Internet corporation for assigned names and numbers (ICANN)', *Telematics and Informatics,* **19**, 159–71.

Leib, Volker and Raymund Werle (1998), 'Computernetze als infrastrukturen und kommunikationsmedien der wissenschaft', *Rundfunk und Fernsehen*, **46** (2–3), 254–73.

Malamud, Carl (1993), *Exploring the Internet. A Technical Travelogue*, Englewood Cliffs, NJ: Prentice Hall.

Mandelbaum, Richard and Paulette A. Mandelbaum (1996), 'The Strategic Future of the Mid-Level Networks', in Brian Kahin (ed.), *Building Information Infrastructure. Issues in the Development of the National Research and Education Network*, New York: McGraw-Hill, pp. 59–118.

McGowan, Francis (1993), 'Trans-European networks: utilities as infrastructures', *Utilities Policy*, **3** (3), 179–86.

McKnight, Lee and Russell W. Neumann (1995), 'Technology Policy and the National Information Infrastructure', in William J. Drake (ed.), *The New Information Infrastructure. Strategies for U.S. Policy*, New York: The Twentieth Century Fund Press, pp. 137–54.

Norberg, Arthur L. and Judy E. O'Neill (1996), *Transforming Computer Technology. Information Processing for the Pentagon, 1962–1986*, Baltimore: Johns Hopkins University Press.

Sandholtz, Wayne (1998), 'The Emergence of a Supranational Telecommunications Regime', in Wayne Sandholtz and Alec Stone Sweet (eds), *European Integration and Supranational Governance*, Oxford: Oxford University Press, pp. 134–63.

Schmidt, Susanne K. and Raymund Werle (1998), *Coordinating Technology. Studies in the International Standardization of Telecommunications*, Cambridge, MA: MIT Press.

Schneider, Volker and Raymund Werle (1990), 'International Regime or Corporate Actor? The European Community in Telecommunications Policy', in Kenneth Dyson and Peter Humphreys (eds), *The Political Economy of Communications. International and European Dimensions*, London: Routledge, pp. 77–106.

Shapiro, Carl and Hal R. Varian (1999), *Information Rules. A Strategic Guide to the Network Economy*, Boston, MA: Harvard Business School Press.
Werle, Raymund (1997), 'Technische Standardisierung im deregulierenden Europa', in Karl-Ernst Schenk, Dieter Schmidtchen and Manfred, E. Streit (eds), *Jahrbuch für Neue Politische Ökonomie, Bd. 16: Neue Politische Ökonomie der Integration und Öffnung von Infrastrukturen*, Tübingen: J.C.B.Mohr, pp. 54–80.
Werle, Raymund (2000), 'The Impact of Information Networks on the Structure of Political Systems', in Christoph Engel and Kenneth H. Keller (eds), *Understanding the Impact of Global Networks on Local Social, Political and Cultural Values*, Baden-Baden: Nomos, pp. 159–85

# 8. European regions and Information Society policy instruments

**Antonio Alabau**

## INTRODUCTION

Since the end of 1993, when the presidency of the European Commission was occupied by Jacques Delors, to nowadays, the European institutions have been insisting on the importance of the Information Society in the social and economic development of Europe. The same idea was also reflected in similar proposals made at the time by the new democratic presidential team in the United States beginning 1993. We can now confirm that the development of the Information Society is becoming one of the motors of the economy and that these early proposals pointed in the right direction. As we enter the new century, the Information Society is, with the participation of private and public sectors, nearly a reality. The interest of private industry in the development of the Information Society became clear during the liberalisation of telecommunication services that concluded in 1998, and grew in the years after, as the increasing use of the Internet reached higher levels.

There is now sufficient perspective to begin a detailed analysis of the role played in this process by the various public administrations: European, national, regional and municipal. This is the principal objective of this chapter. This chapter analyses the role of European regions in the development of the Information Society in recent years. We also study the instruments made available for this end to the regions by the European institutions.

## THE REGIONAL FRAMEWORK OF THE EUROPEAN UNION

Public administrations in the EU are traditionally structured in four territorial and administrative levels: European, national, regional and municipal. Compared to the homogeneity of the powers of national and municipal administrations, an enormous disparity exists in what each country understands by the term 'region'. Nevertheless, the term region is widely used in the Community terminology. It is an essential element in policy - especially those policies related to economic and social cohesion. It is defined in articles 158 to 161 of the Treaty of the European Community.

A region of a State is usually understood as a territory defined by a common historical, cultural, economic, or administrative character. The main difference between the European regions is the range of powers given to their public administrations. Representation of the European regions in the Union is exercised through the Committee of the Regions. It is made up of representatives of the regional and local bodies and is advisory in nature - in accordance with article 263 of the Treaty. As laid down in the Treaty, the committee acts as an advisory body to the Council, Commission and Parliament.

## Administrative Powers of the European Regions

The European regional structure is heterogeneous (Alabau 1997: 761–71). The historical evolution of each State has led to great differences between the regional powers of the different member states, and in some cases, among regions of the same State. In every case, there is a distribution of functions and powers among state and regional administrations. It would be very useful to classify the different European regions – despite the difficulties in comparing diverse types of administrative powers and functions existing across the Union (European Parliament 1993a, 1993b). At the risk of some imprecision, Table 8.1 shows the resultant grouping of regions.

## European Commission Services for Regional Development

The European Commission has a Directorate-General of Regional Policy in charge of European actions for encouraging the social and economic development of the poorer regions. The office's principal power lies in its administration of three large funds: the ERDF (European Regional Development Fund), the CF (Cohesion Fund), and the ISPA (Pre-accession Structural Policy Instruments). The office uses these three funds to co-finance programmes and projects presented by the national and regional authorities. The main instrument for encouraging the growth of the Information Society in the regions is the ERDF - whose characteristics are described below.

The regional policy office has created the Inforegio service (http://www.inforegio.org) to distribute detailed information about the activities of the EU in the framework of economic and social cohesion and activities related to the use of structural funds. It is also worth mentioning the

*Table 8.1 A summary of administrative powers of the European regions*

| Type of Powers | Regions |
|---|---|
| Regions with Broad Administrative Powers<br>. Regional Parliament<br>. Legislative powers.<br>. Budget powers special<br>. Some tax collection powers | - Länder in Germany<br>- Länder in Austria<br>- Regions in Belgium<br>- Autonomous Communities in Spain<br>- The five regions with status in Italy |
| Regions with Low Administrative Powers<br>. Regional Parliament<br>. Low budget powers<br>. Low tax collection powers<br>. Basic financing dependent of central government transfer | - The other regions in Italy<br>- Regions in France<br>- Provinces in Holland<br>- Scotland, Wales and Northern Ireland in the United Kingdom<br>- Departments in Denmark<br>- The two autonomous regions in Portugal |
| Regions without Administrative Powers *<br>. No regional Parliament<br>. No budget powers<br>. No tax collection powers<br>. Financing entirely dependent on central government transfer | - The other regions in Portugal<br>- Regions in Greece<br>- Counties and regions in Ireland<br>- Counties and regions in the UK<br>- Regions in Sweden<br>- Regions in Finland<br>- Districts in Luxembourg |

*Notes*: In some of these states a region is considered as a group of minor entities and, sometimes, the territory under the responsibility of a development agency that does not always coincide with the territory of the ERDF regions, in particular in Ireland and the UK.

*Source*: Own elaboration.

Directorate-General of Employment and Social Affairs, which is responsible for the development and monitoring of European employment strategy. It encourages cooperation between Member States on employment policies, supports and complements their actions, and attempts to give employment a central role in all EU policies.

The Directorate-General of Employment and Social Affairs is responsible for the management of the ESF (European Social Fund). This fund is the main European financial tool for employment strategy and also contributes to social and economic cohesion.

## EU FINANCIAL INSTRUMENTS FOR THE DEVELOPMENT OF THE INFORMATION SOCIETY

### The Community Funds for the Development of Telecommunications and the Information Society

Budget decisions, like all EU actions, are regulated by treaties. The first objective of the EC, from its creation in 1957, has been the creation of an internal market and the maintenance of competition. All economic intervention by public administrations is considered in the light of these principles. Nevertheless, from the earliest days it was believed that the EC should also play an important role - through the community budget - in the levelling of economic inequalities among the member states. With the object of encouraging social integration through training, the EC created the ESF, outlined in Title XI of the Treaty, which covers social policy, education, professional training and youth. The use of the fund was specified in article 136 and the following articles.

The adhesion to the EC of countries with important undeveloped areas, such as Ireland, Greece, Portugal and Spain, showed the need for adjustment measures focused to the less developed areas in order to attain economic and social cohesion. The ERDF was created to meet this need. This was defined in Title XVII of the Treaty, and specifically, article 158.

Simultaneously, the persistent industrial crisis of the 1970s forced the EC to introduce a group of new adjustment measures to encourage technological growth in a pre-competitive stage that was not harmful to free competition. The consequence was the creation of research and technological development programmes; regulated by the XVIII Title of the Treaty, particularly articles 163 and the following articles. Finally, article 308 of the treaty authorises the Council to carry out other measures that may not have been foreseen in the treaty and assign the necessary budgets.

Accordingly, funding for activities specifically related to the development of telecommunications and the Information Society can be found from the following principal sources: structural funds, in particular the ERDF; funds of the Fifth Framework Research and Technological Development Programme; and specific funds for promoting and raising awareness of the Information Society. The following sections summarise the main types of funds available for the development of the information society.

### General Aspects of the Operation of EU Structural Funds

The Council of the European Union, in June of 1999, approved a Regulation for the structural fund for the period 2000–2006 (European Council 1999a). In accordance with this Regulation, the structural fund will contribute to the attainment of three objectives:

- Objective 1: promote the development and structural adjustment of less developed regions, with a GDP per capita less than 75 per cent of the community average.
- Objective 2: support the economic and social conversion of areas with structural deficiencies, as defined by criteria included in the regulation. The Member States propose to the Commission the areas they consider most gravely affected by industrial conversion so that they can be included in Objective 2.
- Objective 3: support the adaptation and modernization of political and education systems, training and employment, in areas that have not been included in Objectives 1 and 2.

In accordance with the structural fund regulations, some 94 per cent of the budget is dedicated to financing actions proposed by areas and regions. Despite the regional nature of these funds it must be remembered that it is the Member States, and not the political or administrative regional bodies, that are responsible to the Commission for the management of the funds.[1]

The activities to be developed in Objective 1 regions of a Member State are listed in the community support framework. The specific programmes for each region constitute the Regional Operational Programme. In the case of Objective 2 and 3 regions, each Member State must prepare a Single Programme document listing all actions receiving structural funds.

In addition to the budget for financing actions proposed by the regions, 5 per cent of the total structural budget is made available to the Commission for the financing of Community Initiatives whose objectives are proposed by the Commission itself. Another 1 per cent is reserved by the Commission for financing Innovation Actions (0.7 per cent), and Technical Assistance for the development of these actions (0.3 per cent). In Table 8.2, the distribution of the budgets of the EU is summarized for the year 2001. The table shows the large budget for structural actions in Objective 1 regions and this demonstrates the willingness of the EU to achieve social and economic cohesion. This is the main source of funding available to European regions for developing the Information Society.

### The European Regional Development Fund (ERDF)

Article 130 C of the treaty establishes the ERDF, as 'dedicated to contribute to the adjustment of the main regional imbalances inside the Community by means of a participation in the development and in the structural adjustment

*Table 8.2 Summary of the EU budget for 2001*

| | € (millions) | | % |
|---|---|---|---|
| 1. Agriculture | 44.100 | | 45.5 |
| 2. Structural operations | 32.720 | | 33.8 |
| Objective 1 | | 20.832 | |
| Objective 2 | | 3.613 | |
| Objective 3 | | 3.575 | |
| Structural measures in the fisheries | | 164 | |
| Community initiatives | | 1.683 | |
| Innovative measures | | 136 | |
| Cohesion Fund | | 2.715 | |
| 3. Internal policies | 6.136 | | 6.3 |
| 4. External action | 4.933 | | 5.1 |
| 5. Administration | 4.860 | | 5.0 |
| 6. Reserves | 916 | | 0.9 |
| 7. Pre-accession aid | 3.259 | | 3.4 |
| TOTAL | 96.924 | | |

*Source*: http://europa.eu.int/abc/doc/off/rg/en/welcome.htm

of the lesser developed regions and in the conversion of declining industrial regions'. The operation of ERDF is regulated by means of Council and Parliament Regulation (European Council and European Parliament 1999), in accordance with the general lines laid down for all Structural Funds and described in the previous section. The ERDF is administered by the Regional Policy Director-Generate of the EC.

## Research and Technological Development Fund (RTD)

In 1986, the European Union Single Act extended the reach of article 130 of the Treaty and established the RTDF (Research and Technological Development Fund). From this moment the EU set as one of its objectives 'the strengthening of the scientific and technological bases of industry and the development of industrial competitiveness'. The result has been the development and the execution of RTDF Framework Programmes. Each programme has a group of agreed high-priority objectives (Guzzetti 1995).

In December 1998 the European Parliament and the Council adopted the fifth RTDF programme for the period 1998–2002. In this programme, one of the main themes was entitled 'An information society whose instruments are easy to understand and use' IST (Information Society and Technology) Program. With this inclusion the European institutions were attempting to guide the community technological effort towards the consolidation of the technological bases for the development of the Information Society.

### Specific Funds for Raising Awareness of the Information Society

During 1998 the Council approved a two-year programme to stimulate the establishment of the information society for the period 1998–2000 (European Council 1998). In article 308 the Treaty empowers the Council to unanimously initiate this type of programme. The programme was endowed with a relatively modest budget of €25m to allow the Commission to launch a number of specific actions to raise awareness of the Information Society.[2]

## REFERENCE FRAMEWORK FOR THE DEVELOPMENT OF THE INFORMATION SOCIETY IN THE EU

From the first moment, since the 1980s, the strategy of the European institutions for the development of the Information Society has been defined and driven by the European Commission. In a rapid analysis of the initiatives in this field we can distinguish three very different phases that coincide, in our opinion, with three distinct phases of Community government, characterized by three different Commission presidencies: the Commission periods under Delors (1985–94); Santer (1995–99) and, finally, under Prodi (1999 to the present).

### Commission Strategy under Delors (1985–94)

The first formal initiatives related to the Information Society were begun by the Commission at the end of the command of Jacques Delors in 1993, and also during the final stage of the process of introducing full competition in telecommunications (Alabau, 1998). As we mentioned earlier, a similar process had begun a year before under the Clinton presidency in the United States.

The first declaration of the need to tackle the creation of the Information Society in the EU appeared in December 1993, in the Growth, Competitiveness and Employment White Paper (European Commission 1993). In the usual way, the European Council, in its meeting at Copenhagen in June 1993, asked the Commission to prepare a White Paper on medium-term strategy for growth, competitiveness, and employment. At the time, Europe was suffering a crisis caused by the fall of the Berlin Wall and the imminent incorporation of central and eastern European nations in the western economy. Chapter five of this White Paper discussed social change and new technologies. It said that the birth of the Information Society offered an enormous potential for economic growth and a combined effort was needed to manage the change.

The White Paper proposed the creation of a European information infrastructure – perhaps inspired by the initiative announced some months earlier by the American government, the National Information Infrastructure initiative (Department of Commerce 1993). To guide the definition of priorities and prepare an action plan, the European Council created a special high-level group and asked it to prepare a report in just three months.

The group was composed of 20 members and presided over by Commissioner Bangemann. It presented its report (European Commission 1994c) and it was, in turn, analysed during the European Council meeting in Corfu at the end of June. It is worth highlighting that among the recommendations, the report proposed leaving the creation of the Information Society in the hands of the private market sector.

The Commission adopted the Bangemann report and in July 1994 it presented an Action plan entitled 'Europe's Way to the Information Society' (European Commission 1994a). The plan indicated what needed to be done to accelerate Europe towards the Information Society and paid special attention to cultural and social aspects. The Commission needed external help in the definition of the key social aspects. The action plan foresaw the creation of a group of high-level experts to propose the necessary steps and the creation of a permanent Information Society forum to act as an advisory body to the Commission.

## Santer Commission Strategy (1995–99)

Between 1995 and 1999 the Information Society proposals developed under Delors were carried out. Perhaps the most noteworthy point was an apparent lack of co-ordination between the various Commission services. Various projects were developed in the Directorate-Generals of Employment, Education, Research, Regional Development and, of course, Telecommunications.

At the European Council held in Dublin during July 1996, the Commission published a new Communication in which it revised the main content of the action plan. In November 1996, the Commission began publishing a so-called rolling action plan which detailed actions already carried out, those being executed, and those being started in the future. Inexplicably, the Commission stopped publishing this document in July 1997 (European Commission 1996a, 1996b).

A year after the 1994 action plan was agreed, the Commission created a Group of High-Level experts to analyse the social aspects of the information society and propose initiatives. The group was reduced in size to 14 members and presented its final report in April 1997, called 'Building the European Information Society for Us All' (European Commission 1997).

Among its conclusions, the group proposed making public services the motor of growth in the emerging information society. For the first time, it was affirmed that the public sector, in particular the national and regional administrations, should play a role in the development of the Information Society.

The Information Society Forum was created in February 1995 and consisted of 130 members. Its task was to carry out a permanent and continuous debate of the work begun by the Group of High Level Experts. During recent years the Forum has been so productive in activities, reports and recommendations that it is impossible to even summarize them in this chapter.[3]

## Prodi Commission Strategy (1999 to Present)

After the rapid end of the Santer team, the new Commission, led by Romano Prodi, gave a new impulse to these policies and made the Information Society one of its main objectives through the eEurope initiative. The Information Society was one of the starring themes of the two European Councils held under Portuguese presidency – the Council of Lisbon on 23–24 March and Santa María de Feira on 19–20 June 2000. In autumn 1999, the European Commission apparently needed to grasp some dynamic incentives and objectives, and so presented the e-Europe Initiative, renamed in Feira as *e*-Europe 2002.

What is the *e*Europe Initiative? It is a group of documents in which the Commission proposes a series of measures and commitments to accelerate development of the information society in Europe (see Table 8.3).[4] The Commission maintained that the development of the Information Society is necessary as the base of the new economy and its construction needs encouragement from the EU. To this end, the Commission made some proposals linked to this initiative.

It seems obvious that all European institutions including states, regions and municipalities should participate in this task. This initiative, which was approved in Santa María de Feira, attempts to encourage states and regions to finally use the available structural funds to co-finance projects related to the information society.

It is important to note that the eEurope initiative did not include a specific budget and is being financed from those community funds mentioned earlier. It is also worth taking into account the effect this initiative will have the preparatory work for the future Sixth Framework Programme for Research and Development for 2002–2006 (RTD 2000; European Commission 1999d).

*Table 8.3 'eEurope' initiative proposals*

| | |
|---|---|
| A cheaper, faster, secure Internet | • Cheaper and faster Internet access<br>• Faster Internet for researcher and students<br>• Secure networks and smart cards |
| Investing in people and skills | • European youth into the digital era<br>• Working in the knowledge-based economy<br>• Participation for all in the knowledge-based economy |
| Stimulate the use of the Internet | • Accelerating e-commerce<br>• Government online: electronic access to public services<br>• Health online<br>• European digital content for global networks<br>• Intelligent transport systems |

*Source*: European Commission (2000b).

## EU REGIONAL ACTIONS FOR THE DEVELOPMENT OF THE INFORMATION SOCIETY AND TELECOMMUNICATIONS

### Regional Actions During the Delors Commission (1985–94)

As we mentioned previously, the main community instruments in the regional policy field are the Structural Funds and, in particular, the ERDF. Therefore, the evolution of the actions of the EU in the promotion of the information society in the regions is intimately linked to the evolution of the structural funds and the possible actions foreseen in each of its successive stages.

ERDFs were started in 1975 (European Council 1975) as a consequence of the incorporation of the United Kingdom and Ireland, and were then modified in 1979 (European Council 1979). The first actions related to telecommunications took place as a result of a second reform resulting from the incorporation of Greece. This second reform was laid down in the ERDF regulation of 1984 (European Council 1984).

This regulation governed the actions of the ERDF during the period 1985–89 and created the community programme that, in turn, allowed the

Commission to launch the STAR programme. The principal aim of this programme was to help equalise the regional imbalances in telecommunication infrastructure.

The STAR programme (European Council 1986), approved in 1986, emerged as a result of the ERDF 1984 regulation and the 1984 telecommunication programme.[5] More than 80 per cent of its budget was dedicated to the correction of telecommunication infrastructure imbalances in Objective 1 regions - as well as promoting application projects for advanced telecommunication services. It should be remembered that public co-financing of telecommunication operators was then possible because their monopoly operation meant competition was not threatened.

The ERDF regulation was modified in 1988 after the incorporation of Spain and Portugal (European Council 1988). This regulation governed the use of the fund between 1989 and 1993 and created the community initiative that is still in use today.

The TELEMATIQUE community initiative arose from the 1988 ERDF regulation and the 1987 telecommunication programme (European Commission 1987), and was developed between 1991 and 1993 (European Commission 1994b). Its objective was to promote the then recently-liberalised value added services in information technology.

Given its nature and the strong relationship with actions taken by the telecommunication operators, both the STAR programme and the TELEMATIQUE initiative were managed by the Commission and Member States with little participation from the regions.

During this period, some regions included in their operational plans various other actions aimed at developing projects related with telecommunications in their territories. These projects were linked with the expansion of services in rural areas, improvement of corporate communications, or the development of information technology projects in the region.

The real possibilities for regional action in developing the information society came about as a result of the new 1993 ERDF regulation (European Council 1993). This regulated actions for the period 1994–99 within the community structural funds, in line with the proposals made by the Commission in their *White Paper on Growth, Competitiveness and Employment* (European Commission 1993).

Within its framework the first proposals emerged for the participation of the regions in the information society – the IRISI initiative (Inter-Regional Information Society Initiative). At the time, the Commission needed to demonstrate some achievements in the development of its embryonic action plan for the development of the Information Society. The Commission intended to present this plan to the European Council in Essen in December 1994. It believed that the regions could be actors in the development of the Information

Society and launched the pilot initiative called IRISI. The funds came from those parts of the structural funds reserved for the Commission – especially ERDF and FSE. These budgets, now termed innovative action funds, were regulated by article 10 of the ERDF regulation and article 6 of the FSE.

The objective of the IRISI was to help an initial group of six regions prepare a regional strategy and action plan for the development of the information society in their territories. During this period the groundwork was being prepared for a future reform of the structural funds under new regulation for the period 2000–2006. The Commission wanted the regions, and in particular the less developed regions, to use a significant part of these funds to contribute to the development of the information society in their territories. In this way, they could help modernise their social and productive infrastructures and better achieve the objectives of social and economic cohesion.

Three of the Commission Directorate-Generals involved in this operation were in favour from the beginning. These were the Directorate-General of Telecommunications because the plan added to its information technology strategy; the Directorate-General of Regional Development; and Directorate-General of Employment and Social Affairs.

## Regional Actions during the Santer Commission Period (1995–99)

The basic work of the Commission during this period was the preparation of the regulations for the structural funds packet 2000–2006 - inside the budget framework derived from Agenda 2000. With the launch of the project for the creation of the Information Society and the imminent disappearance of telecommunications monopolies, it became increasingly obvious that the European regions should play an important role in this process – to avoid the further widening of regional imbalances. From the beginning, the Commission was certain that it would be necessary to convince the regions, especially Objective 1 regions, of the need to use structural funds, especially ERDF, for developing the information society. This experience had begun with the IRISI initiative and continued with the RISI initiative (Regional Information Society Initiative) in which some 22 European regions took part. The results of both initiatives were presented to the Commission between 1997 and 1999.[6]

During this period, various documents published by the Commission stated that public administrations were the motor for the development of the European information society and that the main areas for action should be: education, health, and public administration and services.

## Regional Actions during the Prodi Commission (1999 to Present)

Community action during this period has centred on the use of structural funds for the period 2000–2006 and development of the '*e*Europe' initiative. The article 2 of the ERDF regulations 2000–2006 (European Council 1999b) specifically mentions the activities that can be financed with these funds. They include:

> 1.b. – Infrastructure investments that contribute to increasing economic potential, development, structural modernisation, creating lasting employment, and including investments that help create trans-European networks in the sectors of ... telecommunications
> 2.c. – Development of the Information Society

Therefore, there is not the slightest doubt that regions can include activities related to the development of the information society and telecommunications society in their operational programmes. To help the regions prepare their operational programmes, the Commission published guidelines for structural funds for the period 2000–2006. These guidelines included the principal criteria that regions should take into account when preparing applications (European Commission 1999c).

The principal doubt the Commission had was whether these funds could be used to co-finance telecommunication infrastructure where free competition was unable to provide. Finally, the Commission accepted this possibility – providing that free competition was not undermined, and this was reflected in the *Criteria for Programme Evaluation* published in 1999 (European Commission 1999a).

Later, the Commission published a document entitled: *The Information Society and Regional Development*. In this document, the Commission included a set of specific criteria for the evaluation of regional projects, in particular, those relative to infrastructure and telecommunication networks. Regions classified as Objective 1 may include in their regional operational programmes those parts of their regional strategies for the development of the information society that can be financed through ERDF 2000–2006.

To plan the use of structural funds, it is necessary that the actions proposed in an operational programme form part of a wide-ranging strategy for the creation of the information society. The purpose of this requirement is to avoid improvisation when preparing ERDF proposals and ensure coordination between the various departments of regional administrations.

In the same way, the principles of, additionally, complementariness and cooperation, attempt to guarantee that ERDF funds contribute to the development of viable projects which serve the interests of the region. The objective is to prevent projects being launched solely to capture European structural funds. Finally, the principle of monitoring should be taken into account when setting objectives, so that the results can be measured and evaluated.

Those regions that have participated in the IRISI and RISI initiatives have had the opportunity to prepare their regional strategies for the development of the Information Society so they can be included in their respective regional operational programmes.

The European Commission has also participated in co-financing other activities related to the encouragement of the development of the information society in the regions – and a summary appears in Table 8.4. The origin of the funds for financing these activities is diverse and, with the exception of IRISI and RISI, is based on initiatives and projects put forward by the regions rather than the Commission. Generally, these projects have received very little economic help from the EU and are the result of local enterprise.

During the year 2000 the European Commission and Member States negotiated the approval of the community support framework proposals chargeable to structural funds during 2000–2006. Despite a continual effort made by the European Commission it appears that the proposed regional operational programmes have continued to be centred on traditional public works, and requests for funds to develop information society projects were much fewer than expected.

For this reason the European Commission is using the '*e*Europe' initiative as a final attempt to convince the states and regions of the importance of using currently available funds for co-financing projects related to the information society. This was clearly stated in a document approved in June 2000 at Santa María de Feira (European Commission 2000b). However, according to the structural fund regulations, it is the regions and states that must prepare proposals to be included in the operational programmes, and the European Commission must accept the proposals if they meet the eligibility conditions.

To increase the number of requests from the regions, the Commission has decided to spend part of the ERDF funds reserved for innovative actions on specific actions for the development of the information society. This represents a final opportunity for the regions to propose projects that did not fit in their own regional operational programmes. In any event, the total budget for all innovative actions is just 0.4 per cent of the total ERDF budget.

## COMMENTS REGARDING REGIONAL ACTIONS FOR DEVELOPMENT OF THE INFORMATION SOCIETY

The Commission has been disappointed to find that the number of information society projects proposed by the regions for funding from structural funds is very small (European Commission 2000a). This is despite: the undeniable importance to the regions of projects related to the Information Society;

*Table 8.4 Summary of main activities related to development of Information Society in the regions*

| Name | Description |
|---|---|
| IRISI / RISI Inter-Regional Information Society Initiative / Regional Information Society Initiative | These Initiatives are Innovative Pilot Actions supported jointly by the DG for Regional Policy (Article 10 ERDF), Employment and Social Affairs (Article 6 ESF); and Information Society of the European Commission. They aim to integrate the information society into regional development and employment policies. |
| ERISA European Regional Information Society Association | Involves the 28 regions participating in the RISI and IRISI. Its main objective is to support and enhance regional economic development and social cohesion through the information society. |
| ELANET Local Authorities Telematic Network Initiative | This is a specialised trans-national ICT network operating as an executive committee of the Council of European Municipalities and Regions (CERM). ELANET is formed by representatives of the National Associations of Local and Regional Governments, as well as by a selected number of telematic companies and public information institutes supporting the emerging local and regional networks that are based on information and communication technologies. |
| ERNACT European Regions Network for the Application of Communications Technology | The regions of the ERNACT network actively co-operate to develop an inter-regional information society strategy that adds value to their actions. |
| LOCREGIS II Local and Regional Information Society II | It is a project built on the results, recommendations, experience, and methodology of its predecessor – LOCREGIS. It aims to: maintain the inventory of local and regional information society projects on regional development; create regional information society profiles; and support the networking of regions. |
| TELECITIES | Open network for planned urban development |

*Table 8.4 Continued*

| Name | Description |
| --- | --- |
| | through telematics. Initiated by the Eurocities Technological Committee in 1993 as a working group of cities co-operating in developing the potential of telematics applications. The aim is to support the economic regeneration and social and cultural development of European cities. |
| TELE REGIONS | Regional network open to all European regions. Created to promote the development of information technology in European regions, as well as European co-operation to enhance regional opportunity in the information society. |

*Sources*: IRISI/ RISI: http://europa.eu.int/ISPO/risi/; ELANET: http://www.elanet.org/; ERISA: http://www.erisa.be/; ERNACT: http://www.burleehost.net/ernact/; LOCREGIS: http://www.locregis.net/; ELE REGIONS: http://www.teleregionsnetwork.org/; TELECITIES: http://www.telecities.org/.

encouragement from the European Commission for regional information society projects; and the existence of community instruments for co-financing projects proposed by the regions.

The reasons are rooted in the advanced nature of projects related to the Information Society and the difficulties in making systematic and coherent plans in this field. Additionally, regional governments continue to give greater priority to traditional spending targets for structural funds – such as infrastructure, transport and the environment.

It is difficult to discover the results of regional actions financed with structural funds. In many cases, the only information available is published by the European Commission services. According to the Directorate-General of Regional Policy (Leyges 2000), during 1994–99, only 1.8 per cent of total structural funds were spent on telecommunications. Of this, 1.5 per cent was spent on improving telecom infrastructure and just 0.3 per cent went on developing applications for the Information Society.

In our opinion, these are very small quantities and totally insufficient to enable the less developed regions to accelerate the modernisation of economic, social and administrative structures. This explains why the Commission has made a major effort to raise awareness so that the regions will increase the percentage of funds aimed at Information Society development in the period

2000–2006. Nevertheless, the regions have problems consolidating their actions in this field – as the following section shows.

## The Process of Preparing Regional Strategies and Plans

The preparation of a strategy and action plan for the development of the information society is a systematic task that involves planning the actions necessary to achieve the desired objective. Telecommunications and technology is unique in some specific points, nevertheless, other sectors can offer a great deal of useful experience in preparing strategic plans.

A significant number of European regions have experience in preparing strategies and action plans for developing the Information Society. Many public and private organisations tend to participate in the development of a regional strategy including: regional governments; town halls; employer organisations; unions; chambers of commerce; regional development agencies; universities; and research centres. After a reasonable effort, a region should be able to produce a document that contains a strategy and regional plan for the development of an Information Society.

One of the key elements to immediately bear in mind when preparing a regional strategy is project leadership. By this, we refer to the organisation, or institution, that assumes responsibility for the task from the beginning and guarantees its continuity. Usually, a project is started with the participation of the majority of local organisations, but with leadership problems.

Leadership for producing a regional strategy is usually assumed by one of the following organisations: a regional government department; a foundation; an institution dependent on the regional or municipal government; a regional development agency; a university department; and even a consultancy company. Experience shows that the likelihood that the strategy defined will subsequently be adopted is strongly conditioned by the nature of the organisation that assumes leadership of the preparation. The closer this organisation is to the regional centre of power, then the greater the probability of adoption. This factor is more important than the number of participating organisations.

The preparation of a regional strategy by a department of a regional administration is not a guarantee that the strategy will be adopted. This is because, in some regional administrations, the responsibilities for issues related with the Information Society are shared between different departments: education; communications; industry; public administration; and so on. In these cases, there is a risk that the strategy prepared by one of these departments will only consider actions under its responsibility. On the other hand, if a department considers actions that are the responsibility of other departments, then they may, in turn, reject these proposals. In addition, in many regions there are added difficulties caused by the distribution of administrative powers between the national, regional and municipal administrations in areas related to the information society.

The viability of a regional strategy depends on the sources of financing available for its application. The true guarantee that a regional strategy will be executed is its appearance in the ordinary regional budget. In many cases, the financing of information society projects is dependent on obtaining community funds such as regional development or the social fund. And to condition the financing of crucial regional projects on the availability of funds from programmes for research and development is a crucial strategic error given the nature of these types of projects.

### Results of the Preparation and Execution of Regional Strategies for Information Society Development

Information regarding actions proposed for structural funding appears in the operational programmes prepared by each region. Copies of these documents are usually kept by the regions, or the governments of Member States, and as a result, it is often difficult to obtain access. Using these documents, the Member States prepare the following: community support frameworks for objective 1 regions; and the single programme document for the regions, as well as the objective 1 and 2 zones. These are presented to the European Commission, and once approved by the Commission, become public documents.[7]

It is not common for the regions, or Member States, to prepare reports on the results obtained – and if published, these reports are not made easily available. As a result, it is difficult to evaluate actions financed with European structural funds. However, it is worth noting that the various regulatory instruments related to structural funds require the Commission to periodically publish evaluations of the results obtained from actions co-financed by Europe (European Commission 2000c and 1999b).

## CONCLUSIONS

As we indicated in the introduction, the European regions must react to the irreversible phenomena of the creation of the Information Society. This reaction will depend on the powers of the regional administration and will be undertaken in cooperation with other public administrations. Their objective will be to contribute to the modernisation and dynamisation of the regional economic, social and administrative fabric. The actions necessary for the development of the Information Society are, doubtless, one of the most important strategic governmental action now being taken - and, as such, attract certain difficulties.

With the objective of helping the less-developed regions, the EU offers economic resources within the framework of structural aid. This aid is aimed at helping achieve economic and social cohesion and is analysed in this chapter. Nevertheless, the development of the Information Society depends on the performance of the political and economic leaders and their ability to take maximum advantage of the resources made available.

## NOTES

1. See www.inforegio.cec.eu.int/wbdoc/docoffic/vm20002006/vademecum_fr.htm for more information on this issue.
2. Details on these funds can be found in the documents published by the Commission. See http://www.ispo.cec.be/ispo/call/opencalls.htm
3. The interested reader can access the original sources through the Internet http://europa.eu.int/ISPO/policy/isf/Welcome.html
4. See http://europa.eu.int/ISPO/policy/i_europe.html
5. See the decision of the Council regarding telecommunications. Brussels, 17 December 1984.
6. There is a website devoted to these initiatives: http://europa.eu.int/ISPO/risi/.
   See also www.inforegio.cec.eu.int/innovating/infosoc.htm;
   www.inforegio.cec.eu.int/innovating/DOWNLOAD/avr99/en_is.pdf
7. See a list in http://www.inforegio.cec.eu.int/wbpro/prord/pro2000_en.htm.

## REFERENCES

Alabau, A. (1997), 'Telecommunications and Information Society in European regions', *Telecommunications Policy*, **21** (8).

Alabau, A. (1998), *La Unión Europea y su Política de Telecomunicaciones*, Madrid: Fundación Airtel Móvil.

Department of Commerce (1993), *The National Information Infrastructure. Agenda for Action*, US Government, September 15.

European Commission (1987), *Towards a Dynamic European Economy - Green Paper on the development of the common market for telecommunications services and equipment*, Brussels, 30 June 1987, COM(87) 290.

European Commission (1993), *White Paper on Growth, Competitiveness, and Employment: The Challenges and Ways Forward into the 21st Century*, Brussels, 5 December 1993, COM(93) 700.

European Commission (1994a), *Action Plan Concerning Europe's Way to the Information Society*, Brussels, 19 July 1994, COM(94) 347.

European Commission (1994b), *TELEMATIQUE, Data communications for Regional Development, Technical Status Report*, DG XIII, Brussels.

European Commission (1994c), *Europe and the Global Information Society: Recommendations to the European Council and the European Commission*, Brussels, 26 May 1994.

European Commission (1996a), *The Information Society: From Corfu to Dublin - the New Emerging Priorities*, Brussels, 24 July 1996, COM (96) 395.

European Commission (1996b), *Europe at the Forefront of the Global Information Society: a Rolling Action Plan*, Brussels, 27 November. Final version, 31 July 1997, COM(96) 607.

European Commission (1997), *Building the European Information Society for Us All, final policy report of the high-level expert group*, Brussels, April.

European Commission (1999a), 'Information Society and Regional Development', *The New Programming Period 2000–2006: Technical Paper 2, ERDF Interventions for the period 2000–2006*, Brussels, 2 August 1999, SEC(1999) 1217.

European Commission (1999b), *Sixth Periodic Report on the Social and Economic Situation and Development of Regions in the European Union*, Brussels, 28 July 1999.

European Commission (1999c), *Commission Communication on Structural Funds and their Coordination with Cohesion Funds, Guidelines for the 2000–2006 Programme*, Brussels, (OJ 1999/C 267/02).

European Commission (1999d), *Towards a European Research Area*, http://europa.eu.int/comm/research/area.html.

European Commission (2000a), *Structural Funds and Information Society in 2000–2006,* Brussels, 15 December, Memo 00/113.

European Commission (2000b), *eEurope 2002. Action plan. An Information Society for All*, Brussels, 14 June 2000.

European Commission (2000c), *Annual Report on the Structural Funds 1999*, Brussels, COM(2000) 698.

European Council (1975), *The European Regional Development Fund*, Regulation 724/75 of the Council, 21 March 1975 (OJ L 73).

European Council (1979), *Modification of the European Regional Development Fund*, Regulation 214/79 of the Council, 9 February 1979 (OJ L 35).

European Council (1984), *European Regional Development Fund*, Regulation 1787/84 of the Council, 28 June 1984 (OJ L 169).

European Council (1986), *Creating a Community Programme for the Development of Given Regions by Improving Access to Advanced Telecommunications. STAR Program*, Regulation 3300/86 of the Council, 31 October 1986 (OJ L 305/1).

European Council (1988), *European Regional Development Fund*, Regulation 2052/88 of the Council, 15 July 1988 (OJ L 185).

European Council (1993), *European Regional Development Fund*, Regulation 2083/93 of the Council, 31 July 1993 (OJ L 193).

European Council (1998), *A Community Programme to Stimulate the Establishment of the Information Society in Europe*, Council Decision 30 March 1998.

European Council (1999a), *Laying Down General Provisions on the Structural Funds*, Regulation 1260/99 of the Council, 21 June 1999.

European Council (1999b), *European Regional Development Fund*, Regulation 1261/99 of Parliament and Council, 26 June 1999, (OJ L 161).

European Council and European Parliament (1999), *Regulation on the European Regional Development Fund*, 1783/1999, 21 June 1999.

European Parliament (1993a), *The Organisation of Local and Regional Government in the European Community*, Doc W3, Regional Politics Series, September.

European Parliament (1993b), *The Powers of Regional and Local Authorities and their Role in the European Union*, Doc W4, Regional Policy Series, December.

Guzzetti, L. (1995), *A Brief History of European Union Research Policy*, OPEC, European Commission, Brussels.

Leyges, J.C. (2000), 'La Societé de l'Information. Priorité clé du période 2000–2006',

paper presented at the Conference: *The Information Society and Economic, Social and Territorial Cohesion*, Lyon, 18–19 December.
RTD (2000), *Beyond 2002*, http://www.cordis.lu/rtd2002/

# 9. New technology-based firms in ICT industries: a policy perspective

**Massimo G. Colombo and Marco Delmastro**

## 1. INTRODUCTION

In the 1990s, increasing attention was given by economists and policymakers to entrepreneurship and NTBFs (New Technology-Based Firms). The reason may be traced to the evidence that small and new firms account for a substantial share of the new jobs created in those countries such as the United States that have displayed a strong employment record. According to data from the United States Small Business Administration, between 1992 and 1996 small and medium firms (that is number of employees lower than 500) created 11.8 million new jobs, while larger firms lost almost 650000 jobs, in the United States. In addition, Acs et al. (1999) show that for the five-year period from 1990 to 1995 births of new establishments (inclusive of new branches of existing firms) contributed 25.9 per cent to the net job creation rate of 7.1 per cent. Gross job creation was found to be heavily concentrated among high growth new firms, especially those that are in innovative industries (Birch and Medoff 1994; Kirchhof 1994; Reynolds and White 1997; OECD 1996).

The view has also been rapidly gaining ground that successful high-tech start-ups are an important disciplining and stimulating device for the behaviour of established large companies and thus play a crucial role for the renewal of the economic system. They are also believed to provide the United States with an innovation-based competitive advantage in key sectors of the so-called 'new economy' such as software, e-commerce and communication equipment. Such a view is corroborated by the success stories of Microsoft, Oracle, Cisco, American on line, Yahoo!, and other Internet outfits.

The concern that Europe is a laggard in the NTBF sector triggered a policy-oriented research effort aimed at analysing factors that favour or inhibit the birth of European NTBFs and influence their post-entry performances (European Commission 1996a and 1996b). In particular, a conspicuous body of new evidence was developed on the characteristics of NTBFs and those of their founders in numerous European countries (Storey and Tether 1998a).

Such studies also gave interesting indications as to which policy measures are most likely to support the development of the NTBF sector in Europe (Storey and Tether 1998b). In EU countries, emphasis has been especially placed on the following aspects.

- The creation of Science Parks and BICs (Business Innovation Centers). These are property-based initiatives which generally (though not always) have formal operational links with universities and other knowledge-creating institutions, aim at encouraging the formation and the development of new firms through the provision of business incubators, especially but not exclusively in high-tech sectors, and provide firms located on site with technical and business services. The number of Science Parks and BICs has been rapidly growing in Europe during the 1980s and early 1990s, with France being the single country where the Science Parks phenomenon has attained the largest scale.[1]
- The supply of PhDs and the development of the human capital of would-be entrepreneurs. It is generally understood that having sophisticated technological skills increasingly is an important source of competitive advantage for a NTBF. Such skills often are provided by the entrepreneur himself. As a consequence, enhancing the supply of individuals with the highest educational attainment in scientific and technological fields is among the top policy priorities of all European countries. In addition, there are attempts to bring business skills in science curricula, through the set-up of specialized institutions (such as the Science Enterprise Centres in the United Kingdom).
- The development of stronger linkages between scientific institutions (in particular, universities) and NTBFs. In spite of the fact that in the last decade the linkages between the scientific and academic world and industry have been allegedly strengthened in most European countries, with the rapid diffusion of industrial liaison offices in numerous European universities, much remains to be done as concerns linkages with small or new firms. In particular, most EU countries are trying to increase through specially designed policy measures the likelihood of universities' scientific personnel and students starting their own companies to exploit scientific results. A recent interesting example is provided by France, with the law of 12 July 1999 on innovation and research. The target of such law precisely is the community of researchers, university professors, technicians, engineers and PhD students that aim to create a new enterprise to exploit commercially the results of their scientific activity. For this purpose, they are authorized to participate in the new venture as a manager or a partner for a

maximum period of six years, with their salary possibly being paid by the originating institution and with this period having no negative impact on their original career. At the end of such a period, they have the option either to stay with the firm and give up their initial career or to abandon the firm and come back to their originating institution. This law also includes other measures that are aimed at favouring the temporary transfer of scientific and technical personnel from public research institutions to private enterprises, encouraging consulting activity to industry by scientific and technical personnel, and supporting the establishment of technological incubators and the provision of technical and scientific services on the part of universities and State-owned knowledge-creating bodies. Another measure that is worth being mentioned is the launch of a national competition for the creation of NTBFs, with the winners being allowed financial support to go on with their business idea. A similar programme, the University Challenge Competition, has proved quite successful in the United Kingdom, with the set-up of 15 professionally managed seedcorn funds; involving 37 universities, they are precisely aimed at developing new science- and technology-based commercial initiatives and bringing them to the point where the capital market will take them up.

- The provision to NTBFs of seed and start-up capital. This is an area where Europe is a laggard with respect to the United States, mainly due to the fact that the European venture capital industry is less developed and less focused on NTBFs than its United States counterpart.[2] Nonetheless, in most European countries there are no specific measures addressing the problem. Of course, there are exceptions too. For instance, the above-mentioned French law of 12 July 1999 also comprises measures aimed at encouraging equity investments in the early stages of life of a NTBF. In particular, seed and start-up capital funds benefit of public co-financing. Money is given by the State to *sociétés de valorisations* established by State-owned knowledge-creating institutions to participate in such funds. State funds have to be reimbursed by 12 years, with capital gains being shared equally between the state and the *société* that received the funds; on the contrary, there is no sharing of capital losses, which are deducted from the amount that must be reimbursed. A similar scheme also exists in Germany (the BTU scheme); in addition to co-financing such a scheme also involves guarantees, so as to reduce the risk involved in financing the birth and early development of NTBFs. It is also worthwhile to notice that the European Investment Bank is increasingly supporting venture capital initiatives around Europe, with the creation of the European Investment Fund.

This study intends to add to the above-mentioned stream of literature on European NTBFs. Its first objective is to supplement the available evidence on the characteristics of European NTBFs with comparable data relating to new Italian high-tech firms and their founders. Note that Italy is a very interesting, though underresearched case. On the one hand, propensity towards entrepreneurship is especially high in Italy (Blanchflower and Oswald 1999) and small firms account for a disproportionately high share of total employment.[3] On the other, Italy exhibits a poor performance in high-tech industries; the ratio of research expenditures to GNP now is close to 1 per cent, that is less than half the value of France or the United Kingdom, and has been declining over the 1990s. So the issue of how to promote the creation and development of NTBFs is a key priority of technology policy. In this respect, Italy may be regarded as a 'laboratory', as considerations about the Italian situation may have important implications for other European countries which specialize in medium or low-tech industries.

Secondly, the evidence provided by previous studies on the characteristics of European NTBFs mainly concern manufacturing industries. Nonetheless, it is generally acknowledged that the development of the Internet and its use for commercial purposes offer very interesting opportunities to NTBFs. Sectors such as e-commerce, other Internet services, software and multimedia content are at the core of the 'new economy'. In spite of the fact that such sectors are presently dominated by young, highly successful United States firms, there seems to be evidence that Europe is catching up in this area.[4] Therefore, in this work we will bring to the fore service industries which are directly related to or have been rejuvenated by the development of the Internet,[5] and will compare them with ICT manufacturing industries. Such exercise is instrumental to investigating whether Internet-based NTBFs have special characteristics which differentiate them from NTBFs in other high-tech sectors, a likely situation if one considers the radical nature of the Internet revolution, and so deserve special policy measures.

In order to comply with such objectives, we consider a sample composed of 116 new firms that operate in ICT manufacturing and service industries, are located in Northern Italy and were established between 1984 and 1999. We devote special attention to differences in the characteristics of both firms and their founders according to the sector of operation of the start-up. In particular, we investigate whether firms in Internet-based activities are different from those that operate in other ICT industries (especially in manufacturing).

The findings of the empirical survey show that, in many respects, the characteristics of Italian NTBFs and high-tech entrepreneurs differ quite substantially from established patterns that refer to the United States or to other higher-tech European countries, both large (that is France, Germany and the United Kingdom) and small (that is the Nordic countries). In addition, our findings also highlight significant sectoral differences connected with the Internet. This provides an initial assessment of whether policy measures that are traditionally considered as very effective to support NTBFs also are suitable to Internet start-ups.

Such remarks lead us to the third objective of the chapter. Namely, we aim to reconsider which policy measures targeting NTBFs should be given higher priority, especially in countries like Italy that specialize in low- and medium-tech sectors. For this purpose, it is fundamental to take duly into account the specific requirements of Internet start-ups.

The remainder of the chapter is organized as follows. In the next section we briefly present the empirical survey. In Sections 3 and 4 we analyze the characteristics of Italian NTBFs (for example start-up size, post-entry performances, financial structure) and those of their founders (for example education, previous working experience). We also compare such evidence with the characteristics of NTBFs from the Silicon Valley and some European countries. Section 5 is devoted to Internet start-ups. Lastly, Section 6 illustrates the policy implications of the findings of this work.

## 2. THE EMPIRICAL SURVEY

The data set used in this chapter has been developed at Politecnico di Milano in 1999. For more details about the sample, see Colombo and Delmastro (2001). The sample is composed of 116 Italian NTBFs[6] that operate in Information and Communication Technology (ICT) sectors (both in manufacturing and services[7]) and are located in Northern Italy.[8] We also have information relating to the 241 founders of such firms.

The above sectors can be regarded as representative of the universe of NTBFs, at least in Italy.[9] Only 11.2 per cent of NTBFs in the sample operates in manufacturing, while the remaining 88.8 per cent is in the Internet (23.3 per cent), multimedia content (10.3 per cent) and, above all, software (55.2 per cent). So, most NTBFs operate in services; these sectors either belong to the new paradigm of the Internet or have been recently reshaped by it (as in the case of both software and multimedia content).

Data collection was carried out in 1999 through a mail survey. A questionnaire was sent to 260 firms that complied with the requirements for consideration in the survey. In order to define the target universe we resorted to a variety of sources, due to the absence of official national statistics on NTBFs. These include lists of newly established firms provided by the Milan Chamber of Commerce and national industrial associations (AIIP, ANIE, ANEE), on-line and off-line firm directories (such as Kompass), and lists of participants in industry expositions. The questionnaire has both a quantitative and a qualitative nature. The first section contains information on characteristics of the entrepreneurs such as age, education, prior working experience, and motivations of the self-employment decision. The second section comprises further questions concerning the characteristics of the start-up firms and their post-entry performances in terms of growth and innovative activities. The final (qualitative) section is devoted to factors that promote or inhibit growth and innovation.

## 3. THE CHARACTERISTICS OF ITALIAN NTBFs

Table 9.1 reports some key characteristics of the 116 sample NTBFs. In order to have a benchmark, we have proceeded to compare our findings with those of a sample of 173 United States high-technology start-ups located in the Silicon Valley (Baron et al. 1999). The two samples are homogenous in terms of sample size, industry distribution, ownership status (at firm's foundation) and age profile (average firm ages are 6.14 and 5.23 years for the United States and Italian samples respectively). The findings of Table 9.1 highlight the existence of a country-specific effect. First of all, Italian firms are on average of smaller size at the start-up date than their Silicon Valley counterparts. Indeed, at the year of foundation they have an average number of employees equal to 6 which is significantly lower than 28, the average start-up size of US high-technology firms. Not only do Italian NTBFs start smaller, but they also experience a poorer post-entry performance, with the average growth rate being 211 per cent as compared to a 1034 per cent growth rate for United States NTBFs. Thus, at the date of the surveys the average number of employees had increased from 6 to 12 for Italian firms and from 28 to 161 for United States firms.

In addition, there are marked differences related to financial characteristics. United States' high-tech firms receive a substantial part of their funds both from venture capital (70 per cent of them received venture capital by the survey date, that is by an average time of 6 years from foundation) and the stock market (37.6 per cent of them went public). Instead, the Italian financial system has so far not allowed high-technology start-ups to finance their activities through venture capital (only one out of 116 Italian NTBFs had received venture capital by the survey date) and/or IPO (Initial Public Ofering), so that none went public. This has been due to the absence of a specialized stock market for young technological firms (at least until 1999, the year of the foundation of the so-called 'Nuovo Mercato') that not only precluded Italian NTBFs from going public, but also prevented the growth of venture capital. This latter effect was mainly due to the impossibility for venture capitalists of cashing out participations in young technological

*Table 9.1 Characteristics of Italian and US NTBFs (means)*

| | Italy (1998) | USA (1994) |
|---|---|---|
| Age (years) | 5.23 | 6.14 |
| Start-up size (number of employees) | 5.85 | 28.17 |
| Current size (number of employees) | 12.05 | 161.23 |
| Growth rate (since foundation) | 211 per cent | 1034 per cent |
| IPOs | 0.0 per cent | 37.6 per cent |
| Participation of venture capital | 0.9 per cent | 70.0 per cent |
| CEO turnover | 5.0 per cent | 41.0 per cent |

ventures through IPOs. Therefore, Italian young entrepreneurs generally use their personal savings to finance their activities (Giudici and Paleari 2000). This is indeed witnessed by the high percentage (95 per cent) of sample founders who have financed their start-up using their personal income.

Moreover, when asked to choose factors which had been very detrimental for the post-entry performance of their firms, sample entrepreneurs have indicated financial constraints, such as the absence of a specialized stock market, the high cost of banking debt, the lack of State funds for NTBFs, as the most important constraints. Italian entrepreneurs have also indicated two additional institutional constraints to the growth of their start-ups: the deficiency of the labour market especially as concerned the supply of skilled personnel, and the lack of synergies with research organizations such as universities. As concerned the links between NTBFs and universities, only 10 per cent of Italian entrepreneurs have enjoyed substantial technological spillovers from universities. Instead, Keeble et al. (1998) find that more than 50 per cent of a sample of young technology-intensive firms located in the Cambridge area have benefited from spillovers from the university system.

Finally, in Table 9.2 we have proceeded to compare answers of sample entrepreneurs on factors that hinder the innovative activity of NTBFs with those of a sample of 7553 Italian innovative manufacturing firms (Istat 1997). In other words, by following the Italian 'Survey on Innovation', we have asked the interviewed entrepreneurs to give a mark (by using a 6-point Likert scale) to factors which may hamper the innovative activity of their firms. Selected factors are of four types: (1) financial constraints (that is lack of financial resources, risks and costs connected with innovative activity), (2) problems linked to the labour market (that is lack of a skilled workforce), (3) institutional constraints (that is bureaucratic rules, laws, standards, and absence of a market for new products and services), (4) information issues

*Table 9.2 Factors detrimental for the innovative activity of Italian manufacturing firms and NTBFs (per cent of firms quoting the factor as very detrimental)*[a]

| Factors | NTBF | Italy (ISTAT 1997) |
|---|---|---|
| Lack of financial resources | 50.9** | 41.4 |
| High costs of innovative activity | 25.9*** | 41.5 |
| Lack of skilled workforce | 27.6*** | 14.0 |
| High risk of economic activity | 24.1*** | 13.4 |
| Bureaucracy, laws and standards | 22.4 | 22.8 |
| No market for new products and services | 12.1 | 11.6 |
| Lack of market information | 11.2 | 12.1 |
| Lack of technological information | 7.8 | 8.9 |

*Notes:* [a] Score greater or equal to 4 in a 6-point Likert scale.
**Chi-squared test between the percentage of the two samples significant at 5 per cent.
***Chi-squared test between the percentage of the two samples significant at 1 per cent.

(that is lack of information on market and technology). Finally we have compared rankings of NTBFs and Italian innovative manufacturing firms and run chi-squared tests in order to evaluate the statistical significance of differences. Results are quite interesting. First, respondents (entrepreneurs of both NTBFs and Italian manufacturing firms) in general give a high score to the lack of financial resources. However, scores are significantly higher in the case of NTBFs: 51 per cent of them signal financial constraints as a very detrimental factor against 41 per cent of innovative manufacturing firms, with the difference being significant at 99 per cent. This may be due, as said earlier, to the absence of a specialized stock market for young technological firms and the inefficiency of the Italian venture capital system. Second, new high-tech firms consider hiring skilled personnel as a more severe problem than in traditional manufacturing. Indeed, 28 per cent of interviewed high-technology entrepreneurs indicate this factor as very harmful for the innovative activity of their start-ups against 14 per cent of manufacturing entrepreneurs (the difference being again significant at conventional levels).

## 4. THE CHARACTERISTICS OF ITALIAN NTBF FOUNDERS

This section summarizes major findings on the characteristics of the 241 sample high-tech entrepreneurs. In particular, we focus upon age at the date of firm's foundation, education and prior working experience (Colombo and Delmastro 2001).

The age at which an agent takes the self-employment decision clearly depends on aspects such as his risk aversion, financial constraints and the need for technological and market competencies which may have been acquired through both education and prior working experience (Roberts 1991). Empirical studies show that this choice usually occurs when an individual is between 30 and 40. On the one hand, both risk aversion and the cost of leaving an employment position are positively correlated with age, due to family concerns and career patterns (see for instance the job shopping models of Johnson 1978 and Miller 1984). This effect would decrease the age of the self-employment choice, other things being equal. On the other hand, entrepreneurship may not be an option for younger workers due to both lack of professional and relational skills and liquidity constraints. As to this latter aspect, the older an individual the larger the amount of capital he can build up to start a new business (Evans and Jovanovic 1989).

In high-tech environments, raising capital may be even more difficult because information asymmetries are more severe. So, technology-based starters are generally found to be older than other starters (Donckels 1989). In particular, this effect is likely to depend on the specific nature of the sector in which new firms operate: financial (and knowledge) barriers to entry are influenced by industry characteristics (see Section 5).

Table 9.3 sheds some light on the age profile of European NTBF founders. At the date of the firm's foundation, the average age of Italian high-tech entrepreneurs is 33, which is in line with the international evidence. Indeed, Autio et al. (1989) studying a sample of Finnish founders of NTBFs find an average age equal to 34. In the French case NTBFs' founders are on average 37 year old (GMV Conseil 1989), in the United Kingdom they are between 30 and 50 (Westhead and Storey 1994).

Turning to the education of founders of NTBFs, which is generally recognized as a key element to understand the post-entry performance of

*Table 9.3 Age of high-tech entrepreneurs at firm's foundation: some European evidence*

| | Minimum | Mean | Maximum |
|---|---|---|---|
| Italy | 18 | 33 | 67 |
| Finland | – | 34 | – |
| France | – | 37 | – |
| UK | 30 | – | 50 |

high-tech start-ups (Jo and Lee 1996), international empirical evidence shows that entrepreneurs working in high-tech environments are found to have an excellent education career. Before proceeding with the evidence of educational attainments of Italian and other European founders of NTBFs, a preliminary remark is in order. Italian graduate degrees can be hardly compared to most European degrees. Indeed university education programmes generally are longer: they last for no less than four or five years, depending on the specific topics (four years for social sciences and most scientific degrees, five years for engineering), and the average time needed for graduation is longer than six years (again, it depends on the specific field).

Table 9.4 presents findings on the level of education attainment of Italian and other European technology-based entrepreneurs. The difference between Italian high-tech entrepreneurs and their European counterparts is striking: only 38 per cent of Italian high-tech entrepreneurs have a graduate degree. Conversely, Autio et al. (1989) find that 90 per cent of Finnish founders of NTBFs have followed higher education. Similar results have been found by Westhead and Storey (1994) for UK (85 per cent with graduate degree and 48 per cent with doctorate), Donckels (1989) for Belgium (80 per cent have followed higher education) and Licht et al. (1995) for Germany (more than 50 per cent with an engineering degree).

The low percentage of graduated entrepreneurs may be partially due to the Italian institutional context. However, there could be something more than institutional factors. The low level of educational attainment of sample founders may also be due to industry-specific effects. Indeed, while prior evidence relating to other countries is based on samples of entrepreneurs working in high-tech manufacturing, in this study the overwhelming majority of start-ups is in industries directly (ISP, e-commerce) or indirectly (software, multimedia content) connected with the Internet. Section 5 will be devoted to analysing cross-sectional differences in greater detail.

*Table 9.4 Educational attainments of high-tech founders: some European evidence*

| | Percentage of founders with a graduate degree |
|---|---|
| Italy | 38 per cent |
| Finland | 90 per cent |
| UK | 85 per cent |
| Belgium | 80 per cent |
| Germany | >50 per cent |

In order to complete the picture of the characteristics of high-tech entrepreneurs, we present evidence on the prior working experience of founders of NTBFs. Because high-tech start-ups depend heavily on founders' knowledge and skills, we expect these latter to have developed considerable experience in related technological and market activities before becoming self-employed. In order to gain insights into the working background of Italian technology-based founders, we have divided prior employment status (a) depending on whether the sample entrepreneurs already had working experience or not, and (b) as far as the former group of founders is concerned, according to the sector of operation of the firm in which founders were previously employed. Within ICT we have distinguished between four industries: (1) electronics, (2) computer industry, (3) telecommunications (both the production of communications equipment and the provision of telecommunication services), and (4) software and e-business.

It turns out that 39.4 per cent of sample founders can be defined as spin-offs, given that before founding the firm they were working within ICT industries.[10] Of these, only 13.7 per cent were previously employed in the electronic, computer or telecommunication industry, that is in sectors dominated by large firms and research organizations which are recognized by previous studies as the main incubators (together with public research organizations) of successful high-tech start-ups (Carayannis et al. 1998). Some 25.7 per cent were previously employed in software houses and Internet companies; these usually are, at least in Italy, very small firms.[11] More than 37 per cent of sample founders had prior working experience in sectors outside ICT and publishing, and 20.3 per cent had no working experience.

Even if there is no extensive international evidence to compare our findings, we have clear indications that in Italy the percentage of high-tech entrepreneurs which are spin-offs is relatively lower than elsewhere. Indeed, the study of the GMV Conseil (1989) on a sample of French NTBFs highlights that 76 per cent of high-tech entrepreneurs have previous working experience in the same or related sectors.

## 5. THE INTERNET-BASED SECTORS

Even if previous findings suggest that the institutional context may deeply influence the self-employment decision, especially in high-tech sectors, we think that cross-sectoral differences may also be key in explaining our findings on education attainments and prior working experience. In particular, we shall show that the characteristics of start-ups in ICT manufacturing and the Internet largely diverge. Since prior international evidence on NTBFs is mostly based on high-tech manufacturing, detected differences between Italian and

European high-tech start-ups are not only due to a country effect but also to an industry-specific effect.

As for the age at the start-up, Internet-based founders represent the youngest category (average age equal to 28), whilst entrepreneurs of ICT manufacturing firms are the eldest (40). Moreover, in ICT manufacturing, the level of educational attainment of founders of Italian NTBFs is significantly higher than that of Internet entrepreneurs, even though it still is lower than in other European countries. Forty per cent of the founders are graduates and 72 per cent have followed an ICT education (either through a higher education degree, 36 per cent, or by means of an ICT high school, 36 per cent). Conversely, Internet entrepreneurship is composed of young businessmen with a rather poor educational background: of them only 28 per cent have a graduate degree and 22 per cent have followed an ICT education. Founders of NTBFs working in the software industry or in the provision of multimedia content have an intermediate profile. On the one hand, as concerns higher education, they are similar to those of ICT manufacturing industries: 40 per cent and 50 per cent of founders of firms operating in software and multimedia content provision have a graduate degree, respectively. On the other hand, as to technical competencies, they look very similar to Internet businessmen: only 31 per cent and 15 per cent of them have followed an ICT education, respectively.

Turning to professional experience, founders of Internet companies are mainly at their first working experience (40 per cent); if they have a working background this derives either from software (21.7 per cent) or from a sector other than ICTs (31.7 per cent). Similarly, founders of multimedia content companies and software houses were previously employed in firms operating in the software industry or outside ICT. However, in this case the percentage of founders at the first working experience is significantly lower than that of Internet businessmen (16.2 per cent and 10 per cent for software and multimedia content provision, respectively). Finally, founders of ICT manufacturing firms again have a very different working profile: most (68 per cent) are spin-offs having a prior working experience in an ICT sector, and only 4 per cent of them are in their first working experience.

In sum, a scenario emerges with two opposite types of high-tech entrepreneur. On the one hand, individuals that decide to start an Internet activity are significantly younger, less educated and with few (if any) prior working experience. On the other hand, founders of ICT manufacturing firms are older, more educated (at least as regards technical education) and with more professional experience in ICT sectors.

A thorough analysis of the determinants of these sector-specific differences lies beyond the scope of this chapter. Nonetheless, some preliminary remarks are in order. First, it is worth emphasizing that in manufacturing the minimum optimal scale is substantially higher than in services (especially Internet-based services). Accordingly, the start-up size of sample firms is equal to 18 employees in ICT manufacturing industries and to 4 in the other sectors (in particular, 3 employees for Internet, 4 for software and 5 for multimedia content). Thus, an individual needs a larger amount of financial resources to set up a new firm in manufacturing. As said, entrepreneurs of Italian NTBFs usually use their personal savings to finance their activities; it follows that those that operate in manufacturing industries need to wait longer before being able to leave their previous job, having accumulated sufficient financial resources to found a start-up. This argument helps explain why entrepreneurs in ICT manufacturing industries are significantly older than those that operate in services.

Moreover, the advent of the new Internet paradigm and the associated birth of new markets have created new business opportunities which encourage entry of a large number of new entrepreneurial firms.[12] So, lower entry barriers and business expectations of an expanding market have caused an excess of entry of newly established firms (Camerer and Lovallo 1999), the majority of which is run by entrepreneurs who lack both managerial and technological competencies. In the long run, competition will lead to a shake out, selecting efficient firms and forcing less efficient ones to exit. Also, the Internet is a competence-destroying paradigm.[13] Therefore, technological and managerial knowledge related to previous experience becomes obsolete very quickly, and reproducing consolidated patterns of behaviour may be detrimental to business success. Internet founders are thus more likely to be both less educated than other ICT entrepreneurs and in their first working experience. If one focuses attention on Internet founders that do have prior working experience, they are less likely to be spin-offs. Instead, ICT manufacturing industries are in a more mature stage of the life cycle and enjoy lower industrial turbulence. In addition, they are based on rather consolidated technological knowledge. In this case, competencies acquired through both education and professional experience are crucial.

## 6. SOME POLICY RECOMMENDATIONS

NTBFs have special characteristics and requirements which differ from those of other SMEs; so they need special policy measures. This fact has been acknowledged by previous studies (Storey and Tether 1998b). Nonetheless, one has also to recognize that heterogeneity is great among NTBFs, and there are substantial differences across sectors, as has been shown here for Internet start-ups with respect to new ICT manufacturing firms. Therefore policy measures should be adapted to the specificity of the different industrial settings where NTBFs operate. Developing a coherent policy framework along these guidelines to support the birth and growth of high-tech start-ups lies beyond the scope of the present work. The objective of this section is more limited. First, we will highlight the policy measures which, in the light of the empirical results presented earlier, seem to us as the most promising ones, especially in countries like Italy which do not specialize in high-tech industries. Secondly, we will consider the policy implications of the specificity of Internet-related activities.

## A General Premise

Generally speaking, policy measures aimed at supporting the birth and development of NTBFs should have two main objectives. On the one hand, one has to cope with problems due to information asymmetries between high-tech would-be entrepreneurs and the financial community. Having access to external financial resources in sufficient amount and at the right time probably is the main single problem affecting NTBFs (Westhead and Storey 1997); this holds true especially in those European countries like Italy which lack a well developed financial market. On the other hand, it is important to assure that environmental conditions are conducive to *risk-taking* on the part of individuals equipped with sufficient technical and managerial skills. As to this latter point, measures aimed at influencing the trade-off between the costs and benefits of the self-employment choice play a crucial role.

## Policy Measures in the Financial Sphere

In spite of the fact that there is no lack of funds in Europe which may *potentially* support the birth and growth of NTBFs, access to external financial resources generally is deemed by high-tech entrepreneurs as the most crucial constraint to their activity. In this respect, Italian entrepreneurs are no exception. Being financed mainly with founders' savings and those of their family members and close friends (Giudici and Paleari 2000), Italian NTBFs turn out to suffer from persistent nanism: they are too small at the time of foundation and tend to remain too small afterwards.

Under such circumstances, we think that the role of government is not to substitute for financial institutions: public money should not replace private money. What government has to do is to alleviate information asymmetries.

As is well known, venture capital firms are well equipped to deal with information asymmetries which hamper provision of funds to NTBFs by banks and other traditional financial institutions. However, the European venture capital industry is less developed than its US counterpart. In addition, European venture capitalists traditionally did not devote sufficient attention to

NTBFs (OECD 1997). This holds true especially for countries like Italy which specialize in medium- and low-tech industries. So one of the key priorities of an industrial policy that targets NTBFs should be to create incentives for the provision of seed and start-up capital. This seems to have been acknowledged by some European national governments[14] and also EU authorities, as is witnessed by recent moves by the European Investment Bank aimed at increasing the supply of venture capital to European NTBFs. It seems to us that this is a very favourable time for the introduction of measures of that kind. Namely, in numerous European countries a specialized 'New Market' with regulations more appropriate for small high-tech firms, has been created and is rapidly becoming popular among investors.[15] For the development of venture capital firms efficient exit mechanisms allowing them to divest participations smoothly are critical.

We believe that indirect financial support to NTBFs on the part of governments is more effective than direct provision to NTBFs of public subsidies. Nonetheless, if there is a role left for direct financial support, this should be in the form of co-investment, thus leveraging equity provided by private institutions. In other words, additional public funds should be granted only to start-ups which proved to be able to obtain external equity capital from financial institutions; this allows selectivity and increases the likelihood of successful use of public money. A good example of this kind of policy measure is provided by the BTU programme in Germany.

### Policy Measures Affecting the Costs and Benefits of the Self-employment Choice

At the date of foundation, the distinctive competencies of a start-up, and consequently its likelihood of success, closely depend on the knowledge and skills (both technical, commercial and managerial) of its founders. This argument is especially appropriate for NTBFs. However, it has been highlighted in the literature that highly skilled individuals have a higher opportunity cost of abandoning their employment than less skilled ones. In particular, in most European countries aversion towards entrepreneurial risks is likely to be especially high among scientists, technicians and top executives of large firms and public research organizations, which benefit from rather favourable labour regulations (especially when they are compared to less qualified personnel in SMEs) and a high social status.[16] Therefore, policy measures aimed at ameliorating the economic opportunities of NTBFs are key in increasing the appeal of the self-employment choice for such individuals. Such measures include the following ones.

- Policy measures aimed at alleviating the tax burden of NTBFs in the early years after foundation. It is well known that failure rates are very high among infant firms in high-tech industries. The reason often is not lack of competence or absence of a good entrepreneurial idea, but lack of resources and bad luck. Freezing taxes and postponing their payment to a later stage of development may contribute to increase the chance of survival of high-tech start-ups during such a very turbulent period.

- Changes in the discipline of bankruptcy. Failure is a physiological characteristic of a risky high-tech venture. Nevertheless, in Italy and in most other European countries, sanctions against entrepreneurs that go bankrupt are particularly severe. In addition to sanctions provided by the law, there are social sanctions arising from insolvency. For instance, after bankruptcy, it is very difficult for individuals to raise capital and obtain bank loans for a new venture. The risk of going bankrupt and thus incurring such sanctions is a powerful deterrent for would-be high-tech entrepreneurs.
- Policy measures aimed at encouraging the commercial exploitation by scientists, especially those working in universities and other public research institutions, of their technological knowledge. In addition to the fact that in Europe the traditional culture of such institutions is not oriented towards entrepreneurship, in most European countries there are regulations discouraging or even prohibiting such individuals from exploiting commercially the results of scientific research. On the contrary, we suggest that the creation of spin-off enterprises should be stimulated by European governments through the provision of adequate incentives to both research institutions and individual researchers. Examples of measures of this kind are provided by the New University Challenge Fund in the UK which established seed venture capital funds for universities to commercially exploit scientific results, and the French law of 12 July 1999.

## Policy Measures Affecting the Supply to NTBFs of Highly Qualified Workers

Most factors mentioned in the previous section that discourage the self-employment choice of highly skilled individuals, also hinder their hiring on the part of NTBFs. Namely, NTBFs in our sample mentioned the difficulty of hiring skilled personnel as one of the most serious problems that negatively affected their post-entry performances. Actually, for such individuals, being employed by an NTBF means sharing with founders (a portion of) the risk of the venture. In order for them to be willing to do so, the expected rewards must exceed the (rather high) opportunity costs. This is a very serious problem as human resources are the main asset of a young high-tech enterprise. There are two ways governmental action may deal with it.

- First, the government may try to reinforce the ability of NTBFs to attract and retain qualified workers through targeted subsidies. These may take the form of an ease of the burden of the costs connected with social security regulations (for example tax deduction of the health and retirement expenses incurred by NTBFs that hire highly qualified personnel).
- Second, offering stock-options is an effective means for high-growth NTBFs to recruit and maintain employees at lower salaries. In particular, they allow such firms to attract talented employees while keeping the cash cost of personnel under control. Employee stock option plans are extensively used in the USA, where they are regarded as a driving factor allowing NTBFs to lure away top executives and technicians from incumbent firms (OECD 1999). Their introduction should be strongly supported by European governments through favourable fiscal treatment. This includes for instance exemption of stock options granted to employees from social charges and introduction of a favourable tax rate on the associated capital gains.

## Other Supply-side Policy Measures in Support of NTBFs

Previous works have pointed out that there are other policy measures beyond those analysed in the previous sections which may favour the development of the NTBF sector (Storey and Tether 1998b). For the sake of synthesis, we will confine our comments to two such measures, namely an increase of the supply of PhDs in scientific and technical fields and the set up of Science Parks and Business Innovation Centres.

First of all, it has been pointed out that the potential supply of NTBFs is closely linked to availability in a given country of individuals with high academic qualifications, especially in scientific and technical fields. Founders of NTBFs on average have higher educational attainments than founders of other new firms. However, this is less so in medium–low-tech countries, as has been pointed out for Italy in the previous sections. In addition, it is worth stressing that an increase in the supply of scientific and technical PhDs is no guarantee of greater high-tech entrepreneurship, as PhD programs in most European countries have primarily been oriented towards providing entry into academic careers.

Second, in the last two decades great emphasis has been placed in most European countries on the establishment of Science Parks and Business

Innovation Centres, probably as a consequence of the success experienced by such initiatives in the United States. These can be defined as property-based initiatives aimed at supporting innovative firms through the provision of logistic, technological and other business services; among them, the presence within a park of a technology incubator is deemed as crucial to nurture the formation and growth of NTBFs. Whether the establishment of Science Parks has been beneficial to European NTBFs is controversial. A number of studies, relating especially to the UK experience, show that in spite of the fact that Science Parks act as catalysts for the formation of NTBFs, a Science Park location does not significantly influence firms' innovative behaviour and post-entry performances (see for instance Monck et al. 1988; Westhead and Storey 1994 and 1995; Westhead 1997; Westhead and Batstone 1998). However, the alleged positive impact of Science Parks on NTBFs is contingent on the characteristics of the external environment, especially as regards the availability of top-quality professional services. In countries where the market for such services is less developed, the importance of the creation of SPs is likely to increase. Evidence in line with such a view, which documents a more positive role of SPs than the one which is generally recognized in the literature, is provided by Colombo and Delmastro (2002).

### Policy Measures in Support of Internet-based NTBFs

In the last couple of years, a considerable number of new firms has been established in European countries in Internet-based service sectors (that is e-commerce and other Internet services). Such sectors are at the core of the 'new economy'; even though they still are in their infancy in most of Europe, they will be of fundamental importance for innovation and growth of European economies in this decade. In spite of the advantage that the US enjoys in Internet activities, there is evidence that Europe is catching up; even more importantly, European high-growth NTBFs are going to play a crucial role in such a process. So there is a case for (temporary) targeted public support to such firms, in particular in countries like Italy which have been late in the diffusion of the Internet. It is also important to acknowledge that, as has been shown in Section 5, Internet NTBFs have special characteristics which differ from those of NTBFs in other sectors, even within ICTs; consequently, they also have special policy requirements.

In our view, the most important peculiarity of an industrial policy oriented towards Internet start-ups is that demand-side measures are at least as important as supply-side ones. For a series of reasons which have been analysed elsewhere by the authors (Colombo and Delmastro 2001), we believe that there will be no shortage of Internet entrepreneurs in Europe. First, barriers to entry related to both scale economies (that is size of minimum efficient scale) and the need for specialized technological competencies are relatively smaller in Internet-based sectors than in other high-tech sectors. Second, as Internet services still are in the very early stages of their life cycle, especially in laggard countries such as Italy, there may be excessive optimism about economic perspectives: this encourages entry of new entrepreneurs. For the same reason, we expect no shortage in the supply of funds from venture capitalists, at least in comparison with other sectors. However, the likelihood of success of the new outfits will be tightly contingent on the rapid take-off of a national mass market for Internet-based services, both in the business and private customer segments. On the one hand, there are increasing returns in the supply of such services, due to dynamic economies of scale (that is learning by doing) and bandwagon effects in their consumption. On the other, in spite of the global character of some content (for instance, films, music, financial information), the market for Internet services is segmented on a national basis, due to language differences and cultural specificities of the various countries which, with all else being equal, favour national providers.

There are a series of policy measures which may stimulate demand for such services. There is no room here for a detailed analysis. Examples of such measures, most of which are mentioned in the plans for the take-off of the Information Society developed by the various European countries, include the following ones:

- Support for the use of the Internet on the part of small businesses, professional and residential users through subsidization (in the form of tax deduction) of broad-band Internet access.
- Support for the use of Internet in schools (both secondary and primary).
- Provision of Internet-based public services.[17] As the value to users of having access to Internet depends on the variety of the available services, this measure is key at an early stage of the development of the market for Internet services in order to capture indirect network externalities and induce bandwagon effects.
- Establishment of competitive conditions in the supply of telecommunication services so as to reduce the price users have to pay for being connected to the Internet.

## NOTES

1. In the mid 1990s, there were 35 SPs in France; the 7160 firms that were located on them had more than 145000 employees (see Storey and Tether 1998b).
2. Note, however, that there are signals that things are changing in Europe. For instance, investments by the UK venture capital industry in start-ups and early stage firms increased from £85m in 1995 to £350m in 1999 (see Department of Trade and Industry 2000).

3. In 1992, Italian firms with less than 20 employees accounted for 38.7 per cent of total employment, a value that is five times as large as that of the United States and three times as large as that of the United Kingdom (see OECD 1997).
4. This is indirectly witnessed by the growing attention that the international economic and financial press is devoting to European NTBFs in Internet-based sectors (see for instance the cover stories of *Business Week*, 31.1.2000, 7.2.2000 and 6.3.2000).
5. E-commerce and ISP belong to the former category. The latter one includes sectors such as software and multimedia publishing.
6. In this chapter, an NTBF has been defined as a young firm founded after 1984, which at the date of foundation was independent (that is not controlled by another firm).
7. The following sectors are included: Internet (namely Internet service and access provision and e-commerce), software, multimedia content, and manufacturing industries of ICT (that is communication equipment, computers and electronics). These latter sectors correspond to the following four-digit industries (NACE-CLIO classification): communication equipment 31.30, computers 30.02, electronics 32.20.
8. The decision to confine the analysis to Northern Italy was due to practical reasons; as the identification of target firms was a very time-consuming process, we were forced to concentrate efforts in geographical areas where the likelihood of finding ICT-based NTBFs was sufficiently high. In this respect, note that Northern Italy accounts for over 50 per cent of Information Technology expenses of Italian firms and over 65 per cent of total employment in the industries considered in the present work (see again Istat 1999).
9. The two most important high-tech sectors that were not considered are pharmaceuticals (inclusive of biotechnology) and aerospace. According to 1996 Italian census data (Istat 1999), the number of small and medium-size firms (that is number of employees lower than 500) in such industries is only 1.4 per cent of the number of firms that operate in the ICT industries taken here into consideration. Absent more precise data on the age distribution of firms, there is no reason to believe that such proportion is substantially altered when one focuses attention on NTBFs.
10. If one also considers publishing (indeed competencies deriving from a working experience in traditional and multimedia publishing may be important, at least for entrepreneurs working in the provision of multimedia content) this percentage rises to 42.4 per cent.
11. In 1996, 87 per cent of software houses had five or less employees, versus 41 per cent of firms in the communications equipment sector and only 1 per cent in the computer and other office equipment industry.
12. Note that Italy was a laggard in the development of Internet. For instance, in 1997 the ratio of TLC wired lines to Internet users was almost 40 in Italy, against 2.6 in the US and 7.6 in Europe. However, Italy has been rapidly catching up. In 2002, according to estimates by CIRET, the same ratio is expected to equal 5.3, 3.1 and 1.8 in Italy, Europe and the United States, respectively.
13. For a definition of technological paradigm and technological trajectories see Dosi (1982). On the difference between *competence destroying* and *competence enhancing* technological change see Tushman and Anderson (1986). Finally, for a thorough analysis of the characteristics of the Internet paradigm see Colombo and Garrone (1997).
14. On this issue, see the policy measures mentioned in the Introduction, recently introduced by the French, German and UK governments.
15. European stock markets dedicated to small high-growth firms which adhere to the Euro.NM network exist in Amsterdam, Brussels, Frankfurt, Milan and Paris. Their common trait is that the rules for stock market listing are less demanding than in traditional stock markets. Altogether, by March 2000, 366 firms were listed at such stock exchanges, with a market value greater than 250 billion Euro.
16. In Italy, labour flexibility is substantially higher among small firms due to the existence of different rules governing labour relations according to firm size. The dual characteristics of the labour market may be regarded as partly responsible for the lower qualification in terms of both educational attainments and prior working experience, of Italian high-tech entrepreneurs with respect to their counterparts in other European countries. Of course, also the limited supply of 'incubating' organizations (that is the research laboratories of large

firms and public research institutions active in applied research) plays a key role.

17. An example is provided by the possibility offered to Italians since the year 2000 to fill tax forms through the Internet.

# REFERENCES


Acs, Z.J., C. Armington and A. Robb (1999), 'Measures of job flow dynamics in the US', *Discussion Papers CES 99-1.*

Autio, E., R. Kanerva, M. Kaila and I. Kauranen (1989), *New, Technology Based Firms in Finland*, Helsinki: Sitra Publication Series.

Baron, J., D. Burton and M. Hannan (1999), 'Engineering bureaucracy: the genesis of formal policies, positions, and structures in high-technology firms', *Journal of Law, Economics, and Organization*, **15**, 1–41.

Birch, D. and J. Medoff (1994), 'Gazelles', in L.C. Solmon and A.R. Levenson (eds), *Labor Markets, Employment Policy, and Job Creation,* Boulder and London: Westview Press.

Blanchflower, D. and A. Oswald (1999), 'Measuring latent entrepreneurship across nations', mimeo, University of Warwick.

Camerer, C. and D. Lovallo (1999), 'Overconfidence and excess of entry', *American Economic Review*, **89**, 306–18.

Carayannis, E., E. Rogers, K. Kurihara and M. Allbritton (1998), 'High-technology spin-offs from government R&D laboratories and research universities', *Technovation*, **18**, 1–11.

Colombo, M.G. and M. Delmastro (2000), 'How effective are technology incubators? Evidence from Italy', mimeo, CIRET-Politecnico di Milano.

Colombo, M.G. and M. Delmastro (2001), 'Technology-based entrepreneurs: does Internet make a difference?', *Small Business Economics*, **16**, 177–90.

Colombo, M.G. and M. Delmastro (2002), 'How effective are technology incubators? Evidence from Italy', *Research Policy*, **31**, 1103–220.

Colombo, M.G. and P. Garrone (1997), 'The multimedia paradigm: an evolutionary approach', *Communications and Strategy*, **28**, 215–43.

Department of Trade and Industry (2000), *Excellence and Opportunity: A Science and Innovation Policy for the 21st Century*, London.

Donckels, R. (1989), *'Tech versus Common Starters: Comparison by Means of 32 Case Studies'*, Bruselas: Small Business Research Institute.

Dosi, G. (1982), 'Technological paradigms and technological trajectories', *Research Policy*, **11**, 147–62.

European Commission (1996a), *New Technology-based Firms in Europe*, *EIMS* publication, 31.

European Commission (1996b), *Review of Studies on Innovative Fast Growing SMEs*, EIMS publication, 42.

Evans, D. and B. Jovanovic, (1989), 'An estimated model of entrepreneurial choice under liquidity constraints', *Journal of Political Economy*, **97**, 596–615.

Giudici, G. and S. Paleari (2000), 'The provision of finance to innovation: a survey conducted among technology based small firms', *Small Business Economics*, **14**, 37–53.

GMV Conseil (1989), *La Creation d'Enterprises Innovantes*, Rapport pour la Ministere de l'Industrie, Paris.

Istat (1997), *Indagine sull'Innovazione in Italia.*

Istat (1999), *Censimento Intermedio dell'Industria e dei Servizi.*

Jo, H. and J. Lee (1996), 'The relationship between an entrepreneur's background and performance in a new venture', *Technovation*, **16**, 161–71.

Johnson, W. (1978), 'A theory of job shopping', *Quarterly Journal of Economics*, **92**, 261–78.

Keeble, D., C. Lawson, H. Lawton Smith, B. Moore and F. Wilkinson (1998), 'Internalisation process, networking and local embeddeness in technology-intensive small firms', *Small Business Economics*, **11**, 327–42.

Kirchhof, B.A. (1994), 'Self-employment and dynamic capitalism', *Journal of Labor Research*, **17**, 627–43.

Licht, G., E. Nerlinger and G. Berger (1995), 'Germany: NTBF literature review', *ZEW*, Mannheim.

Miller, R. (1984), 'Job matching and occupational choice', *Journal of Political Economy*, **92**, 1086–120.

Monck, C.S.P., R.B. Porter, P. Quintas, D. Storey and P. Wynarczyk (1988), *Science Parks and the Growth of High Technology Firms*, London: Croom Helm

OECD (1996), *SMEs: Employment, Innovation, and Growth*, Paris.

OECD (1997), 'Small businesses, job creation, and growth: Facts, obstacles, and best practices', http://www.oecd.org/dsti/sti/industry/smes/prod/smes.pdf

OECD (1999), *Regulatory Reform for Smaller Firms*, Paris.

Reynolds, P.D. and S.B. White (1997), *The Entrepreneurial Process: Economic Growth, Men, Women, and Minorities*, Westport, Conn. and London: Greenwood, Quorum Books.

Roberts, E.B. (1991), 'The technological base of the new enterprise', *Research Policy,* **20**, 283–98.

Storey, D.J. and B.S. Tether (1998a), 'New technology-based firms in the European Union: an introduction', *Research Policy*, **26**, 933–46.

Storey, D.J. and B.S. Tether (1998b), 'Public policy measures to support new technology-based firms in the European Union', *Research Policy*, **26**, 1037–57.

Tushman, M.L. and P. Anderson (1986), 'Technological discontinuities and organizational environments', *Administrative Science Quarterly*, **31**, 439–65.

Westhead, P. (1997), 'R&D "inputs" and "outputs" of technology-based firms located on and off science parks', *R&D Management,* **27**, 45–62.

Westhead, P. and S. Batstone (1998), 'Independent technology-based firms: The perceived benefits of a science-park location', *Urban Studies*, **12**, 2197–219.

Westhead P. and D.J. Storey (1994), *An Assessment of Firms Located On and Off Science Parks in the UK*, London: HMSO.

Westhead P. and D.J. Storey (1995), 'Links between higher education institutions and high technology firms', *Omega-International Journal of Management Science*, **23**, 345–60.

Westhead P. and D.J. Storey (1997), 'Financial constraints on the growth of high-tech small firms in the UK', *Applied Financial Economics*, **7**, 197–201.

# 10. European national platforms for the development of the Information Society

**David Sancho**

## INTRODUCTION

In this chapter, we are going to analyse the policymaking styles of four European countries with regard to providing impetus for the IS (Information Society) together with their relationship with the action plans elaborated by the EC (European Commission). First of all, we will study the formulation and the content of government action plans concerning the IS in the 1990s. Secondly, we will analyse how, in recent years, and in particular following the initiative '*e*-Europe', these programmes have resulted in a certain coming together and convergence of policies of a promotional nature carried out by member states.

To begin with, the different governments' action plans regarding the IS took on a very different shape. Some countries based their programmes on state intervention with a global focus via strategic planning, while in other countries, government initiatives consisted of specific plans of action, which were subsequently systemised into plans of action on a wider scale. The timing and sequence of these political plans of actions were very varied, as was the degree of 'anticipation' or 'reaction' of the different national governments. In the chapter we will comment on possible reasons for these differences and we will concentrate on the formulation processes of the policies, given that the relative newness of these initiatives (the late 1990s) means that the evaluation of their implementation and social impact require a time aspect which we do not, as yet, have. For our analysis we have chosen four national cases to study (the United Kingdom, France, Germany and Spain). Our choice was governed by the fact that we wished to compare four clearly different traditional political institutional traditions. As Scott points out (1995: 146), it is difficult to understand variations in political decision-making if we cannot compare these within different institutional contexts.

The different countries have assimilated, be it at different rhythms and to different extents, that the diffusion of ITC (information and communication technology) constitutes the generation of positive externalities in the economy as a whole. In our opinion, the differences between countries have been governed by their form of transition towards the new regime of competition in the telecommunications market. On many occasions the government's role and responsibilities with a view to IS policies in the 1990s took a back seat to priorities such as the establishment of a regulatory framework to ensure competition or the casting of 'national champions' based on former state monopolies. This would, to a certain extent, explain the delay in introducing IS programmes which can be observed in some of the countries analysed, especially those which as we will see placed greater importance on the need to participate actively in the structuring of its telecommunications market.

Apart from this working hypothesis, we will also examine to what extent national policies converged as a result of the copying or 'transfer of policies' between countries and as a result of the impetus provided by the development of European initiatives regarding the IS. From the mid 1990s onwards, there has been a certain exchange, on a national scale, of instruments used in the promotion of the IS through the copying or adoption of those examples of intervention which in other countries have proven successful. We also consider that the definition of strategic national programmes of a promotional nature has also been affected by the impact of the new European IS programmes, especially from the late 1990s onwards, with the emergence of the 'eEurope' initiative.

## AN INSTITUTIONAL FOCUS ON THE DEVELOPMENT OF INFORMATION SOCIETY NATIONAL PLATFORMS

The institutional contrasts between the different countries may influence the strategies of political government action (Zysman 1984; Hall 1986 and 1999; North 1991). Variations in decision-making styles in different countries are therefore influenced by incentives or conditioning factors generated by phenomena such as 'path dependence' (Hall 1986; Immergut 1998; Thelen 1999; Thatcher 2000). The different institutional structures influence the generation of 'policy outcomes' (Pierson 2000; Evans et al. 1885; Steinmo et al. 1992). The area of telecommunications and IS is no exception. Thatcher (2000) shows us how, as a result of differences in institutional environments, differences were generated in the sequence of reform of telecommunications policies in different European countries, although they were subject to similar environmental forces. As far as promotion of the IS is concerned, the decision-making styles which evolved in the United Kingdom, France, Germany and Spain were conditioned to a large extent by their respective institutional traditions, which led to different processes of political interaction. Broadly speaking and depending on the country in question, these processes could be qualified as pluralist, state-controlled, corporate or capture.

In recent years, policymaking in these countries has shown a tendency towards convergence, both in political styles and in policy content, although the differing national traditions have influenced to a certain extent the success or failure of the implementation of like promotional instruments in these countries. The trend towards convergence shows us that the different national institutional systems do not act alone, but rather how they are subject to the influence of processes which come from political structures on a supranational level, as well as to a certain reproduction of experiences of those nations which are considered as examples to follow (Jones 2002). In this sense, DiMaggio and Powell (1991) distinguish between different types of institutional isomorphism, different phenomena which can be detected in the formulation processes of IS policies throughout Europe. First, we will study a 'coercive-type' of isomorphism based on formal and informal pressures from European institutions, whose aim is to facilitate the coordination of IS policies in different countries and secondly, we will examine a 'reproductive-type' of isomorphism involving the imitation of references seen as examples to be followed. National policymakers hence learn from the successes or failures of state intervention in other countries, imitating alternative actions. This type of isomorphism is favoured by the reinforcement of an international network of professionals exchanging knowledge and experience, aiding the spread of 'practices regarded as suitable'.

## EUROPEAN IS PROGRAMMES AS A DETERMINING FACTOR OF POLICIES ON A NATIONAL LEVEL

The European institutions have given rise to the emergence of a common agenda within the area of telecommunications and IS. Since the 1980s, European initiatives have become an obligatory point of reference for politicians and national actors (Alabau 1998) and more importantly, the political level in Europe has led to the establishment of a new space for the representation of interests. This fact has directly contributed to the transformation of the traditional methods of representation on a national level. In general, the way in which interests are predominantly represented on a European level is of a more pluralist nature than of a state or enterprise-controlled nature (Mény et al. 1996). The relationships established between European groups and institutions, particularly in the case of the Commission, are not characterised as being very stable and in contrast they can be qualified as being very open and competitive. For this reason, sectorial agents can take advantage of the European level to 'skip' the system of national representation, or to mobilise additional means of pressure on the state. The extension of the political agenda to a European scale does not, however, mean absolute consensus on how to tackle key issues. What is more, the actors within the national sectorial area should continue 'negotiating' until they manage to formulate alternative actions to implement in each country (Mény et al. 1996). This process of interrelation on European and national scales can be observed in the evolution of the European policy concerning the IS.

After 1979, the first European texts emerged on the concept of IS as a means of scientific development and the key to improvement in economic transition. Later, the Telecommunications Green Paper of 1987 once again stressed the strategic importance of the IS for companies. Another idea which was stressed and extended by European institutions was the need to use market forces as the basis for the development strategy of the IS. In 1993, the Commission edited the White Paper *Growth, Competitiveness and Employment*, which was already using the specific terminology of 'Information Society'. This term was understood as being the generalised use of information technology for social and economic activity. Based on the proposals of the White Paper, the 'Bangemann Report' appeared in 1994 (European Commission 1994a). This proposed the liberalisation of the telecommunications services as an instrumental factor in triggering the evolution of the IS. In the report, private initiatives were considered to be a key factor for the funding of new communications infrastructures, while it was understood that European institutions should concentrate on the creation of a regulatory framework to facilitate the development of the sector.

In July 1994, following the recommendations of the Bangemann report, the Commission designed its action plan 'Europe towards the Information Society'. This plan, which designed different initiatives was an initial attempt at bringing the IS closer on a global level (European Commission 1994b). It was based on four lines of action: first, the adaptation of the regulatory framework of telecommunications to facilitate the liberalisation of infrastructures; secondly, the facilitating of networks, services and content applications on a transeuropean scale; thirdly, the recommendation, backed up by economic reasoning, to foster the social and cultural impact of the IS; and lastly, concrete initiatives for the promotion of the IS were programmed. This document played a fundamental role in triggering and dispersing the concept of 'consensus' on the role which states should adopt in promoting the IS (Alabau 1998). The plan was updated in 1996 on a similar basis (European Commission 1996). This dynamic was reinforced by the institutionalisation of meetings of experts and the setting up of open debates on the subject. In 1995, for example, a group of leading experts was put together with a view to specifically analysing the social repercussions of the development of the IS.

With a similar objective in mind, that is, of encouraging a sectorial debate, the Information Society Forum was set up in the mid 1990s with a view to encouraging the participation of public and private agents in the definition of alternative public action. Along the same lines, a Ministerial Conference was held in Bonn in 1997 with 29 European countries participating in the debate of aspects related to the use of global information networks. During these years, promotion of different programmes related to the IS continued, such as the Telematics Application Programme, the Advanced Communication Technology Services, and the Information Technology.

In 1999, the new Commission, headed by Romano Prodi, established as one of its top priorities intervention in the area of the IS. This priority emerged as a programme called '*e*Europe: An Information Society for All', and it symbolised a qualitative change as far as the previous stage was concerned. Through an agreed and coordinated process of definition, specific objectives, commitments to action plans and deadlines were considered for the first time. It was a far-reaching plan of action which employed a method of open coordination between states and included a comparative evaluation of national initiatives. One of the key factors of *e*Europe was to obtain state consensus to carry out activities to promote the IS following predetermined schedules. Hence the *e*Europe initiative implied the acceptance of political commitments on the part of States. The objectives of eEurope could only be achieved if the member states, the European Parliament and the European Commission coordinated the formulation of priorities and plans of action. In this way, an initiative by the European Institutions combined different national plans on a global scale. As we will see in the case studies, the *e*Europe initiative led to strategic planning of IS promotional activities in member states. Apart from this, the content of *e*Europe also served as a model for the design of promotional activities on a national scale and was based on three central ideas for action: (a) to introduce all European citizens to the digital age and facilitate their access to the web; (b) to spread digital literacy throughout Europe and above all to introduce it into the business culture; and (c) to ensure that the introductory process of the IS was socially inclusive and adhered to the trust and safety of the citizen. These important central ideas took practical shape through ten areas of priority action, which were carried out during the year 2000 through an implementation programme called the '*e*Europe Action Plan', and covered areas from education to transport, healthcare to social services (see Table 10.1).

The *e*Europe initiative demonstrates that the European institutions work as a unifying force as far as the content of IS national programmes is concerned, promoting learning from experience and facilitating consensus on priority lines of action. This has encouraged a kind of isomorphism with regard to the adoption of IS policies by states. This contrasts with the effect of the European

*Table 10.1 Principal lines of action of the 'eEurope' initiative*

| Priority areas of action |
|---|
| 1. European youth into the Digital Age |
| 2. Cheaper Internet access |
| 3. Accelerating e-Commerce |
| 4. Fast Internet for researchers and students |
| 5. Smart cards for secure electronic access |
| 6. Risk capital for high-tech SMEs |
| 7. eParticipation for the disabled |
| 8. Healthcare online |
| 9. Intelligent transport |
| 10. Government online |

*Source*: European Commission (1999).

influence on telecommunications policies based on coercion through the creation of binding regulations and directives for states, in the promotion of the IS the influence from European institutions has been based more on the encouragement of consensus, on the coordination of different national initiatives, on the creation of a common approach to the IS and on the establishment of pilot schemes which serve as an example to follow.

## INFORMATION SOCIETY POLICIES IN THE UNITED KINGDOM, FRANCE, GERMANY AND SPAIN

The convergence of European policies in the area of the IS does not imply absolute harmonisation, but rather the progressive emergence of a common set of principles of action. The European institutions do not possess an adequate structure for the implementation of these policies, which is why this remains in the hands of the member states, which still have ample room for manoeuvre. We will see how this room for manoeuvre has evolved through IS initiatives in the United Kingdom, France, Germany and Spain.

### United Kingdom

The United Kingdom was one of the first countries to advocate the importance of the use of ICT for economic and social development. At the end of the 1970s and at the beginning of the 1980s, several initiatives were already underway, although government priority was given to the process of liberalisation and deregulation of the telecommunications sector. Later, in the mid 1990s, a new institutional agenda on the area of IS promotion made a reappearance through the collaboration of private companies.

At the beginning of the 1980s, Margaret Thatcher named Kenneth Baker Minister of Information and Technology, and in 1982 a document by the Information Technology Advisory Panel was already recommending the development, in conjunction with the private sector, of a cable network to facilitate the extension of advanced telecommunications services. In 1984, the United Kingdom prepared to connect the principal higher education institutions through a network called JANET (ESIS 2000). Following these initial programmes concerning the IS, the government turned its attention to the deregulation process of the telecommunications sector. BT was set up in 1981, and three years later entered a process of privatisation and a break from public control, a process which ended in 1997 (Thatcher 1999). OFTEL (The Office of Telecommunications - a semi-independent regulator) was created in 1984, while the introduction of competition spread from terminal equipment and the existence of a duopoly (in the form of a second operator) in the 1980s to free competition at the beginning of the 1990s. The regulatory process thereafter concentrated on the preservation of effective competition and the protection of consumers, a strategy directed by OFTEL (Thatcher 2000).

In the mid 1990s with the liberalisation process already at an advanced stage, priority was again given to promotional strategies for the IS. In 1994, the government published a document called 'Creating Superhighways of the Future: Developing Broadband Communications in the United Kingdom', where the role of liberalising telecommunications was once again highlighted as being an essential requisite for the development of the IS. During this time, different advisory documents and IS initiatives appeared, but they did not respond to the need for a global action plan (ESIS 2000). The documents centred on underlining the need for a stable regulatory framework, conceiving the private sector as a leader in the development of the IS, and the defining of the role of public policies as a motivation factor with regard to the stimulation of competition in infrastructures and services. This idea of the public role as a motivator was, as we will see, gradually accepted and assimilated by the other European countries. As part of this action strategy, the British govern-ment funded 23 pilot programmes, and in 1995 different national programmes were set up to introduce ICT to the sectors of healthcare (National Health Service Net) and education (Education Department's Superhighways Initiative).

One of the first coordinated actions within the IS area was that directed by the Department of Commerce and Industry in 1996 in the guise of a project called ISI (Information Society Initiative), The objective of this project was to give global coverage to the different initiatives already underway in the United

Kingdom. The ISI, which was scheduled to last for five years, was divided into an extensive number of programmes which were further subdivided into specific action projects, where both public and private agents played a part (ESIS 2000). Amongst the most relevant of these programmes was the programme 'IT for All'. The principal objectives of this programme were: to publicise and increase social awareness of the need to introduce the use of ICT to companies, to establish a national network of advisory centres on the area of IS and to adhere to the programme 'Improving Access to Cultural Heritage' in order to study the impact of the IS on cultural issues and the Green Paper 'government.direct'. This latter led to a debate on how to improve access to public services through the Internet. The creation of a government plan which brought together actions by various state departments was an important innovation, and had as its aim the guarantee that a horizontal implementation, something necessary in IS policy-making, could be effectuated to avoid the duplication of efforts and the lack of coordination between different initiatives.

The next step was taken by the new Labour government, who on coming into power established the intensification of IS development as one of their priorities of action. In 1998, the Prime Minister presented the document 'Our Information Age, the Government Vision'. Once again, it defended the fact that state control should not substitute private initiatives in the development of the IS, but instead it should become a promotional or motivational force through the adoption of different strategies. At the same time, it recognised the need to coordinate government action in the area of IS through interdepartmental collaboration and also through public and private sector interaction. This government strategy was complemented by the publication of different reports and white papers such as the 'Modernising Government White Paper', 'Our Competitive Future' or 'e-commerce at its.best.uk'. In the year 2000, the Prime Minister introduced three specific objectives: to facilitate the provision of all public services on the Internet by the year 2005, to ensure that all citizens had access to the Internet by this year and to introduce the strategy of e-business to the public sector.

These proposals also had an organisational implication, which led to the naming of an e-Minister to take charge of coordinating the government agenda regarding IS issues. Secondly, an IS interministerial committee was set up to ensure that the different initiatives of the various governmental departments shared a common vision and action strategy, while at the same time looking to create coherent government action regarding relations between the business sector and public opinion. Thirdly, an Envoy Structure (e-envoy) was created, which reported directly to the Prime Minister and which, through its 'Central IT Unit', promoted e-commerce and the modernisation of the public services, with a network of coordinators placed in the different government departments and agencies. There were also other new organs set up called the 'Information Age Government Champions Group', which brought together 36 heads of Central and Local Administration to advise different levels of government on e-government-related issues, and the 'Information Age Partnership' - a forum for relations between the government and the principal companies in the ICT sector.

At the end of the year 2000, the Government presented the annual report 'UK on Line', developed in conjunction with industry, NGOs, trade unions and consumer organisations. This report detailed the new governmental strategy consisting of a programme of 95 initiatives with a view to developing the IS in the United Kingdom (see Table 10.2).

British policymaking in the area of the IS was characterised in the early days by the fragmentation of public programmes, a fact which led to the generation of a large number of initiatives which were poorly coordinated and did not meet the need for large structural plans. The second stage was characterised by the resolution to generate coordinated action through planning programmes on a global scale and the creation of organisational structures favouring participation and consensus between public and private agents. The policy-defining process was also characterised by the incorporation of extensive consultation and negotiation processes between public authorities and sectorial agents, primarily through flexible and informal mechanisms aimed at establishing consensus on the policies to be implemented.

## France

A genuine public policy for the development of the IS did not evolve in France until the mid 1990s. The first French political initiatives came about in response to IS projects in existence in the USA and European Institutions and particularly in response to the Commission's White Paper *Growth, Competitiveness and Employment* in 1993. French politics at this time was passive and centred on considerations related to industry and macro-economics. The main preoccupation of the time was not focused on the needs of citizens nor on the social utility of infrastructures but rather on how to achieve a favourable position for French industry in the newly emerging global market (Vedel 1997).

The DGT (Direction Genérale des Télécommunications) controlled the telecommunications services from within the ministerial structure up to the 1980s. The French government had traditionally developed its strategy of *grands projects* in the sector of telecommunications through the design of programmes and the implementation of services, taking responsibility for the design and execution of policies from a position of management and control.

*Table 10.2 Objectives for action on the IS in the United Kingdom*

| Area | Objectives |
|---|---|
| Modernise markets | Establish the UK as the best environment in the world for electronic commerce by the year 2002 |
| Guarantee ITC user access and trust | Guarantee secure access to the Internet for the whole population by the year 2005 |
| Company and IS | Extend the use of electronic commerce especially within small and medium-sized companies<br>Make the United Kingdom world leader in business-to-business and business-to-consumer transactions |
| On-line government | Provide 100% of public services on line by 2005<br>100% public contraction by Central Government on line by the year 2002 |
| Guarantee international competitivity of British IT companies | Improve productivity of IT companies and content in relation to countries such as the USA, France, Germany or Japan |
| Leadership in IS-coordination initiatives | Improve government coordination systems to place the United Kingdom in a leading position with regards development of integrated systems in the implementation of IS initiatives |
| Evaluation of IS-promotion policies | Develop informative and evaluative systems of the impact of IS-promotion policies |

*Source*: eMinister (2000).

These initiatives aimed to strengthen French industry (Cohen 1992). At the end of the 1980s, governmental policymaking in the sector was very control-oriented, with an entrepreneurial state directly developing the provision of telecommunications services through a monopoly regime.

At the beginning of the 1990s, the first structural changes came about in French telecommunications. The DGT became France Télécom and no longer formed part of the ministerial structure. It became an independent institution within the public sector and subject to government control (Gensollen 1991). Privatisation was not initiated until 1997, the year in which a new semi-independent regulator the ART (Autorité de Régulation des Télécommunications) was set up. During this time, the telecommunications sector had slowly opened up to competition, first in the area of added value services and mobile telephones, and by 1998, competition had extended to land-line services.

It should be pointed out that as far as IS policies were concerned, several significant reports were published in the mid 1990s, for example reports by Thierry Breton (1993) or Gérard Théry (1994), General Director of Telecommunications at the time. This latter report pointed out the importance of state intervention as an element of support, both in the area of infrastructure and the development of services for the IS. The Théry report assumed that the development of the IS was to be inevitable and on a global scale. It established a series of objectives, among which the proposal to connect all families and companies to the Internet by the year 2015 stood out. The report considered that access to the Internet should be total in order to prevent discrimination against social groups or residential areas. Secondly, it also proposed the massive development of infrastructures of high-speed data transmission and lastly, the fostering of pilot projects in which the private sector was to participate.

However, the government did not adopt any plan of action which followed the recommendations of the Théry report. Its policy strategies took on a more modest form through a process of funding pilot programmes to be carried out by private entities. As a result, at the end of 1994, the Ministry of Commerce, Industry, Post and Telecommunications announced a tender for the development of experiences in new services and content and applications platforms which used information technologies extensively (Chevallier 1996).

This new governmental role began to transform the traditional French concept of state control. Moving from a role of management and control, the government's specific actions centred on three new areas which became evident in the second half of the 1990s: the adaptation of a regulatory framework to permit greater competition in basic telecommunications services, the promotion of private initiatives related to IS, and finally the promotion of a public debate on the IS (Thatcher 1999). As Vedel (1997) points out, this movement from a management-style leadership to a pragmatic stance was influenced by a series of structural factors: a new liberal and ideological position, the failure of cable development in France - attributed by various authors to excessive control by the authorities - the lack of public resources which impeded the prioritisation of investment in the IS, and finally, the resistance of France Telecom to adopt a leading role in the development of the IS, instead preferring to reserve its strength to adjust itself to the new liberalised environment. In this sense, France Telecom's reaction to the Théry report was quite negative since the operator preferred to support specific applications for groups of users through agreements limited to specific suppliers rather than to advocate a universal position.

It was not until 1997 that the Prime Minister Lionel Jospin made clear his intention to design a global plan for the Information Society, the coordination of which was assured through an interministerial committee. In January 1998, the government presented its PAGSI (Programme d'action gouvernmental pour préparer l'entreé de la France dans la Societé de l'Information) in which the French state presented itself as a catalysing agent for citizen and company initiatives, facilitating the removal of obstacles for the use of ICT. Hence, together with the government's traditional position as a market regulator, the PAGSI understood that the government should play a leading role by providing incentives and demonstrating exemplary behaviour concerning the use of ICT for companies and citizens. The Plan was based on six principle lines of priority actions and various initiatives for action (see Table 10.3).

From 1998 onwards, the different Ministries developed the governmental action programme through specific plans of action (PAMSI) and an

*Table 10.3 Objectives for action on the IS in France*

| Action priorities | Some anticipated initiatives |
|---|---|
| 1. Education | - Introduction of ICT to schools<br>- Training of teaching staff<br>- 'On-line' training<br>- Creation of multimedia educational material |
| 2. Culture | - Creation of multimedia services<br>- Protection of French culture on the Internet<br>- Reinforcement of the presence of France and the French language |
| 3. Public Services | - Facilitate access to Public Services through the Internet |
| 4. Companies | - Promote the introduction of ICT to small and medium-sized companies<br>- Promote electronic commerce<br>- Facilitate the diffusion of strategic information for companies |
| 5. Research and Development | - Promote innovation<br>- Rationalise investment in R&D<br>- Promote development of the Internet<br>- Promote new communication technologies in France |
| 6. Regulation | - Promote secure systems in communications<br>- Guarantee national security<br>- Adapt legislation to the new reality of the IS |

*Source*: CISI (1998).

interministerial committee, called CISI (Comité interministériel pour la Société de l'Information) was created. In line with this initiative, other coordination structures were established, such as an interministerial committee specialising in technological matter, an interministerial delegation to promote the use of new communication systems by Public Administration and a department responsible for studying the technical and legal aspects of information and communication. The implementation process of the PAGSI also presented an opportunity to promote the participation of different social and economic agents in the redefinition of ministerial programmes of action. Therefore, over the years to come, consultation processes were opened up, the formulation of reports by experts was promoted and the dynamics of negotiation and consensus on priority action in conjunction with local and regional authorities (ESIS 2000) were extended. It was observed that there were still problems concerning unequal access to the information networks both on a geographical and a social scale. This situation led the government to design a new top-level strategic committee on the Internet and information technology with a view to facilitating more dialogue between the public and private sectors and research centres.

It was not until the end of the 1990s that a coordinated plan of action regarding the IS was formulated, and when this was completed it incorporated a large number of the points which had appeared in European documents on IS promotion. The French stance with regard to the liberalisation of telecommunications therefore changed until its acceptation became inevitable (Thatcher 1999). The French policy regarding IS promotion also changed: moving from an initial rather control-oriented position to a new government role which was based on facilitating private initiatives in the area of IS (Vedel 1997).

**Germany**

We have witnessed a transformation from a control-oriented style to a much more open pragmatic style in France in terms of promotion of IS. Similarly, for years, the German government's stance was quite passive towards the concept of incorporating a strategic horizontal vision of IS policies. This, as we will see, led to a delay in the emergence of promotional plans which lasted until the end of the 1990s.

In the 1970s, the DBP (Deutsche Bundespost) formed part of the ministerial department of telecommunications and postal services. The restructurisation of the German telecommunications sector was initiated in the 1980s with liberalisation policy restricted to equipment and terminals. The public status of the DBP was maintained by political pressure coming from the stances of trade unions, equipment suppliers and directors of the DBP (Schneider and

Werle 1991). The DBP had established a close economic relationship with certain industries which manufactured telecommunications equipment and this situation facilitated the creation of a corporate coalition which defended the maintenance of the status quo. Therefore, at the end of the 1980s, Germany presented a model of sectorial policymaking of an enterprise-oriented nature (Thatcher 2000), with a firm interaction between the state monopoly and certain sectorial agents.

Until the 1980s, the style of government in this sector excluded a part of the industrial sector, or in other words, confined it to a restricted network, offering only limited access to certain agents. The state played the role of the authoritarian 'facilitator' in this interaction. The legal and institutional structure which this political style upheld was based on the deeply rooted enterprise-oriented German tradition (Van Waarden 1992) and was reinforced by the fragmentation of public power resulting from the German federal structure. For this reason, the emergence of open instruments for sectorial participation was complicated in Germany, as was the development of interactive dynamics to facilitate a greater openness in the process of policymaking (Thatcher 2000).

From the 1990s onwards, changes came about in the structure of the implementation of telecommunications policies and in the style and instruments of German politics. These instruments were now aimed at seeking wider consensus, with increased collaboration on the part of more agents in a way which was increasingly more open. Apart from this, in 1990, the DBP was divided into three public corporations, one of which took over responsibility for telecommunications - Deutsche Telekom. Deutsche Telekom's privatisation was subsequently initiated between 1996 and 1998 and in 1998 a semi-independent regulator was created with the aim of promoting competition and controlling the dominant position of DT. However, even at the beginning of the 1990s, the federal government seemed reluctant to take on a leading role in the process of global promotion of the IS (Kubicek 1997) even though it received criticism from German industry, which called for greater political action as regards technological promotion on a federal scale (Thatcher 2000). Finally, at the end of 1994, the government announced a plan to organise dialogue between industry, the scientific sector and the government in areas of technological research, development and innovation. The Council for Research, Technology and Innovation was thus created in 1995, in which universities, the ICT industrial sector, trade unions, four federal ministries and a regional government took part. The government also created a work group to study new reforms, and a series of meetings with authorities of the *Länder* was programmed to modify regulation in the area of media.

In 1996, the various government initiatives were incorporated into a programme called 'Info2000: Germany's Way to the Information Society', which was based on an earlier study carried out by the previously mentioned Council for Research, Technology and Innovation. This action plan emphasised the need to increase liberalisation and to create a legal space on a federal scale which would favour the emergence of greater demand for ICT. Along with this, emphasis was given to four relevant aspects: first, the need to develop training and educational policies to create a critical mass of qualified workers in the area of the IS; secondly, the establishment of technological research and development initiatives through specific programmes developed by the Ministry of Education, Research, Science and Technology; thirdly, the incorporation of the IS into Public Administration in order to provide improved services; and finally, the need to develop IS policies based on cooperation and closely connected to EU initiatives in this field (ESIS 2000). With a view to facilitating dialogue and consensus on the implementation of different IS initiatives the BMBF created a discussion forum called 'Forum Info 2000' at the end of 1996 in which industry, trade unions and social organisations participated. At the same time, during the period 1996–98, the telecommunications market was further opened up, and various Ministries developed numerous initiatives of a specific nature. The most significant of these were related to telecommuting and support programmes for small and medium-sized companies (through the Ministry for the Economy). There were also programmes aimed at connecting schools to the Internet.

When Gerhard Schröder assumed power in October 1998, the new federal government adopted a more proactive attitude towards promoting the IS. They made it a political priority to ensure that Germany did not fall behind in a globalised society, in which ICT was gaining increased importance in economic transactions. As a result of this stance, the Ministry for the Economy, in conjunction with the Ministry for Education and Research, elaborated a new plan of action called 'Innovation and Work in the Information Society of the 21st Century', which was scheduled to be implemented by the year 2005. The plan had a dual objective – first to place Germany at the head of development in information technology at a European level and secondly to fight against unemployment by promoting this sector from an economic and social angle (ESIS 2000). The new plan defined four strategic lines of action: to facilitate access to ICT; to guarantee secure transactions on the Internet (by increasing citizen and company confidence in the use of new media); to guarantee the modernisation of the state, and to promote the participation of public and private sectors in innovation processes. These strategic lines of action were also developed through programmes which defined a number of more specific objectives (see Table 10.4).

The objectives of the action plan were implemented through initiatives originating from different Ministries and federal organs, as well as from the private sector and different social agents. It should also be added that the

*Table 10.4 Objectives for action on the IS in Germany*

| Fields of action | Objectives |
|---|---|
| 1. Increase social access to ICT | – Increase access to the Internet by 9% between 1999 and 2005<br>– Increase access to the Internet for small and medium-sized companies so that it matches access percentages of large companies. |
| 2. Eliminate unequal access to the Internet among social groups | – Increase access to the Internet by 50% for women<br>– Increase the number of companies set up by women by up to 40% by 2005, especially in the area of ICT |
| 3. Consumer protection | – Guarantee the creation of legal regulations to guarantee the same level of security in transactions on the Internet as in non-telematic transactions. |
| 4. Education | – Equip all schools with multimedia systems by 2001<br>– Provide training software and programmes through the Internet<br>– Ensure interconnection of all universities through computerised networks |
| 5. Research and Development | – Ensure interconnection of research groups through high-speed networks |
| 6. Infrastructures | – Ensure that all homes have access to fibre-optic cable by the year 2010<br>– Develop infrastructure and multimedia mobile services by the year 2005<br>– Free access to the Internet by cable by 2002 |
| 7. Work | – Create 40000 training places in ITC by the year 2002<br>– Create 250000 workers specialised in ITC by the year 2005<br>– Double the number of telecommuters by the year 2002<br>– Double the number of multimedia companies by the year 2001 |

*Table 10.4 Continued*

| Fields of action | Objectives |
|---|---|
| 8. Ecology and Sustainability | - Use ICT to meet sustainability objectives established in the agenda 21 |
| 9. Modernisation of the State | - Extend the use of ICT in the Federal and e-government Administration by 2001<br>- Electronic public contraction by 2001<br>- Electronic tax declarations by 2000 |
| 10. European IS and international cooperation | - Promote cooperation on a European and international scale to reduce inequalities in access to and use of ICT. |

*Source*: ESIS (2000.)

*Länder* are becoming more and more involved in the development of IS-related policies as independent agents, a factor which has enriched and diversified the means of state intervention in this area within the country.

**Spain**

Spain's adoption of IS-related policies came about through a fragmented process which was quite heavily influenced by the top-down factor of European initiatives. The predominance of Telefónica in the Spanish telecommunications sector and its close historical links with the government (being a private company under public control) meant that sectorial agents had limited access to the defining process of policymaking in the area of IS and telecommunications until well into the 1990s (Jordana 1998). For this reason, Spain's IS policy was characterised for many years by Telefónica's independent initiatives such as the promotion of new programmes in this sector through a foundation of theirs called Fundesco. This situation was quite convenient for the government and at least until 1996–97 the introduction of competition to the telecommunications sector in Spain and the promotion of a 'national champion' led to a certain forgetfulness with regard to issues related to the promotion of the IS. Leaving aside Fundesco's activities, government action, without being completely inexistent, was characterised by a certain dispersion of initiatives carried out by different ministries and the emergence of a nucleus of promotional activities within the General Management of Telecommunications.

Moving back in time, it should be pointed out the earliest initiatives concerning the IS appeared in Spain in the mid 1980s, and were closely connected to policies concerning industrial promotion. Telefónica played a key role in stimulating industrial telecommunications policies, a fact which is exemplified by their participation in the objectives of the first National Electronic and Computer Plan of 1984. At this time, Fundesco worked as a platform for the debate and promotion of studies on ICT, and developed numerous training programmes and research and development projects, constituting an observational role for pilot schemes in the area of IS. Apart from funding studies and pilot schemes, Fundesco also promoted social debate through work groups, opinion-exchanging sessions and public acts, in which representatives from different sectorial agents participated. One of the most significant activities carried out by Fundesco during this period was its management of the IRIS programme. This was a programme geared towards the provision of Internet services and the maintenance and future development of the communications infrastructure of research centres.

At the beginning of the 1990s, the Spanish government initiated some of its own programmes aimed specifically at promoting the IS. Of particular interest were the programmes ARCO/TELEMÁTICA (1992–94) and ARTE/PYME (1995–99). These programmes aimed at helping small and medium-sized companies, by co-funding projects which involved the use of advanced telecommunications services. There were also specific research and development initiatives for the promotion of telecommunications technology and equipment (PlanSAT 1994–97, PlanTVD 1996–98) and an initiative to promote and identify the Emerging Advanced Telecommunications Services (PISTA and PISTA-Cable). This initiative promoted the use of ICT in various sectors such as education, healthcare, administration, industry or transport through pilot schemes. However, as we have already mentioned, in the 1990s the IS activities spearheaded by the different ministries were dispersed and uncoordinated. These, and similar programmes, were technology-oriented and suffered from the lack of an integrated plan to take advantage of economies of scale, which might have resulted in their coordinated management.

The chance to participate in the definition of the need for state action on the IS, which had traditionally been associated with technological actors, started to open up at the end of the 1990s. In 1998, the Ministry for Industry and Energy promoted the creation of a advisory group responsible for developing studies and putting forward recommendations for the development of the IS in Spain. This group was made up of experts from different sectors connected to ICT. Their first assignment, which was published in July 1998, presented a series of recommendations, emphasising the need to promote the demand for services, with a heavy emphasis on the use of ICT in education, leisure or through electronic commerce, the establishment of means to fund innovation projects, the creation of a forum for the IS and the need to establish improved interministerial coordination with regard to the IS. In October 1998, the Ministry for Industry and Energy established a forum for the Information Society, to advise on and propose promotional lines of action. The intention was to open up the exchange of opinions between representatives from the ICT, audiovisual and telecommunications sectors and the government.

An attempt to achieve integrated planning of IS-related policies appeared for the first time in 1999, when the government decided to set up a process to define the national strategy for IS development, thus preventing the duplication of uncoordinated efforts by the different Ministries. In line with this plan of action, the Interministerial Commission of the Information Society and New Technologies was set up, incorporating representatives from different Ministries. Apart from this, an inventory of the different initiatives which had to this date been carried out by the different government institutions was drawn up. Finally, towards the end of 1999, the Government passed a plan called 'INFO XXI: The Information Society for All' for the period 2000–2003. This plan consisted of numerous initiatives (more than 300 actions and projects) which were to be carried out by the different ministries, using their own budgets. At the same time, an attempt was also being made to set up projects requiring the support of the private sector. With a certain rhetorical tone, different objectives, deadlines, leaders, collaborators and means of funding the principle action lines making up the initiatives of the action plan were established. In all probability, the elaboration of the Plan Info XXI represented a direct reaction to the proposals of the e-Europe initiative, passed in the same year.

The Plan Info XXI had three important underlying concepts, which were a reproduction of the model for action analysed in other European countries: the promotion of the telecommunications and IT sector, the creation of a market and competition and the strengthening of electronic administration and access by all to the Information Society. Hence, by copying the philosophy of the 'e-Europe' initiative, both the concept of an economic IS was promoted and a social perspective was also included to justify the government's role in this sector. Finally, as in the other countries analysed, Info XXI covered measures of a regulatory nature as well as specific plans of actions and projects for promotion.

In short, it is clear that Spanish initiatives regarding IS policies were influenced until at least 1996, by Telefónica's traditionally privileged position with relation to public institutions. In the mid 1990s, a government action plan began to emerge. This plan was characterised by fragmentation and dispersion and centred on the promotion of business and industrial development. The chance to participate in sectorial decision-making was still restricted and this only began to open up partially at the end of the 1990s through various

*Table 10.5 Objectives for action on the IS in Spain*

| Lines of action | Priority action |
|---|---|
| Education | - Infrastructure and equipment for schools<br>- Educational portals on the Internet<br>- New training models through the use of ICT<br>- Training of teaching staff<br>- Promotion of education in Spanish especially focussed on South America |
| Creation of jobs | - Promotion of training for workers in the use of ICT<br>- Incentives for the purchase and maintenance of ITC equipment<br>- Incentives for telecommuting |
| Innovation | - Elaboration of experimental networks with a high communication capacity<br>- Simplification of regulations and economic incentives to facilitate innovation in small and medium-sized companies<br>- Encouragement of Spanish companies to participate in EU innovation programmes<br>- Programmes related to cable, television and computer applications infrastructures<br>- Creation of an observatory for industry in the information area |
| Promoting efficiency | - Introduce digital services to the Internet<br>- Guarantee a digital signature<br>- Train state employees in ICT<br>- Create an observatory for outstanding on-line services<br>- Promote B2B and B2C services<br>- Develop information systems for environmental issues |
| Social cohesion | - Introduce ITC to the area of justice<br>- Elaborate services procedure guidelines for citizen information<br>- ITC for the education of social sectors with problems<br>- ITC for the elderly<br>- Develop information systems for job hunting<br>- Telemedicine and communications networks for hospitals |
| Quality of life | - Programmes for secure communications<br>- Connect remote areas of population<br>- Promote public library networks<br>- Train library staff |

*Table 10.5 Continued*

| Lines of action | Priority action |
|---|---|
| | - Promote services in the area of tourism<br>- Publish 20000 books by Hispano-American authors on the Internet<br>- Improve museum catalogues and set up virtual exhibitions |
| Culture and exterior image | - Standardise and develop the Spanish language on the Internet<br>- International initiatives for the development of the Internet in Hispano-American countries<br>- Offer cultural and artistic services |

*Source*: Ministerio de Ciencia y Tecnologia (1999).

institutional mechanisms aimed at the participation of sectorial agents (Sancho 2000). Without a doubt, the influence of the European IS-promotional programmes played a fundamental role as a conditioning factor for the Spanish position: first, by acting as a stimulus for various actors through specific programmes, secondly, by encouraging institutional change through sectorial liberalisation and thirdly, the generation of isomorphism in sectorial policies by presenting a model of planning to follow concerning IS-promotion policies.

## FROM DIFFERENTIATION TOWARDS CONVERGENCE IN INFORMATION SOCIETY PROMOTION POLICIES

The four countries studied clearly show differing starting points as far as the development of their sectorial policymaking in the areas of telecommunications and IS politics was concerned. These transnational differences can be understood by considering how their respective traditions influenced the generation of policy-formulation processes. Table 10.6 summarises the main characteristics of sectorial governing and the different styles of interaction seen in the formulation process of IS policies by the four countries analysed. To this end, we have identified a series of variables in the role played by the different states in these policies, and we have summarised the most relevant factors previously analysed.

In the mid 1990s in some cases, and the late 1990s in others, different European countries promoted coordinated plans to promote the IS – more

*Table 10.6 Different forms of sectorial governing*

| | France | The United Kingdom | Germany | Spain |
|---|---|---|---|---|
| Role of the State | Authority | Arbiter | Mediator | Non-intervention |
| Dominant orientation | Look after national interest Economic perspective | Look after private interests Economic perspective | Incorporate conflictive interests of different groups Economic perspective | Protect dominant interest Economic perspective |
| Means of interaction | Management, control based on hierarchy | Competition and negotiation based on the establishment of winning coalitions | Negotiation and reconciliation to reach consensus | Client-based action |
| Dominant actors | Government actors | Government actors and a large number of groups or parties | Governmental actors and recognised functional associations | Dominant pressure group |
| Level of political action | Centralised and planned | Centralised based on the consideration of concrete issues | National or subnational depending on area | Centralised |
| Government attitude | Passive | Proactive | Passive | Highly passive |
| Moment of introduction of coordinated plans on IS | Mid–late 1990s | Mid 1990s | Mid–late 1990s | Late 1990s |

Own source.

sophisticated than their initial interventions in this area – and at the same time they extended their strategy to create participatory organisms in which the main sectorial agents of each national environment were widely represented.

The real impact of these plans, or of the participating institutions, was not the same in all countries, but in general terms it led to a common path which opened the way for a certain pluralism in the process of public decision making. This trend towards similitude, based on the transfer of policies, has not replaced the traditional form of intermediation of interests in each country but it has contributed to its transformation (Albert 1991; Soskice 1991; Milgrom and Roberts 1992). Moreover, the influence from Europe, which involved renewed and more ambitious initiatives from 1999 onwards, altered the role of the state actors, reinforcing the position of those actors who were more involved in overcoming resistances to the change of the dominant sectorial groups. As far as the state's relationship with agents in the sectorial network was concerned, this influence also transformed its role to the figure of partner, mediator and go-between (Kohler-Koch 1999).

The IS-promotion strategy of European institutions encouraged a reproduction of IS-policy formulation on a national scale. Working on principles of a complementary nature, the intention was to stimulate the development of national programmes to promote the IS. This was done by fostering pilot programmes to serve as an example for the different states given that the global nature of IS-related problems meant that the different countries faced similar challenges. An organised exchange of experiences promoted imitation and convergence in the development of policies. Hence, the 'need' to plan IS-related programmes in an integrated way was progressively accepted, leaving behind fragmented and dispersed actions by different departments. The strategic plans and the interministerial organs of coordination were a common answer to this challenge in the countries analysed. The *e*Europe initiative supposed a further step in the European strategy to coordinate the formulation of priorities for national action and action plans, by meeting political commitments laid down in an agreed schedule for action.

Technological change also brought about the reconfiguration of the positions and preferences of the agents present in the different national arenas (Thatcher 2000). The technological evolution facilitated the entry of new service providers and the readaptation of the former dominant operators who were faced with a new reality. However, their initial participation was poor due to the fact that their priorities were centred on the consolidation of their positions in the new global telecommunications market. In any case, once the rules of the game had been redefined, and the new positions of the group of actors consolidated, governments began to give shape to their new role as a stimulus in this new sectorial area, although there were differences in time and rhythm (Hayward 1995). What were the predominant characteristics of this new style of government regarding the IS? In Table10.7 we have summarised the main elements which were present in the majority of the countries examined.

*Table 10.7 Elements of convergence in national styles*

| Role of State | Activator |
|---|---|
| Dominant orientation | Coordinate interests by interrelating them<br>Economic, social and cultural perspective |
| Means of interaction | Multilateral negotiations to bring positions closer |
| Dominant actors | Governmental actors, supra- and sub-national, interest groups, users associations, trade unions, management |
| Level of political action | Functional, horizontal via specific agreements having effect at different levels of government |
| Government attitude | Proactive |
| Means of action | Planning: incorporation of initiatives into the framework of a global programme |

Own source.

The policymaking which to a certain extent characterised policies for the promotion of the IS present a group of particular characteristics. In the first place, the existence of a large number of organised subsystems, with difficulties to interact. Secondly, the transformation of the government's role towards the role of 'activator', facilitating negotiation structures to varying extents according to the areas in question and in which the different actors also participate according to the issue in question. Thirdly, the fact that it is not merely government agents who are capable of negotiation, but also private actors, which is why the state remains an important leader but no longer the only one. Finally, the government assumes as a basic function that it must provide a framework to reduce transactional costs and provide stability to self-regulation agreements. The government tends to be the actor who organises the area to facilitate the exchange and generation of agreements.

This study has brought us to the conclusion that though there are still certain distinctive characteristics in how IS-promotion policies are developed on a national scale, a certain politico-institutional convergence can be detected on three levels: first, in how the establishment process of public national agendas has changed under the influence of the European political agenda; secondly, in how interests are represented, with an encouragement of the opening up of national systems in which a more competitive type of representation has appeared as well as institutionalised mechanisms promoting participation; and finally, in the convergence of policy content by government agents and in the acceptation of the need for horizontally integrated planning and implementation, through systems of interdepartmental coordination reducing the fragmentation of public initiatives.

## REFERENCES


Alabau, A. (1998), *La UE y su política de telecomunicaciones*, Madrid: Fundación Airtel.

Albert, M. (1991), *Capitalisme contre capitalisme*, Paris: Seuil

Breton, T. (1993), *Les téléservices en France. Quels marchés pour les autoroutes de l'information?* Paris: La Documentation française.

CISI (1998), *Programme d'action gouvernemental 'Préparé l'entrée de la France dans la Société de l'information'*, Paris: Comité interministeriel Société de l'information.

Cohen, E. (1992), *Le Colbertisme 'High Tech',* Paris: Hachette.

Chevallier, J. (1996), 'La nouvelle réforme des télécommunications: ruptures et continuites', *Revue Française de Droit Administratif*, **12** (5), 909–51.

DiMaggio, P. and W. Powell (1991), *The New Institutionalism and Organization Theory*, Chicago: University of Chicago Press.

ESIS (2000), *Public Strategies for the Information Society in the Member States of the European Union*, DG Information Society, EU.

eMinister (2000), *UK on line Annual Report*, London: Crown copyright.

European Commission (1993), *White Paper on Growth, Competitiveness, and Employment: The Challenges and Ways Forward into the 21st Century*, Brussels, 5 December 1993, COM(93) 700.

European Commission (1994a), *Europe and the Global Information Society: Recommendations to the European Council and the European Commission*, Brussels, 26 May 1994.

European Commission (1994b), *Action plan concerning Europe's way to the information society*, Brussels, 19 July 1994, COM(94) 347.

European Commission (1996), *The Information Society: From Corfu to Dublin – the New Emerging Priorities*, Brussels, 24 July 1996, COM(96) 395.

European Commission (1999), *eEurope. An Information Society for all*, Brussels, COM(1999) 687final.

Evans, P., T. Skocpol and D. Rueschemeyer (1985), *Bringing the State Back In*, Cambridge: Cambridge University Press.

Gensollen, M. (1991), 'Les réformes institutionelles et réglamentaires des télécommunications en 1990', *Communications and Stratégies*, **3**, 17–34.

Hall, P. (1986), *Governing the Economy: The Politics of State Intervention in Britain and France*, Cambridge: Polity Press.

Hall, P. (1999), 'The Political Economy of Europe in an Era of Interdependence' in Herbert Kitschelt et al. (eds), *Continuity and Change in Contemporary Capitalism*, Cambridge: University Press.

Hayward, J. (1995), *Industrial Enterprise and European Integration*, Oxford: Oxford University Press.

Immergut, E.M. (1998), 'The theoretical core of the new institutionalism', *Politics and*

*Society*, **25** (1), 5–34.
Jones, E. (2002), *The record of global economical development*, Cheltenham: Edward Elgar.
Jordana, J. (1998), 'La Política de Telecomunicaciones en España: del Monopolio a la Transición al Mercado', in R. Gomà and J. Subirats (eds), *Políticas Públicas en España*, Barcelona: Ariel.
Kohler-Koch, B. (1999), 'The Evolution and Transformation of European Governance', in B. Kohler-Koch and R. Eising (eds), *The Transformation of Governance in the European Union*, London: Routledge.
Kubicek, H. (1997), 'Multimedia: Germany's Third Attempt to Move to an Information Society', in B. Kahin and E. Wilson (eds), *National Information Infrastructure Initiatives*, Cambridge: MIT Press.
MCyT – Ministerio de Ciencia y Tecnología (1999), *Plan de acción 'Info XXI': La Sociedad de la Información para todos*, Madrid: Ministerio de Ciencia y Tecnología.
Mény, Y., P. Muller and J.L. Quermonne (1996), *Adjusting Europe*, London: Routledge.
Milgrom, P. and J. Roberts (1992), *Economics, Organization and Management*, Englewood Cliffs, NJ: Prentice-Hall.
North, D. (1991), *Institutions, Institutional Change and Economic Performance*, Cambridge: Cambridge University Press.
Pierson, P. (2000), 'Increasing returns, path dependence, and the study of politics', *American Political Science Review*, **94** (2).
Sancho, D. (2000), 'Politics and institutional networks in Spanish telecommunications policy', *South European Society and Politics*, **5** (1), 25–53.
Scott, R. (1995), *Institutions and Organizations*, London: Sage.
Schneider V. and R. Werle (1991), 'Policy Networks in the German Telecommunications Domain', in B. Marin and R. Mayntz (eds), *Policy Networks. Empirical Evidence and Theoretical Considerations*, Frankfurt: Campus.
Soskice, D. (1991), 'The Institutional Infrastructure for International Competitiveness: A Comparative Analysis of the UK and Germany', in A. Atkinson and R. Brunetta (eds), *The Economics of the New Europe*, London: Macmillan.
Steinmo, S., K. Thelen and F. Longstreth (1992), *Structuring Politics*, Cambridge: Cambridge University Press.
Thatcher, M. (1999), *The Politics of Telecommunications*, Oxford: Oxford University Press.
Thatcher, M. (2000), 'Cross-national Linkages and Regulatory Reform in Europe: The Case of Telecommunications', Annual Meeting of the American Political Science Association, Washington, August–September.
Thelen, K. (1999), 'Historical Institutionalism in Comparative Politics', *The Annual Review of Political Science*, **2**, 363–404.
Théry, G. (1994), *Les Autoroutes de l'Information. Rapport au Premier Ministre*, Paris: La Documentation Française.
Van Waarden, F. (1992), 'Dimensions and types of policy networks', *European Journal of Political Research*, **21** (1), 29–52.
Vedel, T. (1997), 'Information Superhighway Policy in France: The End of High Tech Colbrertism?', in B. Kahin and E. Wilson (eds), *National Information Infrastructure Initiative*, Cambridge: MIT Press.
Zysman, J. (1984), *Governments, Markets, and Growth: Financial Systems and the Politics of Industrial Change*, Ithaca, NY: Cornell University Press.

# 11. The dilemmas of an inevitable relationship: democratic innovation and the information and communication technology

**Joan Subirats**

## INTRODUCTION

In a conference on the new information society, the rector of the Open University, John Daniel, said 'Ladies and gentlemen, the new technologies are the answer. What was the question?'. The phrase is a good way of expressing the great expectations generated in many different areas of our lives by the prospect of the application of ICT (information and communication technology), but at the same time the prevailing disconcertion over their possible uses and impacts. The remark recalls the comment made by one of the fathers of wireless communication, Marconi, when a collaborator, flustered by the discovery, said, 'We can talk with Florida', to which Marconi responded: 'But do we have anything to say to the people in Florida?'. Similarly, we can say that not a day goes by that we do not meet someone filled with enthusiasm for the possibilities opened by new technologies in the field of democracy and the functioning of the political system. But we should first think about the problems facing us today and in the potential and real uses of these ICTs. The present work aims to first point up the deficiencies of the current functioning of European democratic systems, and to later explore to what extent ICT can contribute to processes of innovation and improvement.

It has been said that modernity can be defined politically by democratic institutions and socially and culturally by the civilization of technology (Barber 1998). But the relations between these two components are not free of ambiguities. While some, like Jean-Jacques Rousseau, have always been hesitant about the effects scientific progress would have on privacy and on equality in political relations, others such as Karl Popper or Bertrand Russell understood that there was a close relation between the spirit of science and the success of democratic institutions. But what is ever more present is concern about how to relate the proliferation of ICT with the processes and values of democracy (Hoff et al. 2000; Bellamy and Taylor 1998). Simplifying somewhat, we could say that there are at least three interesting (and not necessarily exclusive) possibilities for ICT in relation to political democracy. They could aggravate the problems parliamentary democracy now presents, help to solve or overcome these problems, or create new problems they are not capable of resolving.

Some are of the opinion that if first-generation media (radio, television) have made politics into something almost virtual (Holmes 1997), this will be enormously strengthened in second-generation media (interactive electronic networks) (Poster 1995), leading to a sort of apotheosis of sharply directorial political forms. To complete this pessimistic scenario, it is predicted that ICT will allow exhaustive control of data and sophisticated political marketing, and will offer great possibilities for manipulating information, with little margin for generating change. Other authors consider that ICT could favour easier access by the citizenry to the activities of the government, transforming it into a more controllable entity with fewer possibilities of exercising hierarchical control without adequate checks and balances (Dutton, 1999). At the same time, the new forms of communication among citizens, parliaments and governments may come to balance or compensate for the current power of the media, pressure groups and parties, who shape the political agenda and 'format' the issues of the system. This would be a hopeful vision of democratizing and power-balancing effects in relation to institutions and elites that are now rather closed to society.

But in the sphere that interests us here, we must note that the modus operandi of ICT and that of the political system do not seem to coincide overmuch. While democracy leads us to a scenario of deliberation, prudence and parsimonious interaction, with a great investment of time, the technological revolution is characterized by the speed it imparts to everything it touches. While the digital form of reasoning is very simple, binary, always seeking a choice between A and B, between Yes and No, political reasoning seeks to delve into complexity, bringing to light nuances and various ways to see the problem. Before the dilemma of A or B, it can look for such answers as 'both', 'neither', 'these are not answers to the problem', or even 'this is not the problem'.

We should therefore treat with a certain caution the topic of the incorporation of ICT into the field of democratic institutions and their forms and procedural rules, since the starting points are quite different. We have no reason to cleave to a certain technological determinism that tells us it is a waste of time to worry about whether use of ICT in democratic systems of government is appropriate or not, since it is simply inevitable (Grossman 1995). We are interested in analysing the real difference that might be generated by the use of ICT on what were considered problems or deficiencies of democratic systems, in order to find useful connections between the two worlds, from positions that are not free of normativism, since we are interested in what reinforces democracy and broadens its spaces of civil participation. And we will do so trying to carry the debate into the European context of parliamentary democracies, with relatively well organized, centralized parties, with a strong presence in intermediation of interests and with well established and notably hierarchical administrations.

## DEFICIENCIES IN THE FUNCTIONING OF DEMOCRACY?

We find ourselves at a curious moment. Never in the history of humanity has the complexity of rules and mechanisms of plural representation, participation and control that historically have made up the concept of democracy been so widespread. From this point of view, we would say that democracy seems to be living through halcyon days all over the world. Nonetheless, there is still a growing dissatisfaction with how it works. The foundation of this criticism can be found in what Bobbio (1984) called 'unkept promises'. But it is also evident that democratic decision-making mechanisms show little capacity for resolving problems. Formalism, distance between representatives and the represented, opacity, and asymmetry in theoretically equal resources are some of the criticisms in political debate which are directed at the current functioning of our democratic systems.

In recent years a strong base of empirical evidence has been gathered for this group of perceptions, which some have defined as a phenomenon of disaffection of the citizens towards the political players and institutions of each country (Norris 1999; Newton and Norris 2000). It is not so much a distancing from democracy as a system of government (this being an aspect in which a reduction of legitimacy is not seen, just the opposite), but a marked decline in public confidence in how representative institutions operate and perform. There are no signs of preference for non-democratic or authoritarian governmental alternatives, but it is noted that public attitudes towards parties, parliaments and governments express more and more mistrust.[1]

This tendency may be considered significant, since we are not talking about changes in popular confidence in any governments or parties in particular but in the representative institutions that have characterized the model of political governance in the contemporary history of the Western world. What could explain this tendency? Is it, as has been suggested, simple disaffection or disagreement with how the modern world is evolving? Is it a response to the perceptible inability of public powers to control an economy ever more heedless of borders and regulations? Is it a product of the growing individualization of lifestyles that weakens social bonds and community participation, and therefore decreases confidence in everything that representative institutions of collective action are? Or is it simply a loss of credibility and recognition of the way each government operates and the concrete actions it takes, its real ability to resolve the problems posed by living together in society?[2]

We would therefore have a scenario in which the democratic system appears to be enjoying good health, since its legitimacy has increased everywhere, while the alternatives that historically have been set in motion have ended in resounding failures. It has even been argued that the criticisms of how it really functions from country to country are part and parcel of the mechanism of continuous perfecting that democracy sets up. According to this vision, there is at bottom no problem. The thing to do is to go on improving what exists without calling into doubt its essential parameters: representative power chosen in competitive elections among parties, participation and channels of controlling legitimately constituted power. Yet, as we have mentioned, growing dissatisfaction with the 'quality' of this democracy is observed.

The questions connected with these observations immediately arise. Does disaffection towards democratic institutions produce a decline in the mechanisms of conventional participation? Or are these mechanisms what do not satisfy citizens' expectations, leading them to use them less and less and to mistrust representative institutions? Or is it both things at once? There is abundant literature on the subject, which we will not enter into here.[3] But in general there are problems of dissatisfaction with the systems of selection of the representative elites; excessive ritualism in the channels of representation; the quasimonopolistic position of political parties in the scenario of political participation (facing which the voiceless can only walk away); and the difficulty of seeing reflected in electoral platforms the issues that might be of more direct interest than the debate over who the next prime minister will be, or which political force will gain a sufficient majority to form a government.

Universal suffrage has not brought us to the full realization of the ideal of popular sovereignty but to the development of more sophisticated techniques through which the elites of the parties and the administrative bureaucracies have increased their capacity to control the citizenry. It would then seem that the mixture of constitutionalism and democracy has transformed parliamentary institutions more into instruments of government than channels of representation and popular expression. If we add to this the confluence of interests and organizations brought about by the consolidation of Keynesian welfare options and the use of mass media, we can say that space for a public sphere of debate and opinion, truly autonomous from the state apparatus, has been disappearing. Our democracy, apathetic and alienated, has become more 'managerial' than anything else (Luadon 1977).

## WHAT IS TO BE DONE?

The alternatives under this type of diagnosis are unclear. If one of the principal concerns is democratic regimes' lack of performance, one might think of strengthening their performance by authoritarian options following the logic of 'less participation, more efficacy'. Increasing the 'decision' capacities of the system at the cost of reducing the capacity of control and citizen action ('delegative democracy' in O'Donnell's expression), or trying to depoliticize the system through trusting in 'captains of industry' and figures who make 'common sense' their ideological banner (Perot, Berlusconi, Fujimori), and others who present themselves as 'cleaners' of the rot of 'politics as usual' (Chávez). Less traumatically for the values and rules of democracy, the idea has been taking hold that it should be isolated from institutionalized politics in certain spheres of public action considered 'sensitive matters'. The solution would be to create independent authorities, agencies and organisms to make legitimate their actions and capacity to make decisions, not according to the principles of popular representation but according to their capacity to 'solve', based on professional and technical criteria of authority and representativeness (and therefore legitimacy). It is in this line that independent authorities have been appearing in securities trading, electrical regulation, the environment, nuclear power, control of competition, and sports discipline, not to mention the increasingly important influence and independence of the authorities of the central banks (Majone 1996).

We do not believe these alternatives are in the line of combining reinforcement of democracy with increased capacity of representation and credibility of democratic institutions. In a meliorist line attempts have been made to find new formulae in the traditional systems of representation and participation. Thus work has been done on improving the forms of candidate selection, whether through primaries, open list systems or reforms of the electoral systems (with a combination of proportional and majority formulae), which increase the capacity of choice and involvement of the electorate in the selection of candidates and accentuate the responsibility of the representative to the citizenry. Other formulae on which more emphasis has been placed recently have been those referring to improvement of communication channels between institutions and citizens and between parties and citizens. Initiatives to offer windows of institutional information from parliaments and governments at all levels continue to proliferate. At the same time, these institutions and parties use surveys and other instruments for measuring public opinion to compensate for lack of feedback on their policies and proposals between elections.

At the essentially local level, there has been enormous development of the participation of very diverse entities and associations, with essentially sectorial bases (seniors, youth, women, the environment, sports and so on), but also territorial ones (neighborhood, district and so on). It seems undeniable that the large expansion of public administrations' areas of action has been generating the presence of more and more players in debate over policy formulation and implementation and has also caused the loss of the hierarchical and *super partes* role that characterized their traditional action. Thus, it is not strange that in many of the policies pursued by governments there has been a tendency to create specific spaces for encounters and information exchange between institutions and entities. In general, these are councils or fora in which policies are agreed on, problems are anticipated and pacts are reached on implementation or even co-management, functioning with more or less formalized rules.

Little by little we have also been seeking or recovering formulae of direct participation of the citizenry in public decisions. The most traditional mechanisms of direct democracy, such as referenda or popular legislative initiatives, have been complemented with other more complex formulae of citizen involvement in public decisions such as 'citizen councils'. It seems clear that in recent years the use of this type of participatory formulae has notably increased. In the case of referenda, we have examples at the nation-state level (in France and Denmark on questions of European integration, or the habitual ones in Italy on legislative abrogation), and they also proliferate on the local scale when especially significant conflicts or decisions considered strategic are faced. Experimentation with involvement in new ways of participation and popular consultation is also increasingly frequent, especially on the local scale (citizen councils in the Basque Country and Catalonia, fora in Great Britain, participatory budgets in Latin America, deliberative mechanisms in the United States, participatory formulae linked to Agendas 21, and so on) (see Font 2001, endnote 9). The reasons that explain this proliferation of citizen involvement and the dissemination of direct participatory experiences, whether in a classic or an innovative format, are linked to the deficiencies of the traditional ways of participation foreseen in representative democracy, especially their inability to link the global legitimacy obtained in electoral processes with the legitimacy necessary in the day-to-day, facing specific issues, freighted with meaning, for which reason extra legitimacy is sought in these new participatory forms.

## THE COSTS AND PROBLEMS OF PARTICIPATION

Skepticism towards these new alternatives, or towards the search for a more lively democracy and the citizenry's involvement in decision-making processes, is very widespread among the political elite. The reasons alleged are very diverse. Some allude to the costs of time and resources entailed by these processes, while others refer to the dangers of 'capture' by special interests. It is usually mentioned how all this erodes the indispensable legitimacy of parties and institutions for good democratic praxis, and also mentioned is the lack of 'added value' (because of the unpreparedness of citizens for the problems posed) that many of these mechanisms end up producing. Connected with all this is the widely held and well founded opinion that we cannot confuse these 10 per cent who are more less intensely interested, in a manner inconsistent with the political decision-making process, with the rest of the population, who only in certain circumstances enter a world they consider foreign and the province of specialists. In this context, it is said, we wind up confusing the citizenry with a very restricted part of the population, that which organizes, mobilizes, and says it represents the rest.

The political elite, while publicly deploring this lack of participatory enthusiasm, or declaring their concern over the increase of abstention in elections, later do not show themselves especially keen to support non-conventional openings for participation (popular legislative initiatives, autonomous referenda and so on), nor to accept the legitimacy or binding force of more novel forms of citizen participation in public decision-making processes. As Flores d'Arcais has said, a sort of vicious circle of shirked responsibilities is created: citizens experience the political system as foreign, turning their backs on it (contrast with this the vitality of new social movements or campaigns based on a single issue), getting what little they can out of it, and globally criticizing something in which they do not feel involved. While politicians say they are hurt by citizens' lack of understanding and complain publicly of the lack of participatory life, they take advantage of a conception of politics that is more and more a thing for initiates and professionals.

The problem is knowing whether, in this context, the democratic system requires or can do without greater and more extensive doses of popular participation, and knowing what mechanisms can contribute to this without overloading (with time and transaction costs) the citizenry's already tired shoulders. We have taken a cursory look at the difficulty and skepticism that surround this issue. The ever greater complexity of the decisions in the public sphere and the habitual inconsistency between citizens' opinions (for example, simultaneously asking for increased social services and reduced taxes) offer new handles for old elitist conceptions. We think, however, that it is more and more difficult to maintain positions of this type, whether because of the enormous diffusion of information and access to education that have come about in many countries in the past few decades, or because of the sophistication in scientific progress that leaves us with ever fewer unequivocal responses from the technical point of view on how to solve problems.[4] In many of these criticisms of more direct forms of citizen participation lie skepticism and suspicion about the very bases of democracy (Budge 1993).

Certainly those of us who think that we should advance in looking for and experimenting with new mechanisms of participation, as a way of improving the quality of democracy and its capacity to resolve the problems generated by living together, should be able to demonstrate that participation and efficiency are not contradictory concepts but are increasingly complementary concepts, and to seek out and experiment with instruments and mechanisms of participation that avoid or at least reduce the existing risks and minimize the problems noted.

As for the presumed complementarity of participation and efficiency, we would like to point out that increasingly often we face problems that are more global and interconnected, and therefore more difficult to segment, define, and approach from the specializations we have been constructing. In such contexts, we cannot fall into the error of confusing technical feasibility with social feasibility, and we will have to work in both directions to address problems on which there is often no consensus, not even on whether there is a problem and what kind of a problem it is. Many of the difficult decisions to be made, which affect deeply rooted social interests, can reach important consensuses in the technical sphere, but they will find it hard to advance if debate is not opened and there is discussion and comparison of costs and benefits, alternatives, and solutions with the whole of society; since people will be able increasingly to accept and share decisions that even affect some of their interests negatively if they consider legitimate the route by which a decision was reached. From this point of view, efficiency and participation are not contradictory but absolutely complementary, and will become more and more inseparable.

How is the complexity of public decisions to be shared with as many citizens as possible? We do not pretend to give a single response to such a complex issue. We believe that the skepticism and danger that surround the world of participation have to be analysed and treated specifically, and can be better or worse resolved according to the participatory mechanism used. There are no universal recipes or ad hoc solutions. We must clarify the dilemmas posed, the limitations that exist and the conditioning factors that make up the case, determine who the most affected parties are, and collaborate with them in trying to find the best participatory formula that broadens the debate and gives it a way out. Here, as we are trying to show in this work, the use of information and communication technologies can be very significant.

## THE ROLE OF ICT BEFORE THE PROBLEMS OF DEMOCRACY: THE VARIOUS STRATEGIES

It is obvious that the possibilities of using ICT are manifold, but it is not the same to work in them from the internal logic of the current system of representative democracy, from the prospect of constructing, with the aid of the new technologies, the old ideal of direct democracy, or trying to imagine new forms of articulation and collective governance.

We can operationalize the question attempting to relate in Table 11.1 the alternatives that relate the use of ICT with the processes of democratic innovation. A first broad option would be to try to apply ICT in the more specific field of policies and their management or in the field of polity and relations between institutions and the citizenry. We have a second broad criterion of distinction if we consider only processes of improvement and innovation within the current constitutional and political framework characteristic of modern European parliamentary democracies, or if we are willing, in a democratic framework, to explore alternative ways of making decisions, thinking, and managing in policies that incorporate the citizenry more directly and accept the pluralism inherent in an open conception of collective responsibilities and public spaces. Crossing the criteria, we have four political strategies or discourses on how to relate ICT and democratic systems and their processes of decision and management.

We will briefly explore each of the alternatives furnished by the table, understanding them not as closed models but as discourses or strategies, sometimes simultaneous, developed in the intersection between ICT and the way democratic systems operate.

## The Consumerist Option

This strategy's starting point is situated in the liberal universe, with absolutely no intention of calling into question the way constitutional and parliamentary democracy operates, with its mechanisms of participation centred essentially on parties and elections. According to this vision, what is failing are the mechanisms of information at the citizenry's disposition, so that they can exercise their possibilities of choice more completely and efficaciously and have more power in their relations with the public bureaucracies. The greater strength or influence of the people would come not so much from their greater capacity for involvement or letting their voice be heard in processes, as from their greater capacity to choose, to change providers, and to express their preferences clearly. Somehow it is understood that the process of collective consumption of resources derived from public policies has no reason to be connected with 'high politics', with values, and is expressed only in efficacy and capacity to satisfy citizens' needs.

How can ICT serve these objectives? It seems clear that the demand for more and better information jibes well with the most evident potential of ICT. There are many varied examples of how ICT has improved relations between

*Table 11.1 Processes of democratic innovation and use of information and communication technologies*

| | | Use of Information and Communication Technology | |
|---|---|---|---|
| | | Policy | Polity |
| Degree of democratic innovation and acceptance of participatory and pluralistic processes | Low | 1<br>consumerist mechanisms | 2<br>changes in democratic elitism |
| | High | 3<br>pluralist networks provision of services | 4<br>processes of direct democracy |

citizens and administrations, and abundant literature that tries to analyse and propose improvements in this area. Not a day goes by that we do not hear of new advances in administration–citizen interfaces that allow or will allow online resolution of what are now complex and costly procedures of obtaining permits, renewing documents, settling taxes or getting information. The advances in the security of these processes through the acceptance of electronic signatures and the growing coordination among different levels of administration are a good example of this. In similar fashion, one observes ceaseless efforts by public entities or services to put ample information online for citizens on the services they have access to or the rights they can exercise, as well as explicit presentations of who is responsible for what, and how to locate specific employees or supervisors in each process or service.

The values that implicitly or explicitly govern these processes of change and the use of ICT are those of economy, efficiency and efficacy, which served to put in motion the processes of administrative modernization of the 1980s and 1990s ('new public management'). New public managers who wished to implement in public administrations systems of management closer to those of the private sector and politicians who sought renewed forms of legitimization in an improvement of the administrations' capacity to provide service, and the growing accessibility and transformative potential of ICT coincided in time and in their expectations. The strategies of 'citizen charts' and 'total quality' are examples of this. Furthermore, the dynamics of 'flattening' structures and decentralizing management, seeking closeness and more personalized service, found in the new information systems the necessary levers for avoiding misgovernment and buck-passing, through contractual systems and establishment of management guidelines and ad hoc organizational charts. ICT seem to offer the realization of a long-sought dream: maximum decentralization without abuse of discretion or loss of control or responsibility. In this way, we are probably witnessing the transformation of many European bureaucracies into 'infocracies'.[5]

However, the problem is that these improvements in the method of managing policies and in communication channels between the citizenry and public administrations not only do not offer new solutions to the problems of democratic disaffection but introduce certain problems in handling the large flow of information that ICTs allow us to store and process with extraordinary ease. It seems clear that we are talking about processes that are to some extent depoliticized, in which the reason for the services or to whom they are directed are not questioned or evaluated, only the best way to provide them. Nor is it a matter of redefining policies or questioning the design of their implementation. We could thus ask ourselves (obviously without disdaining the increases in effectiveness and efficiency that are achieved), whether with these new forms that incorporate ICT into the provision of public services we are really responding to the problems of democratic disaffection mentioned at the beginning of these reflections (Raab 1998).

Attention has also been drawn to the perverse effects that may be produced by large volumes of information about persons and their behaviour, preferences and habits accumulated by administrations through the use of ICTs. Besides processing large quantities of administrative data, the growing use of video surveillance with the new programmes for detecting suspicious persons, and so on, although able to improve the efficacy of security policies, pose problems of the potential violation of the privacy of certain information. A situation is being caused in which the administrations' growing capacity to give service and the increased personalization of that service are inevitably accompanied by a large volume of information on these citizens in the hands of the administrations.

This type of link between processes of innovation via ICT, very much linked to policies and processes of services, will definitely not change in the slightest the technocratic and top-down logic characteristic of well established democratic systems in the second half of the twentieth century. Rather than strengthening the presence and participation of the citizenry in collective affairs, the use of ICT could end up reinforcing the control and authority of institutional elites.

## The Improvement of Representative and Elitist Democracy

We have commented that various ways have been sought to improve communications between democratic political institutions and the citizenry. It would not be so much a matter in this case of improving efficacy in the provision of services, in the outcomes of the system, as of strengthening the legitimacy of government institutions, trying to avoid the sensation of detachment and to reduce the perception of distance between those who decide and the ones they say they represent.

We are not talking about a scenario occupied only by professional politicians. The webs of interests and players formed around politics have been creating a demo-elitist conglomerate basically concerned with flows of information and influence between voters and representatives, between representative institutions and government, between government and external elites, and between elites and interest groups.

It is in this scenario that attempts to apply ICTs in various spheres of parliamentary democracies have been made. These initiatives have been concentrated on such questions as improvement of the internal functioning of parliaments, executives and administrations; better informing the citizenry about parliamentary and governmental activity; or improving and expanding the possibilities for interaction between parliaments, governments and citizens. In Europe, the examples are significant, within individual countries and in the institutions of European Union.[6] We do not wish to nor could we review here the multitude of initiatives of this type that are taking place in Europe. We will limit ourselves to covering their principal characteristics and establishing certain critical elements that allow us to fit them into our analytical scheme.

In the relationship between parties and electors, numerous initiatives have been implemented for improving channels of information with party activists and contact with sympathizers and voters using ICT. Besides the usual electronic newsletters, there have also been interesting experiences in the systems of selecting candidates (as in the Arizona primaries, where Democratic voters could exercise their right over the Internet, which has served as an example for other initiatives), of debate over programme alternatives, and online advocacy, with the presence of groups and individuals who express their interests through the network.

Governments and parliaments have undertaken many projects for using the potential of ICT essentially for facilitating the citizenry's access to institutional information. Through institutional websites, citizens' requests or complaints can almost always reach the government, or in the case of a parliament, proposals of individuals or groups, so that they can be channelled by the parliamentary groups who deem it advisable.[7]

In general, it may be said that the parties and institutions that have taken up ICT have done so without overly predetermined strategies. There are substantial reasons to highlight an organization or institution's symbolic values, and there is also a desire to show that it is up-to-date and modern. The flow of information is usually one-way, and even when the possibility of two-way flow exists, control of the medium and the decision on whether it is opportune to take outside opinions into account fall to the party apparatus rather than the directors of the institution. In this case it is not a question of giving more options to citizens–consumers, but of generating consensus towards the organization, or facilitating the work of advocacy or lobbying from the outside, but always understanding that there are 'experts' in the institution who will decide what should be borne in mind, what should be accepted and what not.

The dominant logic, not so much by design as a result, has been that of trying to use ICTs as a mechanism to allow greater adaptability of the political system to a shifting environment, without a change in the functional paradigm. The types of applications arising from the new ICT (websites, electronic newsletters, mailing lists, information systems, small consultations, electronic voting, and so on) have been devoted to relegitimizing and reorienting political and government institutions, through sophisticated methods of information management, segmentation of the public, and marketing and political communication.

We could definitively say that the type of instruments in the service of objectives such as those described contribute to reinforce the most elitist aspects of the representative democratic system (strengthening the capacity to process and control information flows, becoming nodes of resources and information, strengthening horizontal and vertical interrelations, with non-public players and with other political institutions and organisms and so on), while the more strictly democratizing aspects of the system (ability to respond and to account for themselves, transparency, channels of citizen involvement, and so on) remain in the background. Once again we wish to emphasize that we should go beyond the use (as gadgets) of ICT in democratic systems, and before speculating about what procedural, electoral, parliamentary or control aspect we can use these new technologies in, think about what conception of democracy we are putting them in the service of (Barber, 1998).

We could say that in the two strategies of using ICT we have mentioned, consumerist and elitist-democratic, there is no desire to go beyond a conception of democracy centred on procedural rules and a very strict vision of the principle of representation, without much willingness to experiment with forms of relation between elites and citizenry that would mean altering traditional hierarchical positions.

The two strategies we will now analyse in a necessarily schematic manner relate to ICT from a different conception. Here it is not a matter of improving relations and communication between representative elites and the citizenry. Nor is there a concern much centred on improvement of the capacity to provide services or on expansion of choice for consumers/citizens. In the two strategies we will analyse lies concern for quality of participation and capacity of involvement of people in collective affairs at the micro political level as well as the macro. The starting hypothesis is that of an active citizenry, involved in collective affairs not only as a necessary way to defend their interests, but also as a way of understanding democracy, a relational and participatory democracy.

## The Fabric of Civil Society

One of the most significant characteristics of the new societies in which ICT is gaining ground and developing is the growing opening and existence of spaces of autonomy and new relational networks, where plural communities flourish which make difference, their micro- or macro-identities, their point of reference. The explosion of communication that has come with ICT has facilitated and now facilitates this continual emergence, and allows a reconstruction of politics from parameters different from the usual ones.

We are witnessing the birth of a society in which relationship forms an intrinsic part of communication, and is not a mere result thereof, or a communicative subproduct. The two key elements are the growing subjectivity of the players and the great ease of communication provided by ICT. In this context, there is a great demand for autonomy which goes beyond the traditional freedom-control scheme of modern society (Donati 2000), alternative markets emerge, new social networks and groupings appear, and new cultures emerge that make difference their added value. In the traditional perspective (which covered the strategies examined above), public institutions started from a concept of freedom very much bound up with the freedom to vote, while control was related to obeying laws that emanated from the people's will and were expressed through the representative mechanism. In the new social context we are describing, freedom is based on an idea of reciprocal exchange, while control is entrusted to the rules of associative exchange themselves. These two spheres, state and social, interact with the spheres of the market and the family and other informal networks, generating multiple possibilities of relationship and communication.

In this context, ICT is simultaneously one of the fundamental factors with which to explain this new reality and the natural framework allowing its development, autonomy and constant possibilities for innovation and articulation. Thanks to ICT it is possible to begin to speak of reticular pluralism and the promotion of social autonomy able to generate inclusion and cohesion outside means of uniformity and the abstract rights of citizenship. The welfare mix is not, in this framework, an instrumental response to problems of sustainability of welfare policies, or a simple organizational adaptation to better implement citizenship on a state or public–institutional basis. Rather, a specific form of social citizenship is emerging that finds its values in the associative and civil fabric being woven, a communitarian citizenry, territorialized or not, which has great potential and advantages to develop in the ever better established framework of the communication society.

Politics is becoming more diffuse, acquiring different characteristics in each sphere, and can no longer be considered a state monopoly or the private preserve of public organisms. Political institutions no longer occupy the centre or vertex of the conditions of citizenship and welfare but are increasingly founded on relational goods. It is precisely this autonomous and relational aspect that characterizes this new social fabric. And these same characteristics are those that, at the same time, give it its fragmentary character, of multiplication of isolated groups, in which it can be difficult to articulate or recognize a 'society' as such. In this fragmentation, full of potential and possibilities, it may be difficult to reconcile pluralism with justice, diversity with belonging, and democracy with difference (Bellamy 2000). Furthermore, it should be remembered that the weight of public and commercial organizations on the network is very significant, and generates new hierarchies. In spite of this, the civil and associational reality and weave grows ceaselessly in the shadow of ICT, creating new real and virtual communities, developing new identities, new spaces and public spheres, and increasing political reflection and new social autonomies (Poster 1997; Burbach 2001; Webster 2001). What does all this have to do with democracy and its dilemmas? It is still somewhat early to draw too many conclusions, but it seems indubitable that new forms of 'cyberdemocracy' are taking shape.

## Is Direct Democracy a New Alternative?

Another of the possible strategies in the use of ICT before the current dilemmas of democracy is recovering the old ideal of direct democracy. This is not the time or place to survey democracy and its historical traditions (Bobbio 1990), but perhaps it should be remembered that throughout the nineteenth century, discussion of democracy, from the liberal conception of the state, developed principally from Constant's famous discourse on the freedom of ancient peoples and that of modern peoples. The former, understood as direct participation in public decisions and in the formation of laws through the political body expressed by the assembly of citizens, is understood as not only no longer possible due to expansion of the *demos*, but also perhaps even counterproductive. The freedom of modern peoples implies the recognition of fundamental political rights, with political participation understood as one more political freedom, manifested in the rights of free expression, assembly, and organization to influence a country's politics, as well as the rights to elect their institutional representatives and to be elected as such. Against Rousseau, de Tocqueville and Mill defended the idea that the only form compatible with the liberal state is representative and parliamentary democracy. The so-called democratization of the state, though it expanded the right to vote to more and more social sectors and multiplied representative organs, did not imply any essential modification of this liberal and representative conception of democracy.

Representative democracy has always been defended as a 'viable' (Mill) and 'efficient' (Dahl) alternative to direct democracy or democracy by assembly. The fundamental reasons adduced are, as we know, the size of the population called to gather and participate and the nature of the problems to be dealt with, which go beyond what small units of population can take on. In spite of this, it is recognized that representative democracy has its 'dark side' (Dahl 1998), a price to pay: the enormous discretionary power on very significant decisions that citizens delegate to their representatives. We know that the representative elite must move within the institutional and procedural limits proper to democratic regimes, but we also know that these limits are usually wide, and as the mechanisms of control and popular participation are not very robust or constant, the fact is that the elite's latitude to interpret its mandate of representation, even in decisions of strategic content or great significance, is quite notorious. Therefore once the principle of representation is accepted, the emphasis is on establishing the necessary checks and balances to control this latitude as much as possible and to fix periodic renewal of confidence and clarification of responsibilities through elections.

What changes can the appearance of ICT produce in this scenario? While it is still true that all the citizens of each country cannot meet face to face, it is now possible for them to communicate at a distance through the networks offered by ICT. Therefore, with all the necessary caution, and conscious that the forms of deliberation in an assembly are different from those that take place by telephone or in a virtual forum, one may at least think about at what point we are beginning to see the conditions to advance towards forms of electronic democracy in which it is possible to approach the old ideals of Rousseau without the stumbling block of the size of the *demos*, and seeking efficiency in decision-making.

But what direct democracy are we talking about? We do not think it necessary to insist on the problems generated by a conception of direct democracy by referendum, based on instant decision-making, without deliberative or institutional mediation. In a provocative work, the magistrate of the Italian Constitutional Court, Gustavo Zagrebelsky (1995), points out the discrepancy between the deliberative precepts of democracy, and the haste, not free of demagoguery, surrounding referenda of the 'Barrabas or Christ' type. The extensive literature on deliberative democracy (Elster 1998; Nino

1996; Bohman 1996) shows the extreme importance deliberative and participatory processes have in a full conception of what a liberal democracy is. Following Habermas, it is said the decisions in a democracy take on value and meaning more on the basis of the transformation that follows deliberation than from the simple aggregation of preferences. All incorporation of ICT into public decision-making processes should therefore bear in mind this profoundly deliberative character of democracy; otherwise these decisions could be notably inconsistent among themselves, or too affected by passing emotional situations. We should make it possible or imaginable to use the potential for communication and collective decision-making presented by ICT, already tested in private or organizational contexts,[8] without losing deliberative capacity and quality throughout the new decision-making process inspired by an approach to the values of a direct democracy that has always been seen as theoretically preferable, but not feasible.

If we combine the potential of ICT to advance towards previously unexplored forms of direct democracy with the need for mechanisms that assure deliberation and channel opinions and debates towards pragmatic and efficient ways of making decisions, we should rethink our current democratic institutions. Parliaments, governments and parties are today central elements in the democratic system. From our point of view, it is the political parties who now play the key role of mediation and control between the population and the government - with the constant amplifying collaboration of the communications media - and who supply the content and are the protagonists of parliaments.

From these premises one can imagine a system (Budge 1993) in which the government would be elected through mechanisms similar to those now in place, a system in which the decisions now made by a parliament and others considered significant enough would be subjected to direct referenda by all the citizenry with the right to vote, using those instruments offered by ICT and its future developments. These decisions would be concentrated on certain dates, and public debate would be held in the previous periods, animated by political parties who should orient their functions toward 'brokerage' and articulation of interests and alternatives, backing off their current emphasis on occupying institutional spaces. Thus we are sketching a system in which direct voting would not take place without mediation or deliberation. We are therefore not talking about a simple plebiscitary democracy. Direct voting would have the indispensable mediation of parties, configuring a pragmatic option that would allow alliances with the current leaders of processes of intermediation and representation of the people's will.

It is important to bear in mind that formerly existing institutions have tended to use and model ICTs as mechanisms for reinforcing their positions of power. It is thus not surprising that political and democratic institutions have sought to apply ICT to their routines without breaking previous paradigms of communication and power. In this strategy, there is a recomposition of the prevailing correlation of forces, with an indispensable relocation of political parties as a key element of continuity between one situation and the other.

Now it is obvious that political parties should change significantly their current modus operandi. Their work would become less sure, and it would probably be necessary for them to substantially modify their functions and the type of recruitment they now engage in. Parties are now organisms or entities which are relatively closed and very much caught up in the occupation of institutional spaces, their predominant vision centred on the presence in the media of their leaders, who constantly communicate messages to party members, voters, sympathizers and the citizenry in general. The kitchen work is done with little transparency, centred on the elites, the political cadres and the organization, together with the interests channelled or represented. In a scenario such as the one we were sketching, parties should network much more, with more flexible organization, with an emphasis similar to the current one on the communications media, but with a much greater capacity to articulate interests and opinion on the ground. The role of ideas, of the capacity to convince the immediate social network would be essential, and the role of party discipline and the organized activists would be reduced.

It seems clear that in this strategy, in which ICT would play a central role in the configuration of a democratic system based on the direct vote of the citizenry without the intermediation of traditional representative institutions, there are significant problems. One of the foremost would be the role of parliaments in this new scenario, although some already speak of postparliamentary democracy (Holmes 1997; Tsagarousianou et al. 1998). But if we refer more concretely to the problems that can crop up in the implementation in the proposals for direct democracy we have reviewed, some of the most significant are the lack of continuity and defined strategy in the opinion of the citizenry, the lack of information and sufficient debate, without assumption of responsibilities for the effects of the decisions made, the danger of lack of participation that would permit control of the vote in certain decisions by minorities with very definite interests, excessive complexity in the policies or decisions to be made, and problems deriving from the very use of ICTs, their control, guarantees, and so on.

The point that alludes to the citizenry's lack of preparation to confront the complexity of the issues that feed legislative debates is probably the most telling. Schumpeter ([1942] 1987) and Sartori (1987) have stated that the citizenry does not have enough interest to follow debates closely or to get involved in topics not very connected to their most immediate interests. They also argue that the technification of many of the debates on alternatives to concrete problems distances the citizenry from their possible involvement in decisions, which could only affect the quality of the result negatively. This argument seems difficult to maintain in moments when although the unequivocacy of technical responses is ever more in doubt, one hears more talk about the social construction of risk or about technology assessment, alluding to the need to incorporate lay opinions in questions of significant technical complexity but which are difficult to resolve without the visions of non-experts (López Cerezo and Luján 2000; Mironesco 1997). One is left thinking that arguments against direct democracy based on citizens' lack of sufficient education for making decisions could serve just as well for arguing against democracy itself, generically defined.

The problems deriving from the form in which ICT has been developed (very much linked to business and economics perspectives), control over the network and over software production, inequality of access; and the possible problems of control and guarantees posed by their use, are clear and are going to be with us for some time to come. Much more concretely, there are problems with the very way in which electronic voting should be developed (Fundació Jaume Bofill 2000). None of this can be denied. However, returning to the first sections of this chapter, it is still important, in spite of all of that, to ask ourselves what democracy we are advancing towards and what democracy we would like to approach. The picture of seemingly extending democratic disaffection argues for advancement, even if experimental, to detect strengths and weaknesses.

## CONCLUSIONS?

At the beginning of this chapter, we said that we were interested in analysing the real difference that might be generated by the use of ICT on what were considered problems or deficiencies of democratic systems. We also said that our reflections were not free of normativism, since from the premises set forth we are interested in what reinforces democracy and broadens its spaces of civil participation. All this has been done trying to carry the debate into the European context of parliamentary democracies, with relatively well organized, centralized parties, with a strong presence in intermediation of interests and with well established and notably hierarchical administrations.

We started from the idea that the new forms of communication and information furnished by the technologies influence and can influence still much more the current processes of restructuring and redefinition of the principal variables of European political systems. New models of democracy, of processes of innovation, or simply of the improvement of democratic systems' functioning are spoken of. In this work, we have tried to simplify the many alternatives and tendencies being sketched in relation to these issues, establishing four broad strategies or discourses of change, which in this context coexist with or counteract one another. The first criterion we have used is taking into consideration the degree of strategic ambition or ambition to modify the system in its essential parts each discourse may have. The other criterion, much more substantive, refers to willingness to use ICT within the limits of representative democracy (improving its functioning or the relationship between the citizenry and representative institutions), or exploring new ways of understanding citizenship and democratic politics based on the potential that ICT offers.

We have seen how, in the first two strategies analysed, consumerist and demo-elitist, which are situated in the framework of representative democracy, the communicative elements proper to ICT take precedence over the relational aspects also present in the new technologies. Improved communication between institutions and citizens is sought, whether to make them more loyal consumers of public services or to legitimize more intensely the representative system as a whole. In this vision, the use of ICT does not seem to give rise to new ways of relating, of approaching the relations of hierarchy or representation, or of promoting new mechanisms of participation. Assuming that the representative mechanism is the basis of the only possible democracy, all that is sought are improved communication and reciprocal information, always making clear the responsibilities and roles of all parties.

In the other two discourses or strategies analysed (civil and direct democracy), the components that are alternatives to the representative status quo appear as the most significant. We believe we see that in these discourses the relational elements take precedence over the strictly communicative ones when referring to the potential uses of ICT. The relationship, the new ways of understanding the interests and responsibilities of each party, and the effects of the new technological opportunities have a value in themselves that goes beyond the communicative or informative aspects, which obviously are also present. When we refer to these discourses or strategies, we have referred to the emergence of new communities, new forms of conducting politics, another way of understanding collective responsibilities and the construction of citizenship. We have also referred to the new demands on political parties, which would generate a situation in which mechanisms of direct democracy would function. Political parties take shape as indispensable instruments for the construction of networks, social relationships and new groupings around the issues.

It is obvious that the questions posed when we refer to these two strategies in the use of ICT are much more abundant and profound than those that can be posed when we refer to ICT as a potential way of improving what already exists. A no less important question is whom we are to ask to take responsibility for the decisions that will be made.

There is no doubt that a superficial examination of what is underway indicates that the greatest intensity of efforts and concrete experiences (with the growing interest of businesses and consultants) is in what we have called consumerist discourse. One also notes growing attention to aspects of improvement of the representative democratic system as a whole. Attempts to work in what we have called civil or direct democracy are much more scarce, contradictory and inconsistent. Only at the local level is it easier to find experiences and cases that allow more - horizontal or comparative - analyses. All this is normal, given the initial parameters. What is most worrisome is the apparent disconnection between the two logics. While groups, communities and individuals are increasingly disaffected and disconnected from representative democratic institutions, seen as alien to their lives and life stories, these institutions and their elites are still worried about improving and taking advantage of the old and new communications and information media. New political identities and communities emerge, outside a political system understood as traditional and ever more obsolete. But what seems less clear is that in any of the scenarios analysed ICTs hold a central role. This could be a point of connection to keep exploring.

## NOTES

1. In 18 of the world's 20 best-established democracies, among them all the best-established European democracies, voter turnout has fallen an average of ten points over the past ten years. See Putnam et al. (2000).
2. This last hypothesis is the one that has found most statistical and empirical support in recent works on the question. See Pharr and Putnam (2000).
3. See Font (2001) for a panoramic view of the issue.
4. To cite only one reference, see Lindblom (1990).
5. See Van de Dok (2000). See also the emphasis with which the OECD is insisting on this type of vision: *Focus. Public Management Newsletter*, OECD Public Management Committee.
6. In relation, for example, to the use of new technologies in the functioning of representative assemblies, see Bellamy and Raab (1999), and Dutton (1999).
7. See the interesting experience in Spain of the Fundació Jaume Bofill and its www.democracia.org, specialized in following the activity of the Catalan Parliament. The Fundació's website offers numerous links on electronic democracy.
8. Experiences vary, but in Spain one of the closest at hand is that of the student co-operative at the Open University of Catalonia, or the election of the president of the Instituto de Ingenieros Eléctricos y Electrónicos. See Fundació Jaume Bofill (2000).

## REFERENCES

Barber, Benjamin (1998), *A Passion for Democracy*, Princeton: Princeton University Press.

Bellamy, Ch. (2000), 'Modelling electronic democracy', in J. Hoff, I. Horrocks and P. Tops (eds), *Democratic Governance and New Technology*, London: Routledge.

Bellamy, Ch. and Ch. Raab (1999), 'Parliamentary Democracy and New Technology: Reform, Reinforcement or Replacement?', paper presented in the colloquium *Les Parlaments dans la Societé de l'Information*, Paris: mimeo.

Bellamy, Ch. and J.A. Taylor (1998), *Governing in the Information Age*, Buckingham: Open University Press.

Bobbio, Norberto (1984), *Il Futuro Della Democrazia*, Turin: Einaudi.

Bobbio, Norberto (1990) 'Democrazia', in Bobbio, Mateucci and Pasquino, *Dizionario di Política*, Milan: TEA-UTET, pp. 287–97.

Bohman, J. (1996), *Public Deliberation*, Cambridge: MIT Press.

Budge, I. (1993), 'Direct Democracy: Setting Appropriate Terms of Debate', in David Held (ed.), *Prospects for Democracy*, Cambridge: Polity, pp. 136–55.

Burbach, R. (2001), *Globalization and Postmodern Politics*, London: Pluto Press.

Dahl, Robert (1998), *On Democracy*, New Haven: Yale University Press.

Donati, P. (2000), *La Cittadinanza Societaria*, Bari: Laterza.

Dutton, W. (ed.) (1999), *Society on the Line. Information Politics in the Digital Age*, Oxford: Oxford University Press.

Elster, Jon (ed.) (1998), *Deliberative Democracy*, Cambridge: Cambridge University Press.

Font, Joan (ed.) (2001), *Ciudadanos y Decisiones Públicas*, Barcelona: Ariel.

Fundació Jaume Bofill (2000), 'La votació electrònica: un debat necessari', *Debats Aula Provença*, Barcelona: Fundació Jaume Bofill.

Grossman, L.K. (1995), *The Electronic Republic. Reshaping Democracy in the Information Age*, New York: Viking.

Hoff, J., I. Horrocks and P. Tops (eds) (2000), *Democratic Governance and New Technology*, London: Routledge.

Holmes, D. (ed.) (1997), *Virtual Politics. Identity and Community in Cyberspace*, London: Sage.

Lindblom, Charles (1990), *Inquiry and Change*, New Haven: Yale University Press.

López Cerezo, J.A. and J.L. Luján (2000), *Ciencia y Política del riesgo*, Madrid: Alianza.

Luadon, K. (1977), *Communications Technology and Popular Participation*, New York: Praeger.

Majone, Giandomenico (ed.) (1996), *Regulating Europe*, London: Routledge.

Mironesco, Ch. (1997), *Un Enjeu Democratique: Le Technology Assessment*, Geneva: Georg Editeur.

Newton, K. and P. Norris (2000), 'Confidence in Public Institutions: Faith, Culture or Performance', in S. Pharr and R. Putnam (eds), *Disaffected Democracies*, Princeton: Princeton University Press.

Nino, C.S. (1996), *The Constitution of Deliberative Democracy*, New Haven: Yale University Press.

Norris, P. (ed.) (1999), *Critical Citizens*, Oxford: Oxford University Press.

Pharr, S. and R. Putnam (eds) (2000), *Disaffected Democracies*, Princeton: Princeton University Press.

Poster, M. (1995), *The Second Media Age*, Cambridge, Polity Press.

Poster, M. (1997), 'Cyberdemocracy: the Internet and the Public Sphere', in D. Holmes (ed.), *Virtual Politics: Identity and Community in Cyberspace*, London: Sage.

Putnam, R., S. Pharr and R.J. Dalton (2000), 'What's Troubling the Trilateral Democracies?', in S. Pharr and R. Putnam (eds), *Disaffected Democracies*, Princeton: Princeton University Press.

Raab, Ch. (1998), 'Electronic Confidence: Trust, Information and Public Information', in Suellen and Van de Dok (eds), *Public Administration in an Information Age: A Handbook*, Amsterdam: IOS Press.

Sartori, G. (1987), *Teoría de la Democracia*, Madrid: Alianza.

Schumpeter, Joseph ([1942] 1987), *Capitalism, Socialism and Democracy*, London: Unwin.

Tsagarousianou, R., D. Tambini and C. Bryan (eds) (1998), *Cyberdemocracy: Technology, Cities and Civic Networks*, London: Routledge.

Van de Dok, W. (2000), 'Infocracy or infopolis? Transparency, autonomy and democracy in an information age', in J. Hoff, I. Horrocks and P. Tops (eds), *Democratic Governance and New Technology*, London: Routledge, pp. 137–52.

Webster, F. (ed.) (2001), *Culture and Politics in the Information Age*, London: Routledge.

Zagrebelsky, G. (1995), *Il «Crucifige!» e la Democrazia*, Turin: Einaudi.

# Index